Curb Your Enthusiasm and Philosophy

Popular Culture and Philosophy® Series Editor: George A. Reisch

VOLUME 1 *Seinfeld and Philosophy: A Book about Everything and Nothing* (2000)

VOLUME 2 *The Simpsons and Philosophy: The D'oh! of Homer* (2001)

VOLUME 3 *The Matrix and Philosophy: Welcome to the Desert of the Real* (2002)

VOLUME 4 *Buffy the Vampire Slayer and Philosophy: Fear and Trembling in Sunnydale* (2003)

VOLUME 5 *The Lord of the Rings and Philosophy: One Book to Rule Them All* (2003)

VOLUME 9 *Harry Potter and Philosophy: If Aristotle Ran Hogwarts* (2004)

VOLUME 12 *Star Wars and Philosophy: More Powerful than You Can Possibly Imagine* (2005)

VOLUME 13 *Superheroes and Philosophy: Truth, Justice, and the Socratic Way* (2005)

VOLUME 19 *Monty Python and Philosophy: Nudge Nudge, Think Think!* (2006)

VOLUME 24 *Bullshit and Philosophy: Guaranteed to Get Perfect Results Every Time* (2006)

VOLUME 25 *The Beatles and Philosophy: Nothing You Can Think that Can't Be Thunk* (2006)

VOLUME 26 *South Park and Philosophy: Bigger, Longer, and More Penetrating* (2007)

VOLUME 28 *The Grateful Dead and Philosophy: Getting High Minded about Love and Haight* (2007)

VOLUME 30 *Pink Floyd and Philosophy: Careful with that Axiom, Eugene!* (2007)

VOLUME 31 *Johnny Cash and Philosophy: The Burning Ring of Truth* (2008)

VOLUME 32 *Bruce Springsteen and Philosophy: Darkness on the Edge of Truth* (2008)

VOLUME 33 *Battlestar Galactica and Philosophy: Mission Accomplished or Mission Frakked Up?* (2008)

VOLUME 34 *iPod and Philosophy: iCon of an ePoch* (2008)

VOLUME 35 *Star Trek and Philosophy: The Wrath of Kant* (2008)

VOLUME 36 *The Legend of Zelda and Philosophy: I Link Therefore I Am* (2008)

VOLUME 37 *The Wizard of Oz and Philosophy: Wicked Wisdom of the West* (2008)

VOLUME 38 *Radiohead and Philosophy: Fitter Happier More Deductive* (2009)

VOLUME 39 *Jimmy Buffett and Philosophy: The Porpoise Driven Life* (2009) Edited by Erin McKenna and Scott L. Pratt

VOLUME 40 *Transformers and Philosophy: More than Meets the Mind* (2009) Edited by John R. Shook and Liz Stillwaggon Swan

VOLUME 41 *Stephen Colbert and Philosophy: I Am Philosophy (And So Can You!)* (2009) Edited by Aaron Allen Schiller

VOLUME 42 *Supervillains and Philosophy: Sometimes, Evil Is Its Own Reward* (2009) Edited by Ben Dyer

VOLUME 43 *The Golden Compass and Philosophy: God Bites the Dust* (2009) Edited by Richard Greene and Rachel Robison

VOLUME 44 *Led Zeppelin and Philosophy: All Will Be Revealed* (2009) Edited by Scott Calef

VOLUME 45 *World of Warcraft and Philosophy: Wrath of the Philosopher King* (2009) Edited by Luke Cuddy and John Nordlinger

Volume 46 *Mr. Monk and Philosophy: The Curious Case of the Defective Detective* (2010) Edited by D.E. Wittkower

Volume 47 *Anime and Philosophy: Wide Eyed Wonder* (2010) Edited by Josef Steiff and Tristan D. Tamplin

VOLUME 48 *The Red Sox and Philosophy: Green Monster Meditations* (2010) Edited by Michael Macomber

VOLUME 49 *Zombies, Vampires, and Philosophy: New Life for the Undead* (2010) Edited by Richard Greene and K. Silem Mohammad

VOLUME 50 *Facebook and Philosophy: What's on Your Mind?* (2010) Edited by D.E. Wittkower

VOLUME 51 *Soccer and Philosophy: Beautiful Thoughts on the Beautiful Game* (2010) Edited by Ted Richards

VOLUME 52 *Manga and Philosophy: Fullmetal Metaphysician* (2010) Edited by Josef Steiff and Adam Barkman

VOLUME 53 *Martial Arts and Philosophy: Beating and Nothingness* (2010) Edited by Graham Priest and Damon Young

VOLUME 54 *The Onion and Philosophy: Fake News Story True, Alleges Indignant Area Professor* (2010) Edited by Sharon M. Kaye

VOLUME 55 *Doctor Who and Philosophy: Bigger on the Inside* (2010) Edited by Courtland Lewis and Paula Smithka

VOLUME 56 *Dune and Philosophy: Weirding Way of the Mentat* (2011) Edited by Jeffery Nicholas

VOLUME 57 *Rush and Philosophy: Heart and Mind United* (2011) Edited by Jim Berti and Durrell Bowman

VOLUME 58 *Dexter and Philosophy: Mind over Spatter* (2011) Edited by Richard Greene, George A. Reisch, and Rachel Robison-Greene

VOLUME 59 *Halo and Philosophy: Intellect Evolved* (2011) Edited by Luke Cuddy

VOLUME 60 *SpongeBob SquarePants and Philosophy: Soaking Up Secrets Under the Sea!* (2011) Edited by Joseph J. Foy

VOLUME 61 *Sherlock Holmes and Philosophy: The Footprints of a Gigantic Mind* (2011) Edited by Josef Steiff

VOLUME 62 *Inception and Philosophy: Ideas to Die For* (2011) Edited by Thorsten Botz-Bornstein

VOLUME 63 *Philip K. Dick and Philosophy: Do Androids Have Kindred Spirits?* (2011) Edited by D.E. Wittkower

VOLUME 64 *The Rolling Stones and Philosophy: It's Just a Thought Away* (2012) Edited by Luke Dick and George A. Reisch

VOLUME 65 *Chuck Klosterman and Philosophy: The Real and the Cereal* (2012) Edited by Seth Vannatta

VOLUME 66 *Neil Gaiman and Philosophy: Gods Gone Wild!* (2012) Edited by Tracy L. Bealer, Rachel Luria, and Wayne Yuen

VOLUME 67 *Breaking Bad and Philosophy: Badder Living through Chemistry* (2012) Edited by David R. Koepsell and Robert Arp

VOLUME 68 *The Walking Dead and Philosophy: Zombie Apocalypse Now* (2012) Edited by Wayne Yuen

VOLUME 69 *Curb Your Enthusiasm and Philosophy: Awaken the Social Assassin Within* (2012) Edited by Mark Ralkowsk

IN PREPARATION:

Dungeons and Dragons and Philosophy (2012) Edited by Jon Cogburn and Mark Silcox

The Catcher in the Rye and Philosophy (2012) Edited by Keith Dromm and Heather Salter

Jeopardy! and Philosophy: What Is Knowledge in the Form of a Question? (2012) Edited by Shaun P. Young

Planet of the Apes and Philosophy (2013) Edited by John Huss

Boardwalk Empire and Philosophy (2013) Edited by Richard Greene and Rachel Robison-Greene

The Wire and Philosophy (2013) Edited by Joanna Crosby, Seth Vannatta, and David Bzdak

The Good Wife and Philosophy (2013) Edited by Kimberly Baltzer-Jaray and Robert Arp

Psych and Philosophy (2013) Edited by Robert Arp

For full details of all Popular Culture and Philosophy® books, visit www.opencourtbooks.com.

Popular Culture and Philosophy®

Curb Your Enthusiasm and Philosophy

Awaken the Social Assassin Within

Edited by

MARK RALKOWSKI

OPEN COURT
Chicago and LaSalle, Illinois

Volume 69 in the series, Popular Culture and Philosophy®, edited by George A. Reisch

To order books from Open Court, call toll-free 1-800-815-2280, or visit our website at www.opencourtbooks.com.

Open Court Publishing Company is a division of Carus Publishing Company.

First printing 2012

Front cover picture of Larry David: Vincent Altamore, Altamore Graphic Design

Printed and bound in the United States of America.

Library of Congress Cataloging-in-Publication Data

Curb your enthusiasm and philosophy / edited by Mark Ralkowski.
p. cm. — (Popular culture and philosophy ; v. 69)
Includes bibliographical references (p.) and index.
ISBN 978-0-8126-9766-7 (trade paper : alk. paper)
1. Curb your enthusiasm (Television program) 2. Jewish wit and humor—History and criticism. 3. David, Larry. I. Ralkowski, Mark.
PN1992.77.C84C87 2012
791.45'72—dc23

2012019643

To my niece Ellie Vaupel and to all of Larry's Bald Brothers!

Dominion over the world, as we know, is divided between angels and devils. The good of the world, however, implies not that the angels have the advantage over the devils (as I believed when I was a child) but that the powers of the two sides are nearly in equilibrium. If there were too much incontestable meaning in the world (the angels' power), man would succumb under its weight. If the world were to lose all its meaning (the devils' reign), we could not live either.

Things deprived suddenly of their supposed meaning, of the place assigned to them in the so-called order of things, make us laugh. In origin, laughter is thus the devil's domain. It has something malicious about it (things suddenly turning out different from what they pretended to be), but to some extent also a beneficent relief (things are less weighty than they appeared to be, letting us live more freely, no longer oppressing us with their austere seriousness).

—Milan Kundera, *The Book of Laughter and Forgetting*

Contents

Pretty Pretty Pretty Far Beyond Good and Evil

> I think we're all sort of split down the middle, good and bad, you know. Good is not funny ... but the bad thoughts are funny because they are unexpressed . . . It's being able to get that bad side, that funny side, out. And that's why people really can relate to it. Because it comes from a place inside that somebody else is expressing.
>
> —"*Times* Talks" interview of Larry David by *The New York Times* reporter Bill Carter in 2006

Have you ever wondered why men don't urinate sitting down, or wanted to yell at a disabled person for driving his wheelchair recklessly? Does it bother you when bald people hide their baldness with toupées, or when teenagers trick-or-treat without costumes? Have you ever wondered whether it's okay to make jokes about Affirmative Action or the size of a child's penis? Do you think some women should never flaunt their bare midriffs, or that no man should wear a thong swimsuit in public? If you've ever wondered any of these things—or been bothered by them or wanted to do them yourself—you should read this book. It's exactly what you've been looking for. Think of it as an opportunity to understand why your friends and family, and even the general public, find you so difficult to live with.

This book is mostly about "Larry David," *Curb*-Larry, the character that the *real* Larry David plays on HBO's popular television series *Curb Your Enthusiasm*. However, if it's true—as HBO once suggested—that we all have a little bit of Larry in us, this book is also about *you*. On some level, in some sense, *you are him*.

Maybe that sounds just about right. After all, Larry often says and does things that most of us wish we had the courage to say and do. We may even fulfill some of our own wishes by watching Larry satisfy his. As Cheryl Hines once said, "I think we all live vicariously through Larry, because . . . if somebody asks you to dinner, you'd like to just say, 'No, I don't really like you that much.' But people don't in real life, you know. But Larry does" ("The History of *Curb* . . . So Far," Season Five DVD Bonus Feature).

We certainly *don't* always live as Larry does. But if Cheryl Hines is right, we wish we could. We wish we were as free as Larry is. That's why it makes sense to say that we all have a bit of Larry in us, even if most of us would never break the rules as happily as he does. We admire Larry because he's free. We're like caged animals watching a member of our species roam unfettered in the wild. Larry doesn't care about the things that ordinary people care about most. And while he may sometimes overvalue things that the rest of us consider trivial, there's usually a playfulness and a carefreeness about Larry's life that's easy to want for yourself.

Even Larry David seems to admire *Curb*-Larry's freedom. As he once said in a revealing interview about *Curb Your Enthusiasm*, his real life "is an act. It's a role." And it's *the show* that allows him to be himself ("The History of Curb . . . So Far"). Think about that. Larry doesn't act while he's doing a scene for *Curb Your Enthusiasm*. He acts while he goes about living his daily life. In other words, the real Larry David, the writer and actor, is in the same position as the rest of us, only he's discovered this other side of himself *that is also in us*, and he's put it on television for everyone to see.

Curb Your Enthusiasm is funny, as every fan of the show would agree. But its subject matter is a lot more than just light entertainment. It's hard not to walk away from a few episodes of *Curb* without thinking about something—like race relations, religion, or social expectations—in a new light. And what we usually see is that, like Larry, we live lives that are sort of dishonest. Each one of us has a role—as a Christian, as a Jew, as a friend, as a man or woman, etc.—and we act it out according to unwritten rules, even when we'd rather not. At its best, *Curb* gives us a glimpse of the truth about what we really think and what we really want.

That's how Larry David and Susie Essman understand the show.

> **SUSIE:** You really like your TV-Larry character.
>
> **LARRY:** Oh, God, I'm so in love with that guy, yeah.
>
> **SUSIE:** I think we all love our characters, and that's because our characters allow us to act out a part of ourselves that we're not allowed to in real life.
>
> **LARRY:** Exactly.
>
> **SUSIE:** And that's why I think it works.
>
> **LARRY:** I'm becoming a little more TV-Larry in my life. I gotta tell ya, it's a pleasure.
>
> **SUSIE:** TV-Larry doesn't care about convention.
>
> **LARRY:** No! Somebody asked me out to lunch the other day. I looked at them and said, "No, I don't think so." It was wonderful, and I never saw a face like that in my life.
>
> **SUSIE:** Do you find that, because of TV-Larry, you can get away with it more as real Larry?
>
> **LARRY:** Yes, that's what I'm saying. Of course!
>
> **SUSIE:** So, TV-Larry is just allowing you to be more honest?
>
> **LARRY:** Yes.
>
> **SUSIE:** Because people think there's a schmuckiness about TV-Larry when really there's a lack of artifice about TV-Larry. Do you know what I mean? He's just out there doing what everybody wants to do but they just play by the convention.
>
> **LARRY:** Right, right, I think that's true. But a lot of people I know don't watch the show because they hate TV-Larry. ("A Conversation with Larry David and Susie Essman Recorded Live at New York's 92nd Street Y," Season Six DVD Bonus Feature)

Larry's final comment here is worth thinking about at length. A lot of people hate *Curb*-Larry, he says. This is fascinating because *Curb*-Larry is *the Larry in all of us*. Which means that to hate him is to hate ourselves. How should we understand this?

On the one hand, it isn't surprising at all. *Curb*-Larry is probably best known for being a pain in the ass, for doing things that people aren't supposed to do. He's so famous for this, in fact, that he's added a new concept to our language, the "Larry David Moment," which the online Urban Dictionary defines as an instance "when a person says or does something offensive to someone else, without intentionally doing so." It's a popular concept. If you do a Google search for "Larry David Moment," you'll get over seventy-five thousand results. You can buy "Larry David Moment" mugs, t-shirts, and magnets. You'll find people blogging about "Monday's Larry David Moment." Others list their favorite instances from the show, and provide YouTube links to videos of the relevant scenes. There's even a Facebook page devoted to the concept.

Without a doubt, it's difficult to be, and to be around, *Curb*-Larry. There's something unbearable about the lightness of his way of life. He's not playing by the same rules as the rest of us. So no wonder some people hate *Curb*-Larry. He isn't paying his dues. He isn't following the social contract. If everyone acted as he does, life would be chaos.

But on the other hand, this creates a puzzle. How can we both love and hate the inner Larry in all of us? Why do some people find his behavior and ideas refreshing, while others find them offensive? Do the Larry-haters resent *Curb*-Larry because he doesn't do what he's supposed to do? Or do they hate him because he reminds them of *how they should be living but don't* because they lack his courage?

The authors in this book try to answer these questions and many others related to them. We think you'll be surprised to discover how much philosophy is present in the world of *Curb Your Enthusiasm*. Most of it revolves around *Curb*-Larry: his values and outlook on life, his unusual ways of interacting with people, his inability or unwillingness to conform to the world, and his relationships with others, including the *real* Larry David who plays him. We try to cover everything. Some of the chapters discuss ethical and existential issues, such as whether Larry is a "bad apple" or perhaps worth emulating. Others talk about sexuality, religion, and race relations. There's a chapter on *enthusiasm* itself, another on giving gifts, and we even discuss the philosophical significance of Larry's piercing stare into other people's eyes.

In "Kamikaze Bingo" (Season Five), Larry asks Kevin Nealon to excuse him for having "a curious mind that asks questions of people." If you share Larry's curiosity, we think you'll love this book. We certainly enjoyed writing it. And, if we may say so, we think it's pretty, pretty, pretty, pretty good![1]

ANONYMOUS [2]

---

[1] I would like to thank Jacob Garber for making the index. And I would like to thank Chris Tennberg who was very helpful during the development of this book, especially at the beginning stages when the pieces were first coming together. One day perhaps he will have a chance to enlighten us with his philosophical meditations on baldness.

[2] EDITOR'S NOTE: "Anonymous" is really Mark Ralkowski.

I

There Are a Few Different Realities Here

1

Deep Inside You Know You're Him

MARK RALKOWSKI

> A real comedian—that's a daring man. He *dares* to see what his listeners shy away from, fear to express. And what he sees is a sort of truth about people, about their situation, about what hurts or terrifies them, about what's hard, above all, about what they *want*. A joke releases tension, says the unsayable, any joke pretty well. But a true joke, a comedian's joke, has to do more than release tension, it has to *liberate* the will and desire, it has to *change the situation*.
>
> —TREVOR GRIFFITHS, *Comedians*

Larry David isn't a good man. Not by ordinary standards, anyway. He steals from corpses and roadside memorials. He digs up graves. He fights with women and he says inappropriate things to homosexuals. He makes fun of the disabled. If he doesn't insult your pet, or take advantage of it sexually, he might kill or steal it. He offends black people and Asians, and he stereotypes Muslims.

Sometimes he sexualizes children, commenting on the size of their genitalia. Other times he fights with them, challenging the prices they charge for their lemonade. He lies constantly. He jokes about the Holocaust and September 11th. He will pledge his faithfulness to his wife *for this life*, but he would like to be free to mess around in the afterlife. He's sacrilegious. He's insensitive to the sick. He breaks up marriages, and doesn't send wedding gifts. He fights with doctors and waiters and the elderly who play bingo. And he's absolutely terrible at showing respect, whether it's for the dead, for friends at their birthday parties, or for teenagers at their Bat Mitzvahs. He simply doesn't fit in well with society.

In fact, Larry David is so bad at being human he often has to apologize for his offensive apologies. So why do we like him so much? How can we?

Sure, He's a Schmuck. But Who Isn't?

Maybe it's something simple. Maybe we just like Larry because he makes us laugh. But does that really say enough? The problem here is that Larry makes us laugh at behavior and ideas that we would normally find shocking and monstrous. So, sure, Larry makes us laugh. The question is, why? Why aren't we simply appalled? And what, if anything, does our laughter at him tell us about ourselves? There are a few philosophical theories about the nature of humor. Maybe they can help us answer these questions.

The Superiority Theory of Humor says that humor involves feelings of superiority over other people or over our former selves. We laugh at other people when they fall down, or have toilet paper stuck to their shoes, or are so overweight that they don't fit between the armrests of their seats. And we laugh at ourselves—at pictures of our teenage haircuts or things we did in college—because we feel we're superior to the irresponsible and inexperienced people we used to be. This theory can be traced back to Plato (429 B.C.–347 B.C.) and Aristotle (384 B.C.–322 B.C.), who thought that in comedy we take pleasure in looking down on subjects who are inferior to us. But it was Thomas Hobbes (1588–1679) who developed the Superiority Theory most clearly. He says, "the passion of laughter is nothing else but a sudden glory arising from a sudden conception of some eminency in ourselves, by comparison with the infirmity of others, or with our own formerly."[1] If Hobbes is right, there's something malicious about humor. It's like the German concept Schadenfreude, which means, "the pleasure derived from other people's misfortunes."

Larry seems to use Superiority humor in every episode of *Curb Your Enthusiasm*. He does this in a variety of ways, since

[1] *Human Nature and De Corpore Politico* (Oxford University Press), pp. 54–55.

Curb invites us to laugh at all kinds of undesirable people, but primarily by showcasing his own character's incorrigible shortcomings. Larry's character on *Curb*, like the George Costanza character on *Seinfeld*, is funny in large part because he's so pathetic, especially in social settings. As Ben Stiller says in "Ben's Birthday Party" (Season Four), Larry "really has a ways to go when it comes to dealing with people." He's out of sync with the world. He doesn't get *it*, and it doesn't get him. He's even out of sync with himself, as we learned when he smoked marijuana and spent time in front of a mirror.

In episode after episode we see Larry fail, and often because he has undermined himself. In "The Interior Decorator" (Season One), for example, Larry is punished for his "elevator etiquette": he holds the door open for a young woman who then uses his courteousness to her advantage by signing in and being seen before him at the doctor's office. When Larry tries to get even and wrestles this woman to the floor the next time they are both in the office, the circumstances change (the doctor has changed the check-in policy on Larry's recommendation) and Larry loses anyway.

This pattern is repeated in many episodes of *Curb*. Larry is victimized by someone or something (such as the weatherman's forecast for rain), and so he makes adjustments to avoid the same fate in the future (instead of trusting the weatherman's forecast and cancelling golf, he will do the opposite). However, despite all of his best efforts, like a character in an ancient Greek tragedy who is predetermined to fail, Larry suffers a second downfall, this one often worse than the first (playing golf in the pouring rain) and sometimes a by-product of his own misguided ideas (attributing nefarious intentions, rather than just limited knowledge, to the weatherman). Larry can't win no matter what he does. It's as if the world is prearranged to foil him, which is amusing.

In some cases, Larry's misfortunes allow us to feel superior to *him*. Think of the countless scenes in which a person, or a room full of people, turns against Larry: for stealing a 5 wood from a dead man in his coffin, for offering edible panties to a conservative orthodox Jewish woman, for appearing to mock Michael J. Fox, for making an offensive joke about affirmative action, for making fun of adopted children from China, for mistakenly thinking a well dressed black man is the valet, for bringing a sex offender to Seder, for making fun of a Holocaust survivor, for not standing up to applaud Leo Funkhouser at his testimonial, for feeding a penis-shaped cake to children, for offending a rabbi who lost his brother-in-law on September 11th, for inadvertently calling people names in sign language, for urinating on a picture of Jesus, for trying to bribe a pharmacist, for hugging a little girl while having "something hard" in his pants, for saving his Blackberry before saving Sammy from drowning, for telling a woman not to "flaunt" her bare midriff, for hanging a mezuzah with a "Christ nail," for violently stomping on a spider in front of children, and so on and so on. None of us is *this* socially deviant! The Superiority Theory of humor would say that we laugh at these scenes because they make us feel superior to Larry. Compared to his deep and pervasive character flaws, our own foibles seem trivial.

In other cases, we may actually identify with Larry and see reflections of ourselves in the bad choices he makes or in the consistently bad luck he can't shake. If you have ever found yourself in a "Larry David moment," not knowing what to say to a mourner or wanting to destroy a fire alarm with a baseball bat, you know what it's like to feel a certain affinity with Larry, even when he's most at odds with the world. The Superiority Theory of humor would say that, in these cases, when we laugh at Larry and his misfortunes, we're really laughing at *ourselves*. We're laughing at the harmless and perhaps endearing fools we used to be or sometimes still are on our worst days. Larry reminds us of these former selves. And then he lets us enjoy their foolishness, their bad luck, their short fuses, and their tendency to buy products that come in impenetrable plastic packaging.

There's a third type of Superiority humor in *Curb*. This occurs when we side with Larry as he fights with the unreasonable people who populate the world of *Curb Your Enthusiasm*. He says and does things that a lot of us wish we had the courage to say and do. We've all experienced sample abusers and people who talk loudly on their cell phones in restaurants. Nobody likes to see an old man in a thong swimsuit, and who wouldn't object to having his bathroom habits documented in the office? When we laugh at these people in these scenarios, we're taking up Larry's point of view as our own and condemning *others* for failing to see the world as we do.

All in all, the Superiority Theory of humor clearly has some virtues, which we can appreciate when we apply it to *Curb Your Enthusiasm*. It helps us see that, in some cases, when we laugh at Larry's outrageous ideas and actions, we're enjoying feelings of superiority over him, over ourselves, or over other people. Countless examples attest to this.

The problem with this theory, however, is that it's too narrow. For example, we often feel superior without experiencing humor. Think of the difference between seeing an ordinary person with toilet paper stuck to his pants and seeing a homeless woman with toilet paper stuck to hers. One is humorous; the other is tragic. But both involve feelings of superiority.

This shows that the feeling of superiority is not a sufficient condition for the experience of humor. A condition that is sufficient for a result is like a trigger: if you have the sufficient condition, you get the result. Superiority doesn't have this relationship with humor. If it did, we'd experience humor whenever we felt superior, but we clearly don't.

And we often enjoy humor without feeling superior to anyone or anything. Think of the joke Marty Funkhouser tells Jerry Seinfeld in "The Table Read" (Season Seven). It's outrageously funny because it's offensive and disgusting, and because it is both of those things to a surprising extent—not because it involves any feelings of superiority. The feeling of superiority also is not a *necessary* condition for the experience of humor. If a condition is necessary for a result, you can't get the result without the condition. But we often experience humor without any feeling of superiority.

If superiority is neither necessary nor sufficient for the experience of humor, the Superiority Theory fails to tell us what humor is in every instance, and we will need another theory if we want to fully understand what it is that we see in Larry's humor.

The Bearable Lightness of Being Larry David

The second theory of humor that we should apply to *Curb Your Enthusiasm* is the Relief Theory. It tries to explain both the nature of humor and the psychological benefits of laughter. According to this theory, which was first developed by Herbert Spencer (1820–1903) and then more famously by Sigmund

Freud (1856–1939), we laugh in order to release excesses of psychological energy. Laughter lets us "blow off steam." But how so?

Freud invites us to consider the process that takes place in a man's mind when he is listening to someone "produce humor."

> He sees this other person in a situation which leads the listener to expect that the other will produce signs of an affect—that he will get angry, complain, express pain, be frightened or horrified or perhaps even in despair; and the onlooker or listener is prepared to follow his lead and to call up the same emotional impulses in himself. But this emotional expectancy is disappointed; the other person expresses no affect, but makes a jest. The expenditure on feeling that is economized turns into humorous pleasure in the listener.[2]

This sounds like a general description of what it's like to watch an episode of *Curb Your Enthusiasm*, doesn't it? First Larry makes us cringe; then he sets us free with a joke or an unexpected twist in the plot. Freud thought he could explain this sort of experience psychologically. An excess of energy is produced, he says, when we realize, thanks to a joke, that a situation or person or thing isn't as serious as we thought, and so doesn't warrant a serious psychological response, such as a strong emotion. However, since our minds have already set aside the energy necessary for a serious response, we experience a sudden surplus of energy, a kind of pressure buildup, which we release in laughter. *Curb Your Enthusiasm* is full of this kind of humor.

Think of the moment in "The Carpool Lane" (Season Four) when Larry gets caught with Monina at the Dodgers game. The two men Larry least wants to see—the stuffy Republicans who run the Beverly Park country club that he and Cheryl hope to join—find Larry sharing a bag of popcorn with Monina. When you watch this exchange for the first time, you expect Larry to be upset. After all, in the previous episode, "The 5 Wood" (Season Four), Larry and Cheryl went out of their way to impress these men, dressing and acting as Republicans. They claimed to own "a schooner," to be members of conservative

---

[2] Sigmund Freud, *Standard Edition* (Hogarth, 1961), pp. 161–62.

social clubs, to drive a Hummer, and to have once volunteered for Ronald Reagan.

This carefully crafted image of the Davids as elitist conservative Republicans was obliterated the moment the men of Beverly Park saw Larry with Monina. As viewers of this scene, we also know that back home Larry is already in trouble with Cheryl and Susie for getting the Davids and the Greenes thrown out of their old country club over the funeral incident involving Larry's 5 wood. In other words, the stage is set for Larry to suffer, and we prepare to suffer with him. We prepare to feel his pain as he tries to explain *this* incident to Cheryl and Susie. But in the end we don't have to. Larry turns the whole thing into a joke: "If you're ever looking for a good blowjob at a reasonable rate," he says to the Beverly Park men, "[Monina] is your gal."

Larry may not save his membership application with this quip, but he certainly changes his situation. Instead of being a victim of his circumstances, he accepts them and transforms his misfortune into something funny. If Freud is right, we laugh at situations like this because the joke releases us from the burden of sympathy. We prepare to suffer with Larry—we might even be anticipating Susie's coming tirade over "fucking up" *this* membership as well: we can already hear her raised voice and profanity; we can see Cheryl's looks of exasperation. But then, suddenly, we don't have to feel anything for Larry. His joke changes the emotional significance of his situation. It's no longer serious. He has stripped it of meaning. This sudden shift from serious to non-serious, Freud says, produces a surplus of energy, and we laugh to release it.

If Freud's Relief Theory is correct, there's something liberating about humor. It changes the way we look at the world and ourselves, and so releases us from our ordinary attachments to both. In its essence, humor says, "Look! Here is the world, which seems so dangerous! It is nothing but a game for children—just worth making a jest about!" From this perspective, all of our projects and interests, including those that wound us most deeply, can seem trivial and unimportant. Humor therefore spares us the "affects to which the situation would naturally give rise and dismisses the possibility of such expressions of emotion with a jest."

This isn't just liberating. It's empowering. It makes us invulnerable to the pressures of life, or gives us a kind of antidepressant against them, because it "refuses to be distressed by the provocations of reality" and "insists that [we] cannot be affected by the traumas of the external world; it shows, in fact, that such traumas are no more than occasions for [us] to gain pleasure." When we take up the humorous attitude toward ourselves, we find our successes and our failures, our earnestness and our pessimism, equally insignificant. We look at ourselves the way a parent looks at a child who is upset or excited about something trivial. And that makes us laugh.

The great virtue of humor, Freud thinks, is that it gives us this insight into the insignificance of human life "without overstepping the bounds of mental health," which is what happens when we adopt "other methods having the same purposes." We don't have to lie to ourselves or posit the existence of another world or a transcendent God from whose point of view our troubles are insignificant. Humor is all we need for this perspective. Freud's example is of a man who, while being led to the gallows to be hung on a Monday, remarks, "Well, the week's beginning nicely." This man isn't resigned, Freud says. He's rebellious. He has changed his situation, relieved himself of the most significant emotional weight, and even experienced pleasure in spite of "the unkindness of the real circumstances" (pp. 161–66). We see Larry do something similar when he "dies" in "The End" (Season Five). His last words are about frivolous and inconsequential things, such as how much mayo to use in a tuna sandwich and who misplaced a Sopranos DVD cover. Like Freud's gallows man, Larry uses humor to triumph over tragedy. His death doesn't amount to much if *life* doesn't amount to much.

We might think that Relief humor is just a form of self-deception or sour grapes that we use to make ourselves feel better about our limitations, our bad luck, and our circumstances. Freud denies this. Relief humor is not delusional, he says. It's lucid in its self-mockery. Neither we nor the world nor our projects in life are as important as the ego likes to think. Larry, of course, takes this insight to the extreme, but the idea's the same: let's not exaggerate our own importance. Insofar as there's wisdom in recognizing this, there's genuine wisdom in humor. It helps us see the world in the right light and value it accordingly. Epictetus, a great Stoic philosopher from the early second century, famously said, "we are not bothered by things, but by our judgments about things." Humor, according to Freud, helps us make the right judgments about things.

There's a second kind of Relief humor, and it is also pervasive in *Curb Your Enthusiasm*. In some cases, such as the one with Monina at the Dodgers game, our relief comes from no longer needing to take something seriously. This kind of Relief humor gives us the sensation of having put down a heavy weight. But in other cases, our relief comes from being able to express certain feelings or desires that we would otherwise repress. This kind of relief is more like the excitement of a child running outside for recess, or of a pet dog getting out of the house to run around after being locked up inside all day. A wild energy is finally free.

Some humor, the kind that taps into our innermost urges, produces a similar sensation in us. Instead of repressing a desire for sex or violence, we express it or have it satisfied in a joke. And the energy we would have used to repress our desire is then released in the form of laughter. These jokes often make us laugh the hardest because they release the greatest amounts of energy.

Think of the unforgettable stomping scene in "The Rat Dog" (Season Six). Larry's dad stands up and yells, "It's a rat," as Jean's little purse-sized dog scurries through the audience of a school play. Moments later we see Larry's "date," a crude heavy-set exterminator in a bad suit, stomping violently, over and over, on this defenseless little animal. If you laughed hysterically at this scene, as many people did, Freud would say it's because you felt liberated from the repressed desire to hurt a dog like that. It's no coincidence that, earlier in the episode, Larry asks Hal, Jean's husband, several times whether he really pets "that dog," whether he lets it sit in his lap, and so on.

LARRY: Oh, hey Hal.

HAL: Hey, how are you doing, Larry?

LARRY: You know what? I'm glad I saw you again, because after you left I made a little comment that maybe didn't go over so well with your wife. I said her dog looked, you know, half rat.

HAL: Really?

LARRY: Yeah, I was joking in my tone. I had a joking tone. But I guess because, you know, she doesn't hear, she's not able to detect tone.

HAL: No.

LARRY: You know, the dog, it's kind of a ratty looking dog. You've gotta admit that.

HAL: She loves that dog.

LARRY: How about you? Do you pet that dog?

HAL: Yeah, I pet it.

LARRY: *You* pet that dog?

HAL: I pet that dog.

LARRY: You *pet* that dog?

HAL: I pet that dog, yes.

This dialogue is preparing us for the stomping scene by eliciting our own deep-seated feelings about these little dogs. Larry knows they're unpopular. Most people like dogs *or* cats. Some people like both. But very few people like little dogs. They look like rodents, as Larry says. They sound awful. They aren't very smart. Who hasn't wanted to smack a little dog that wouldn't stop yapping? But almost nothing is as taboo as hurting a pet, so we repress any such desire and probably have a hard time admitting that we have it at all. Larry sets us free. He let's us laugh it out. When the "rat dog" gets stomped on, we laugh hysterically because we're watching a wish be fulfilled.

Like the Superiority Theory of humor, the Relief Theory is very illuminating when we apply it to *Curb Your Enthusiasm*. It helps us make sense of a common experience people have when they watch the show: feelings of deep discomfort followed by relief and laughter. It also helps us understand, and even justify, our fondness for Larry: he isn't the monster that his critics make him out to be; at his best, he is like an ancient Stoic who helps us make the right judgments about things.

Most of us would never live exactly as Larry does, or completely share his perspective on what does and doesn't matter. But, at a minimum, Larry helps us laugh at ourselves, which relieves us of the emotional burdens we carry when we take our lives too seriously. And this isn't all that Larry does for us. His jokes about sex, death, and violence provide us with a kind of therapy for our repressed desires. Watching *Curb* is cathartic. When we laugh hysterically at the rat dog or the black swan or the joke that Marty Funkhouser tells Jerry, we're expressing and indirectly satisfying repressed natural urges that would otherwise torment us.

Critics of the Relief Theory complain that it tells us why we enjoy laughter (it relieves us of a surplus of energy), and it describes a cognitive benefit we derive from experiencing humor (an appreciation of human insignificance). But it doesn't tell us what humor *is*. It doesn't define the object of humor—the thing we laugh at—as much as it tells us about the psychological byproducts of enjoying humor. And even this account seems problematic, since not every experience of humor involves the release of pent up psychological energy, the reduction of a thing's significance, or a reflective meditation on the finitude of the human condition. Sometimes we laugh at things that are already considered insignificant, and these instances don't seem to involve the release of tension or invite us to take ourselves less seriously. When Larry rejects his doctor's medical recommendation because he disagrees with his restaurant recommendation ("The Hot Towel," Season Seven), we laugh because Larry's assumption is absurd (a doctor's medical opinion is not a matter of taste the way his food preferences are), not because we feel relief or superiority.

But this means we still haven't found what we're looking for. If the Relief Theory is too narrow to define the nature of humor in every instance, as the Superiority Theory is, we still need another theory if we want to fully understand our fondness for Larry's humor.

He Likes to Wear Women's Panties?

The Incongruity Theory, which was originally developed by Immanuel Kant (1724–1804), says that incongruity, not relief or superiority, is the essence of humor. Philosophers often prefer this theory because it focuses on the object of humor—the thing we laugh at—rather than the feelings that motivate our laughter (the Superiority Theory) or the psychological benefits of laughing (the Relief Theory). According to the Incongruity

Theory, humor is the product of people, situations, and things that reverse or clash with our expectations. As Kant says, "Whatever is to arouse lively, convulsive laughter must contain something absurd (hence something that the understanding cannot like for its own sake). Laughter is an affect that arises if a tense expectation is transformed into nothing."[3] We're amused, in other words, when we feel or perceive an incongruity between what we expect and what actually happens.

Incongruity humor is pervasive in *Curb Your Enthusiasm*. Think of a few obvious cases of it, such as Larry proudly displaying "his" women's panties, cousin Andy in bed with a *Playboy* model, Larry's countless fights with the disabled, and Larry's father watching pornography with the volume turned up in his assisted living facility. According to the Incongruity Theory, each of these scenes is funny because it reverses our expectations. We would never expect Larry happily to exhibit women's underwear, and we certainly wouldn't expect him to introduce himself by saying, "I'm Larry David and I happen to enjoy wearing women's panties."

Similarly, cousin Andy is the last person we would expect to score with a *Playboy* model. If there's a type of man who's likely to take a *Playboy* model home, Andy is the opposite. Moreover, we expect Larry to give disabled people special treatment, the way the rest of us do, not to fight with them as if they were just any other people. And when we first hear the sounds of pornography in "Kamikaze Bingo" (Season Five), the last person we expect to see connected to those noises is Larry's father.

In episode after episode, *Curb Your Enthusiasm* sets and then reverses our expectations. One of the funniest instances of this occurs when Larry calls Information to look up Krayzee-Eyez Killa's phone number.

> Yeah, I think it's Knox Road and Silver Lake. Um, Killer. Yeah, that's the last name. Krayzee-Eyez. There might be a hyphen in that. Well, Krayzee I guess is the first name, unless the whole last name is Krayzee-Eyez Killer. K-r-a-z-y. Krayzee-Eyez. What about an "h" at the end of Killer? Did you try that? K-i-l-l-a-h? What about a "z", Eyez, E-y-e-z? Is that possible? No, no, no, that's an optometry place. Okay, all right, thank you. (Season Three, "Krayzee-Eyez Killa")

---

[3] *Critique of Judgment* (Hackett, 1987), p. 203.

Larry's request is hilarious because it's absurd. "Krayzee-Eyez Killa" is an entertainment name, not a name listed in the phone book. Larry is exploiting our background knowledge here. We laugh at this scene because we recognize the incongruity between the names we expect Information to have listed and the name Larry is asking them to look up.

These are classic instances of Incongruity humor because the contradictions are so clear and simple. However, as every fan of *Curb Your Enthusiasm* knows, most of Larry's jokes are not about such mundane issues. Many of them, and perhaps all or most of the fan favorites, deal with the weightiest issues in life, such as love, death, marriage, children, and other things we tend to give a sacred status. In these scenes Larry uses the sacred as a lever for his comedy: the more important something is to us, the more humor he can squeeze out of it by reversing our expectations. Think of the conversation Larry has with his father in "The Special Section" (Season Three), when he comes home from New York and learns some bad news about his mother.

LARRY: Where's Mom?

NAT: (*Larry's father*) Well, your mother, yeah, well, I'll tell you all about your mother, you know. After all, you know, we brought her back. You know, your mother, she got sicker, and we had to bring her back to the hospital.

LARRY: She's in the hospital?

NAT: Yeah, well, not now, not now, that's—but we had to bring her back for a while.

LARRY: Why didn't you tell me? Why didn't you even call?

NAT: She didn't want to bother you. You know how she is. She said, "Don't bother him. He's in New York. Let him enjoy himself." She didn't want to spoil your trip. But she's not in the hospital now, so that's over with. Don't worry about that.

LARRY: So she's feeling better?

NAT: Well, in a way. She did warn me. She said, "If anything happens to me, don't bother Larry, because he's in New York and he wants to enjoy." So, then, after a day or two—nobody goes on forever and ever and ever, and, um—you're not gonna go on, I'm not gonna go on—

LARRY: Is she dead?

NAT: Er, yeah. Dead, dead, she's dead. And she didn't want me to bother you.

As this conversation continues, we learn that Larry also missed his mother's funeral, which was held just a few days before he returned to LA. Out of town relatives were there, but Larry wasn't, and all because his mother didn't want to "bother him" while he was enjoying himself in New York. People probably laugh at this scene for all kinds of reasons, but the real engine driving the humor here is the incongruity between how we feel about death, especially a mother's death, and Nat's treatment of it as a minor thing, a mere distraction.

Larry does something very similar in "The Survivor" (Season Four) when he subjects wedding vows to the same desanctification. He begins by questioning Cheryl's request for a promise to continue loving her "through all eternity." Larry's genuinely confused. He had understood his original vows literally. "This is continuing into the afterlife? . . . I thought this was over at death . . . Isn't that what it said, 'Till death do us part'?" Cheryl puts her foot down and Larry agrees to promise his love for eternity. But then, when the time comes to renew their vows, Larry can't remember what he planned to say, and he forgot to bring his copy of the vows. No problem, the rabbi says. "Just speak from your heart. Just speak to Cheryl, look into her eyes, and it'll come. The words will come." Larry agrees, and this is what comes from his heart.

> Things have been good. It's a very good, uh, relationship. Ten years. Pretty good. Pretty, pretty, pretty, pretty good. And I am your devoted servant—well, I don't know about servant. You know, I'm not a servant. I'll certainly help you, if you ever need help with anything. You know that. I'm in the house a lot—you wanna open a Bridge table or something, you know, whatever you need. I'm not a great handy man, and I'm not good at making plans—that I don't do very well, I have to admit. She makes the plans, you know. She makes good plans. We always have stuff to do . . .

It doesn't get much more incongruous than this. The rabbi asks Larry to look into Cheryl's eyes and speak "from the heart." The Davids' close friends and family are watching.

Cheryl has set the mood with her heartfelt promises to Larry, which the rabbi found "very moving." And so our expectations are locked in. We wait for Larry to say something equally heartfelt. When he doesn't—when he goes in the opposite direction and makes a mockery of the event, talking about helping Cheryl with a Bridge table and complimenting her ability to make plans—it's hard not to laugh hysterically. And, again, it's thanks to incongruity.

Like the other theories of humor, then, the Incongruity Theory sheds light on the comedy in *Curb Your Enthusiasm*. It helps us see that Larry makes us laugh by upsetting our expectations. He constantly surprises us, whether it's about the mundane and everyday patterns of our experience, or the sacred things we value the most. This is how his humor works, because this is how humor in general works. We may laugh without feeling superior, and without expressing repressed desires or releasing surplus energy. But the perception of incongruity is essential to every experience of humor, even the instances that we explained earlier with the Superiority and Relief theories.

This is a big deal. If the Incongruity Theory can account for every instance of humor, and the other theories can't, it would seem that Incongruity is the only theory we need. Unfortunately, however, things aren't quite this simple. The Incongruity Theory has flaws as well.

The first problem is that incongruity, like superiority, is insufficient for humor: we don't always experience humor when we perceive incongruities. Sometimes we feel fear or disgust or puzzlement. For example, if I entered one of my classrooms and found all of my students wielding machetes, soaked in blood, and angrily chanting "down with Ralkowski," this would be incongruous *and terrifying*, not funny. But this means the Incongruity Theory doesn't tell us quite enough. It doesn't tell us why some incongruities are funny while others aren't.

The second problem with the Incongruity Theory is that it doesn't explain why people take pleasure in having their expectations contradicted. As John Morreall puts this point, "Such enjoyment looks psychologically perverse or at least irrational . . . People who enjoy incongruity are like travelers who discover they are headed in the wrong direction—and enjoy that discovery."[4] There's something puzzling about our enjoyment of humorous incongruities. It's not clear why rational animals would ever enjoy the experience of intellectual frustration. That's not how we usually are.

For example, if you had a friend who started acting mysteriously (not showing up for work and not answering her phone), wouldn't you try to understand why, and not simply laugh? As rational creatures, we usually respond to incongruities by trying to resolve them, not by reveling in them. This is true at the level of our everyday experience, but it's also true at the theoretical level. In the sciences, for example, we are puzzled and sometimes disturbed by anomalies—when things don't happen as we expect. If something happens in the natural world that we don't know how to explain, we immediately get to work to make sense of things. Why is humor different? How can it be?

The humor in *Curb Your Enthusiasm* can help us answer these questions, but only if we look more closely at a specific kind of incongruity that Larry David specializes in pointing out for his audiences. These incongruities involve a clash between Larry and what I will call the "unknown known," the things we know but don't know that we know. The basic idea is that jokes teach us. They tell us truths we've always known but never expressed, and they help us discover truths we don't know yet and have never imagined. They don't frustrate our desire to understand. They satisfy it by illuminating the world we live in and helping us imagine how it could be different.

Is Larry David's Examined Life Worth Living?

Two twentieth-century philosophers, Martin Heidegger (1889–1976) and Ludwig Wittgenstein (1889–1951), argued that every culture embodies an understanding of what it is to be human, and that this understanding *isn't conceptual*. It's a kind of know-how, the way being good at a sport is. This non-conceptual know-how, which is pervasive in our lives, is what I will call "the unknown known." Some philosophers call the unknown known "cultural background practices" because they

[4] John Morreall, *Comic Relief: A Comprehensive Philosophy of Humor* (Wiley-Blackwell, 2009), pp. 13–14.

want to stress that it refers to tendencies, skills, dispositions, and practices, rather than beliefs or concepts.

There's something inherently funny about this kind of knowledge, because it's a bunch of stuff that we know, *but we don't know that we know it*. We often need to have it pointed out for us, either by a philosopher or by someone like Larry David.

For instance, everyone knows, and knows without asking, the appropriate distance to stand from a conversation partner. That distance will depend on several factors, such as the age, gender, and relationship of the people who are talking. It will also depend on the purpose of the conversation, such as whether it's for business, to share gossip, to discipline a child, or to make a good impression on a first date. Think about what it means *to know* the differences between these contexts. As Carol White points out, "most of us are not even aware of the variation of distance and would be hard put to conceptualize it in all its nuances even if it is pointed out to us."[5]

This isn't knowledge that we've acquired by reading books or learning theory in a classroom. It isn't even something that we've been told. We've picked it up by living our lives, and now it's simply a part of us. Similar things can be said about our business, political, sexual, verbal, and social behaviors. These practices are shaped and constrained by our background practices, so that, for example, a male executive cannot wear a dress and high heels in the office unless it's Halloween or some other occasion that would let him do so in jest. We have extensive knowledge of this kind that we've never thought about, because this kind of knowledge isn't conceptual when we acquire it, and it usually doesn't come up in conversation.

But then along comes Larry. Many of *Curb Your Enthusiasm's* most memorable moments shed light on, and in some cases challenge, our cultural background practices. We tend to treat the disabled a certain way; we tend to give children a special moral status; we tend to behave with a certain type of respect at weddings and funerals; we tend to take turns paying for dinner checks when we dine with friends, and so on. Larry obliterates these tendencies. And as he does so, he sheds light on us—on how we live, on what matters to us, and on all kinds

---

[5] Carol White, *Time and Death: Heidegger's Analysis of Finitude* (Ashgate, 2005), p. 7.

of things we've never verbalized or consciously thought of. These aren't always small matters. In many cases they are the tendencies and dispositions that make us who and what we are.

John Searle, a contemporary philosopher at Berkeley, has written about the importance of background practices for what he calls the "construction of social reality."

> Our whole mode of sensibility is shaped by forces and influences that are, for the most part, invisible to us—what it is to be male, what it is to be female, what is involved in being a citizen, what is involved in being a professor. Though sometimes these points are made explicit . . . there are all sorts of ways in which they are inexplicit. (*Making the Social World*, p. 159)

There are two ideas here. The first is that background practices account for important parts of our identities. The second is that these practices are usually invisible to us. Together these ideas say that one of the most basic and pervasive features of human experience—a feature of our experience that exercises power over us, determining what is and is not permissible to do and believe—is implicit in our lives. We acquire it without thinking about it, and then it determines our thinking!

We don't have to be told not to wear a shark costume to a job interview, or not to wear jeans to a formal wedding. We know not to eat pistachio nuts while we apologize, and most of us know that the poker game ends when someone related to the host attempts to commit suicide. But these are also things *we know without knowing*!

This is the stuff Larry looks for and writes about. In some cases, the issues he focuses on aren't all that surprising. Nobody was shocked when Marty Funkhouser objected to having flowers stolen from his mother's roadside memorial. If we were shocked at anything, it was that Larry would stoop *that* low. Nevertheless, even in these scenarios, Larry is shedding light on our background practices. He's highlighting something we take for granted, something we know without knowing, by being out of sync with that thing, and by being out sync with the world around him. As he stands out by doing something abnormal, he makes himself into an object of humor *and* allows us to see our background practices with surprising clarity. He sheds light on us by standing apart from us.

Of course, this is only half the story. As any fan of the show knows, Larry isn't always the one who is out of sync. Some of his ideas produce a "that is so true" kind of response in us as we watch *Curb*. Think of the sample abuser in "The Ida Funkhouser Roadside Memorial" (Season Six). Larry gets particularly upset about this woman, and he even describes his own ideas about the unknown known.

LARRY: Let me just say this, okay? She was breaking the rules. The woman was standing in front of the counter, getting sample after sample. She had ten samples! . . . She wasn't following the rules of society.

CHERYL: (*exasperated*) What rules?

LARRY: The unwritten rules that we have as we go about our day.

CHERYL: Like what?

LARRY: Like at night, you tiptoe. That's an unwritten rule. You tiptoe so you don't wake people up. You tiptoe. There's no sign, "Tiptoe." You just have to be smart enough and considerate enough to do it.

There are countless examples of these "unwritten rules" observations in other episodes of *Curb*. In "Funkhouser's Crazy Sister" (Season Seven) alone, Larry makes an issue of 1. being asked to a dinner party at the last minute and without being told who else is attending, 2. the conditions under which it is acceptable for a guest to take food and drinks without asking the host, and 3. the empty gesture we make when we say, "Just let me know if there's anything I can do." *Curb* wouldn't be *Curb* without these issues.

Larry isn't just entertaining us. He's describing how we live, and he's offering the occasional recommendation for how we might do better. He takes what is most familiar to us and he makes it unfamiliar, sometimes simply by making us think about it. He shows us that things could be different, and that there often is good reason for them to change. In Larry's hands, the most ordinary moments in life—checking in at the doctor's office, paying a tip on a lunch check, throwing away an apple while taking a walk through the neighborhood—become extraordinary, problematic, and worth rethinking. This is what comedy is at its best. It changes our perspective on ourselves and on the world, and it lets us imagine both differently.

> Jokes return us to a common, familiar domain of shared life-world practices, the background meanings implicit in a culture ... Humour also indicates, or maybe just adumbrates, how those practices might be transformed or perfected, how things might be otherwise ... In laughing at a joke I am also consenting to a certain ideal image of the world ... In this sense ... humour has a certain messianic power.[6]

The best comedy, in other words, helps us appreciate that the accepted ways of living and behaving, as Mary Douglas says, have "no necessity."[7] They are as arbitrary, and sometimes as "fucking nuts," as the beliefs and practices of the orthodox Jewish girl in "The Ski Lift" (Season Five) or Richard's Christian Scientist girlfriend in "The Benadryl Brownie" (Season Three). We can easily see the contradiction in a Christian Scientist hiring the cable guy to fix her television *while refusing to take Benadryl to relieve her allergic reaction to nuts*. As Larry asks, why not just pray for the television, since that's all she's doing for her allergy?

But the true brilliance of *Curb* is evident when an episode or a joke helps us see that our own commitments to ordinary everyday social conventions are often just as irrational, and sometimes just as emotional. There's no downside to Susie telling Larry who will be at her dinner party, for example. It's "just not done" ("Funkhouser's Crazy Sister," Season Seven). That's all Susie can say, because that's all there is to it.

This is classic *Curb*, but it's also the highest kind of comedy. The best jokes are what Mary Douglas calls "anti-rites." They're like leeches that feed on meaning and value, sucking both out of the daily rituals we take for granted and blindly follow. They describe and then undermine the cultural background practices of a society, which means they describe and then undermine some of the most fundamental elements of our identities. "The anti-rite of the joke," as Simon Critchley says, "shows the sheer contingency or arbitrariness of the social rites in which we engage." And by producing a "consciousness of con-

---

6 Simon Critchley, *On Humour* (Routledge, 2002), p. 90.

7 Mary Douglas, *Implicit Meanings* (Routledge, 1975), p. 96.

tingency" humor can have a "*critical* function with respect to society" (*On Humour*, p. 10). It can see what is usually invisible to us. It can tell bitter truths that we typically avoid. It can express and satisfy repressed desires, and help us see the world from a more objective perspective. At its best, humor can change the world, releasing us from the ordinary significance of things, and showing us both that the status quo is unnecessary and that a different way of doing things might be preferable. Freud found wisdom in humor's capacity to make the correct judgments about things. Larry's humor makes us wiser. The question is not, Is Larry David's examined life worth living? The questions is, How can anyone live without it?

The cover of the DVD box for Season Six of *Curb* features an interesting image. It's a giant portrait of Larry that appears to be hanging in a museum. People are gathered around it: a kid looks closely, as if he sees a kindred spirit; a couple is discussing it, and a solitary man looks on from a distance. This is a perfect choice of images for representing the show, maybe the best of them all.

The portrait of Larry on *Curb Your Enthusiasm*, the one that captivates and disturbs us, functions like a mirror in which we see reflections of our own humanity: truths we wish we had the courage to tell, desires we want to but can't express, and pointless norms we'd prefer to change or live without. This portrait has a magnetic quality. None of us can stop looking at it, even when it makes us cringe. As Virginia Woolf might have said of Larry's portrait, "There is always a crowd before that picture, gazing into its depths, seeing their own faces reflected in it, seeing more the longer they look, never being able to say quite what it is they see."[8]

We see ourselves when we look at Larry's portrait. Our own faces are reflected in it. And while the reflection looking back at us is partly familiar and partly unfamiliar, something in us understands that deep inside each one of us is him.[9]

---

[8] Virginia Woolf, "Montaigne," in *Essays* (Hogarth, 1986), p. 71.

[9] I'm grateful to Beau Schilz, Matt Guillebaud, Matt Giudice, Xochitl Romo, Brian Wright, David Pelavin, Mike Dockins, and Ratna Tandavan for their feedback on earlier drafts of this chapter.

2
Larry David as . . . Himself?

JOSEPH WESTFALL

Curb Your Enthusiasm is among HBO's—and current television's—most successful sitcoms. Without a doubt, the show's success is derived largely from the appeal of its central character, Larry David, as portrayed by Larry David himself.

For anyone who has not seen the show, this must be something of a surprise. Larry David has made a career—not just on *Curb*, but in his early days as a stand-up comic in New York (where he was notorious for insulting the audience and storming off stage), as a writer on the sketch comedy series *Fridays* and *Saturday Night Live*, as a writer and executive producer on *Seinfeld*, and in his various non-*Curb* appearances since the show's inception (on various late night talk shows, the Jerry Seinfeld-produced series *The Marriage Ref*, the Woody Allen film *Whatever Works*, and so on)—of playing the outspoken, insulting, no-holds-barred, nothing-sacred, self-centered, insensitive boor.

The curmudgeon. The cantankerous schmuck. There are many names for it, and it's nothing new to American comedy, but whatever we call it, Larry David has perfected it—and he's given it his own name. Larry David is so intimately associated with this character type that people are generally surprised to learn that the real Larry David isn't like that. At least not all of the time.

"Larry David" is today what "George Costanza" was, before the world knew much about Larry David. Which makes sense, of course, since George Costanza was by all accounts based in part on Larry David. Seeing the connection between George and Larry, however, doesn't simplify things at all—since it was just as surprising that people found George appealing as it is that they're attracted to Larry, and his often offensive words and deeds on *Curb*. George and Larry both are sometimes reprehensible human beings, nearly always inexplicably abrasive, petty, and defensive—especially when their actions are indefensible. People shouldn't like these guys. They shouldn't root for them, or take their side in an argument. But people do.

Larry David has said that the main difference between himself and his character on *Curb* is that the *real* Larry David thinks about but would never do the awful but hilarious things the *Curb*-Larry David does as a matter of course. And this was something of the relationship between the real Larry and the character of George on *Seinfeld*, as well. As Jerry Seinfeld notes,

> The connection between Larry and George is that Larry always wanted to do these crazy things to get back at people or to solve his problems or why would someone say that and what could I do about that. Even though he never did those things in life, his mind always ran along those lines. But in George, we had the perfect little voodoo doll that we could just stick a pin in him and make him do it.[1]

Just as George was an exaggerated version of a Larry David-type of character, *Curb*-Larry is sort of an exaggerated version of real Larry. Thus, real Larry can't always be identified with what *Curb*-Larry thinks, says, or does.

This is a distinction we didn't have to make with George Costanza, since George was just a character in *Seinfeld*, played by Jason Alexander. There is no "*real* George Costanza," and thus we're never tempted to ask, "Is George really like that?" But, as Deirdre Dolan writes in *Curb Your Enthusiasm: The Book*, "Bring up Larry David's name and the first thing everyone wants to know is: 'Is he really like that?' Does he really go through life picking fights with guys in wheelchairs, lesbian receptionists, his father-in-law?"[2]

---

[1] "Jason + Larry = George" (supplementary documentary). *Seinfeld: Season 5*. DVD. Columbia Tristar, 2005.

[2] Deirdre Dolan, *Curb Your Enthusiasm: The Book* (Gotham, 2006), p. 9.

Dolan responds that, in *Curb*, Larry shows us "a side of ourselves we've never seen reflected on television—the real side." And while there's some truth to that—on both *Seinfeld* and *Curb*, Larry David has depicted aspects of everyday life that had never been seen on television before—it's still the case that, when we watch *Curb*, we're watching Larry, not ourselves. We watch Larry, and we watch *because of* Larry, and so it matters quite a lot who Larry David—at least the character on *Curb Your Enthusiasm* named "Larry David"—is.

This Is George Costanza

In an interview recorded as a bonus feature for the DVD release of Season Seven of *Curb*, Jeff Garlin makes a familiar point: "one of the truths of *Seinfeld*, is that George was kind of based on a Larry character."[3] This is relatively common knowledge to fans of the show, but we see it corroborated by Kenny Kramer—Larry David's former neighbor in New York, and the inspiration for Michael Richards's character on *Seinfeld*—when he offers his thoughts on Larry: "We started hanging out, and we became very good friends. I think best friends. It's, you know, unlikely for us two guys to be such good friends because we're very different kinds of people. I'm an outgoing, fun-loving, ready-to-party kind of guy, and, you know, this is George Costanza."[4] I think we're used to hearing what Jeff Garlin says here, that George is based on Larry. But Kenny Kramer offers us something else, and something, I think, far more interesting: that Larry is himself (a version of) George.

George Costanza is, given the popularity of *Seinfeld* and Jason Alexander's pitch-perfect performance, an essential element of television history and American popular culture. There's no getting rid of George, whether you watched or liked *Seinfeld*—or you watch or like *Curb*—or not. From Art Vandelay, to the poisoned envelopes, to Festivus and its "Feats of Strength," George Costanza is here to stay. Which is part of why *Curb* has never been funnier (or more important) than

---

[3] "Larry David as George Costanza" (supplementary documentary). *Curb Your Enthusiasm: The Complete Seventh Season*. DVD. HBO, 2010.

[4] "How It Began" (supplementary documentary). *Seinfeld: Seasons 1 and 2*. DVD. Columbia Tristar, 2004.

when it has brought Larry into some sort of conflict with his *Seinfeld* alter ego or the actor who portrayed him, Jason Alexander. These scenes offer viewers a rare treat: to witness the full force of Larry's critical and antagonistic wit brought to bear against . . . itself. Or, at least, some version of itself. Larry versus Jason, Larry versus George, even George versus George: the ongoing feud and contentious never-quite-working relationship depicted between Larry David and Jason Alexander in the second and seventh seasons of *Curb* contribute not only comic fervor to the series, and bind the fictional *Curb*-Larry to the real Larry, but also raise important philosophical questions about the nature of identity and the relationship between reality and fiction.[5] There is no such person as George Costanza; he doesn't exist. And yet, watching some episodes of *Curb*, it seems like there are *two* George Costanzas—one named "Jason Alexander" and the other "Larry David."

One episode in particular, "The Car Salesman" (Season Two), brings this strange and fascinating triangle—Jason-George-Larry—to the fore. There, Larry discovers that the man from whom he's trying to buy a house is in fact Jason Alexander's new talent agent. The agent, Jay Schneider (played by Matt North), notes that Jason is having trouble finding work after *Seinfeld*. After learning that Jay represents Jason, Larry asks after his friend:

LARRY: How's he doing?

JAY: Honestly, he's kind of struggling right now.

CHERYL: Is that right?

JAY: Everybody wants George Costanza.

LARRY: You know what, he's nothing like George.

JAY: He's nothing at all like—he's the antithesis, 'cause Jason is brilliant, and George is an idiot, just an imbecile and, you know, it's just tough to branch out with that. I mean, the range of characters this guy can do.

[5] The relationship between reality and fiction is explored to some extent also by William Irwin in his "Jerry and Socrates: The Examined Life?" *Seinfeld and Philosophy: A Book about Everything and Nothing* (Open Court, 1999), pp. 3–5.

LARRY: (*Pause*) You think he's an idiot, huh? George?

JAY: It's the classic barnacle. But every sitcom needs that.

The humor in this brief scene lies in the fact that, although Jay's description of George is an accurate assessment of the *Seinfeld* character, Larry takes it as a personal critique. George isn't just another character to Larry; he's *Larry's* character, in both the sense that he is Larry's creation, as well as the sense that he stands in for Larry on *Seinfeld*. Larry is upset to hear George called an idiot, because Larry kind of confuses himself with George. For *Curb*-Larry, there is no meaningful difference between George Costanza and himself.

Hey, Costanza! Hey, Jackass!

The same point is made later in the same episode, when Larry sits down with Jason Alexander to discuss possibilities for working together again in the future.

LARRY: So, this is good, how's everything going?

JASON: Things are, you know, things are good. I don't know, I've got this set up, and did some directing and trying to produce some stuff. You know, the acting thing is, frankly, coming a little hard. I'd love to go back to TV, that seems good. But I can't shake this George thing.

LARRY: Really?

JASON: They all see me as George.

LARRY: I mean, the thing about it is that you're not even close to George. I tell this to people all the time: "You can't imagine what a great actor this guy is. He is nothing like that character."

JASON: Thank you.

LARRY: Nothing.

JASON: I know. I go in and talk to them and, you know, I try to present differently. But they see the idiot. They see the schmuck, so, I don't know.

LARRY: What do you mean "schmuck"? I don't get that. What do you mean "schmuck"?

Jason: The yutz, the idiot. You know.

Larry: No, frankly, I don't know. I don't know how you can say he's a schmuck, a yutz, and an idiot. I don't see him that way at all. I just see him as funny.

Jason: I mean, of course, it was funny. But he was the fall guy, the jackass role. You know, this is the guy that never got the girl and he finally gets the girl and he kills her with the envelope. Doesn't know what he wants.

Larry: That's funny, that's not schmucky. That's funny.

Jason: What is more jerky or putzy than going to a girl's house and stealing a tape out of her answering machine?

Larry: I stole—I went to a girl's house and took a tape out of an answering machine.

Jason: Larry, he's eating éclairs out of a garbage can?

Larry: Yeah, so what, I ate an éclair out of a garbage can!

Jason: And masturbation contests, four people agreeing—

Larry: I was in a contest and you know I was in that masturbation contest.

Jason: All right, fine, fine.

Larry: So, I'm a schmuck for being in a masturbation contest?

Jason: It's not an incredibly noble experiment, was it?

Larry: Well, I'm sorry that you hate the character so much.

Jason: I don't hate the character, I'm a little tired of it. I mean, I'm an actor. I have a range of characters that I can play. (*Frustrated à la George*) Why am I relegated to this? Everywhere I go on the street, "Hey, Costanza! Hey, jackass!"

Here, again, Larry's confusion about the difference between himself and George results in conflict with Jason, who has what seems to be the more levelheaded understanding of the character. And yet . . .

It remains true that the real Larry David did draw from his own real experiences in crafting many of George's stories on *Seinfeld*, including the ones Jason and Larry argue over in the scene in *Curb*. While Jason's right to call George a yutz, I think, George's yutziness is derived from Larry's yutzy actions—and Larry resents being called a yutz. "Hey, Costanza!" might as well call out Larry—"Hey, David! Hey, jackass!" This episode, "The Car Salesman," seems to solidify the fact that, if George is a jackass, *Curb*-Larry is a jackass. And, in getting into such violent arguments with Larry about George, Jason Alexander seems to have a bit of the jackass in him, too. They are, all three of them, jerky-putzy-schmucky-yutzy-idiotic jackasses, who can't get their identities straight. And *that's* funny.

The Glasses Are a Little Off

The confusion between George and Larry—at least, as it appears from Larry's perspective—continues in the Season Seven finale, "Seinfeld." There, Larry has decided that he might be able to win back the affections of his estranged wife, Cheryl, by writing a *Seinfeld* reunion show and casting her in it. This is the story arc for the whole season, culminating in the actual and fictional reunion of the cast of *Seinfeld* on *Curb*. Cheryl is cast to play George's ex-wife, Amanda, and as the filming of the reunion show progresses, Larry begins to worry that Cheryl and Jason Alexander are growing too close—that Jason will win Cheryl's love, undermining Larry's schemes. Finally confronting her, Larry bursts into Cheryl's dressing room—and Larry sees that Jason has jumped out of the window and is running away. Cheryl protests her innocence, but Larry doesn't buy it.

Larry: Something is going on, otherwise he wouldn't be running away.

Cheryl: Well, you're intimidating him.

Larry: Really?

Cheryl: Yeah, he's very sensitive, by the way.

Larry: Oh, is he?

Cheryl: Yes.

Larry: Jason's sensitive?

CHERYL: He's sensitive. He's funny. He's a little neurotic, so things like this can get under his skin.

LARRY: Are you kidding? That's George. That's not Jason.

CHERYL: That's Jason.

LARRY: That's George. That's all George. And that's me. I wrote that stuff. You're not attracted to him, you're attracted to me. I'm George.

Here, *Curb*-Larry agrees with Kramer (Kenny, not Cosmo): Larry David *is* George Costanza. But the George whom Larry claims to be is, in fact, not the same George fans of *Seinfeld* came to know so well. *Seinfeld*'s George was in fact petty and insensitive through and through, as was perhaps best demonstrated by his reaction to and behaviors in the aftermath of the death of his fiancée, Susan. *That* George, cheap-and-deadly envelope George, isn't "sensitive," or "funny," or "a little neurotic." Cheryl sees all of these qualities in Jason; Larry sees them, not in Jason, but in his own, somewhat self-serving picture of George—a picture in which he sees himself as the sensitive, funny, slightly neurotic fellow he imagines himself to be.

This other George—with whom Cheryl identifies Jason Alexander, and Larry identifies himself—is the George Larry defended earlier, in his Season Two argument with Jason. While everyone else seems to see in George only the idiot, and thus to identify something idiotic about Larry as represented in George, Larry sees in George only sensitivity and humor and neurosis—traits he sees in himself, and which he presumably tried to depict in the creation of George.

What's funny about all of this, of course, is that neither George nor *Curb*-Larry is sensitive, funny, and neurotic in the ways Larry describes. Larry's wrong about that. But Cheryl isn't right, either, since these same qualities are no more applicable to Jason Alexander as he appears on the show—"*Curb*-Jason"—than they are to George or to Larry. Cheryl is wrong about Jason; Larry is wrong about George; and Larry is wrong about himself. *Curb*-Larry, anyway.

Larry's molding of George into an ideal image of himself takes other forms in this episode, as well, however—subtler forms, really only observable to fans of the show familiar with

Larry's idiosyncrasies. To take just two examples, both from *Curb*-Jason's portrayal of George in the *Curb* episode, "Seinfeld": in one of their first scenes together as George and Amanda, Jason and Cheryl are approached by Larry, who wants to have a word with Cheryl. As Jason gets up to go, he offers Larry a compliment on the quality of the script: "It's really good. It's really good." He then moves to depart, noting, "I'm done. I'm gonna go talk to the prop guy. The glasses are a little off" (Season Seven, "Seinfeld").

This apparently unnecessary, throw-away line draws our attention to the glasses Jason has been wearing when playing George, however, and the fact that they are not the glasses—or anything like the glasses—Jason wore as George on *Seinfeld*. They are, in fact, copies (or near copies) of the unusual glasses Larry David wears, both in real life and on *Curb*—and, despite his intention to "talk to the prop guy," Jason wears them when playing George throughout the *Curb* episode. To be sure, this is a minor change from the original series, and not very much to hang an interpretation on. But for the loyal viewer of *Curb*, that the glasses are "a little off" highlights the fact that *Curb*-Jason's George is at least a little bit more like Larry than he used to be.

In a similar vein, later in the episode we see a scene from the fictional *Seinfeld* reunion in which George meets Amanda again (now played by the fictional actress, Virginia, who is played by the *real* actress, Elisabeth Shue) for the first time since their divorce. Seated in the old familiar booth at Monk's Diner, Jerry points out to George that Amanda has just walked in. George seems ambivalent about Amanda's presence, but is forced to talk to her when she approaches the booth.

AMANDA: George.

GEORGE: Hey.

AMANDA: How are you?

GEORGE: Pretty pretty pretty pretty pretty good. (Season Seven, "Seinfeld")

Casual viewers might miss it, but for the *Curb* fan, George's line here is the obvious incorporation of one of Larry's trademark bits on *Curb* into the universe of *Seinfeld*. It's not something George ever said on *Seinfeld*, and it's only something that it makes sense to the viewer for George to say after Larry has said it on *Curb Your Enthusiasm*. George is quoting Larry, but quoting *Curb*-Larry—which is, strictly speaking, impossible, since for the characters in *Seinfeld*, there is no such person as Larry David and no such television program as *Curb Your Enthusiasm*.

George's quotation of Larry, like the change in his eyewear, indicates not only a new closeness or confusion between Larry and George, but also a blurring of the lines between reality and fiction—or, at least, between two different, mutually exclusive fictions. The "*Curb* world" is a fictional world of Larry David's creation; within the fictional *Curb* world, however, Larry remains the co-creator of *Seinfeld*. As such, the "*Seinfeld* world" is a fictional world that exists as fiction within the *Curb* world. And yet, there is another "*Seinfeld* world," the *real* work of fiction that the *real* Larry David co-created with Jerry Seinfeld for NBC. *Seinfeld* is a work of fiction; *Curb* is a work of fiction; and the episode of *Seinfeld* that is presented within this episode of *Curb* is a work of fiction: a work of fiction within a work of fiction, the show within the show. But the show (the *Seinfeld* reunion) within the show ("Seinfeld," from Season Seven of *Curb*) is not the show (*Seinfeld*). This is obviously very confusing. But it's worth thinking about as well, and that's where a little philosophy can become useful to us as fans of *Curb*.

There's a Few Different Realities Here

Wayne Knight, the actor who played the character of Newman on *Seinfeld*, captures something of the complicated nature of the situation. Talking about the show-within-a-show aspect of the "Seinfeld" episode of *Curb*, Knight notes, "I think what's really different about this is that the levels of interaction, when you're doing a scene, and you're thrown back into sitcom world and doing a scene within a sitcom. And then Larry enters with the verisimilitude of the world of *Curb* that crosses paths with the world of *Seinfeld*, and that's never been really seen."

Picking up on the same theme, *Seinfeld* executive producer George Shapiro notes, "It's a show within a show, it blends back and forth, so it's amazing. Now I'm sitting in the same chair that you sit in during the readings, and then I don't know which show is on. Luckily, Jeff Garlin is sitting next to me—Jeff Greene, I don't know if it's Jeff Garlin or Jeff Greene. But then they say we're rolling and cut, I said, is that a real cut? What show are we on? Are we on *Seinfeld*? Are we still doing *Seinfeld*? Are we on *Curb*? So it's very crazy."

Perhaps Jerry Seinfeld—the *real* Jerry Seinfeld—puts it best when he notes, "there's a few different realities here."[6] It's this notion—of multiple realities at play in a work of fiction—that I find philosophically interesting. Shapiro's comment, that "it's very crazy," doesn't begin to sum up the difficulties inherent in trying to sort out where reality and the different fictions meet up.

The result, naturally, is a sort of confusion. In a group interview with Larry David and the *Seinfeld* cast, this confusion seems to have been prevalent even among the creators and performers of the show.

Larry David: It was very confusing. One side of the line I was on *Curb*, and on the other side of the line I was on *Seinfeld*.

Jason Alexander: It's *Curb*, it's *Seinfeld*, it's—we're playing Jason, and Julia, and Michael, but we're not, they're like sort of Larry's idea of them.

Michael Richards: I'm here as myself, but even that is heightened reality. It's a character on *Curb Your Enthusiasm* called Michael Richards. It's not really who I am.

Larry David: They're playing themselves the way I'm playing myself. Nobody's really playing themselves. They're called by their names, but—but, no, Jason Alexander is nothing like Jason Alexander.[7]

For Jason, Michael, Julia, and Jerry, there are three very distinct realities in which each is participating when filming the *Curb* episode, "Seinfeld."

---

[6] "The *Seinfeld* Reunion: It Could Only Happen on *Curb*" (supplementary documentary). *Curb Your Enthusiasm: The Complete Seventh Season*. DVD. HBO, 2010.

[7] "The *Seinfeld* Reunion: It Could Only Happen on *Curb*."

- ***Real* Reality**, wherein Jason, Michael, Julia, and Jerry are guest stars in the television series, *Curb Your Enthusiasm*, playing the roles of Jason, Michael, Julia, and Jerry. Each was also a regular cast member on the television series, *Seinfeld*, playing the roles of George, Kramer, Elaine, and Jerry, respectively;
- ***Curb* Reality**, wherein Jason, Michael, Julia, and Jerry were regular cast members on the television series *Seinfeld* (1989–1998), each of whom is resuming his or her role for a reunion episode in 2010; and
- ***Seinfeld* Reality**, wherein George, Kramer, Elaine, and Jerry are four friends sorting through the mundane and often ridiculous details of life in New York City, and have been doing so continuously since, it would seem, some unspecified time in the 1980s.

Each actor is confronted with the task of really performing two characters (their *Seinfeld* character, and their *Curb* character), sometimes simultaneously (in *Curb*'s "Seinfeld," Jason Alexander plays Jason Alexander playing George Costanza). While in each of these realities, Jerry is a comedian and comic writer named "Jerry Seinfeld," he is so differently in each reality (the fictional Jerry of *Seinfeld* Reality seems to have written only the pilot episode of the eponymous television series, *Jerry*, for example, whereas the real Jerry was a highly successful writer and producer of the 180 episodes of the eponymous television series, *Seinfeld*). As such, the situation for Jerry doesn't differ dramatically from the situations of Jason, Michael, and Julia.

John, Paul, George, and Larry

For Larry, however, the situation is somewhat different, since although Larry did perform in some *Seinfeld* episodes, none of his *Seinfeld* characters (the original Newman, Frank Costanza's lawyer, George Steinbrenner) reappears in the *Curb Seinfeld* reunion. Thus, Larry does not exist in *Seinfeld* Reality. For Larry, the different realities are:

- ***Real* Reality**, in which Larry David is the highly successful co-creator of the television series *Seinfeld*, and creator and star of the television series *Curb Your Enthusiasm*; and

- ***Curb* Reality**, in which Larry David is the highly successful co-creator of the television series *Seinfeld*, including a 2010 *Seinfeld* reunion episode.

This creates a kind of metaphysical conflict at the roots of the episode, "Seinfeld," since when George, Elaine, Kramer, and Jerry are, Larry is not; but where Larry is, Jason, Julia, Michael, and Jerry are, as well. While I don't mean to say that Jason, Julia, Michael, and Jerry are *more real* than Larry (*Curb* is, in some sense, all Larry and nothing but Larry), it is true that Jason/George, Julia/Elaine, Michael/Kramer, and Jerry/Jerry are real *in more ways* (in *Curb*) than Larry is. Which, as any fan of *Curb* might have been able to guess, is not something that would sit well with Larry.

This brief sketch of the different realities at work in *Curb*—two fictional, one really real—helps us to understand the significance of what is arguably the most brilliant moment in the "Seinfeld" episode. Larry, entirely dissatisfied with what he perceives as the growing intimacy between Jason and Cheryl, rewrites the ending of the reunion show to keep George and Amanda from getting back together. The rewrite compromises *Curb*-Jason's artistic integrity, and as Larry refuses to restore the original ending, Jason quits the show. This leaves *Seinfeld* Reality incomplete, as Jason plays George and, given Jason's departure in *Curb* Reality, George would become inexplicably absent in a way that threatens the very foundations of *Seinfeld*. Larry, however, seems ready with a solution—which, naturally, everyone else finds unsatisfactory.

MICHAEL: So, what are we doing?

JERRY: I don't know. We're not doing anything.

MICHAEL: Larry, what do you want to do?

LARRY: I'll play George.

JULIA: What?

LARRY: I'll play George. I'll play George.

JULIA: What?

LARRY: Yes, I can do it.

JERRY: You'll play what, George's butler? What do you mean?

LARRY: No, I will play George Costanza. I can do it. I know I can. I wrote it. The character is based on me. There were two Darrens on *Bewitched.*

JERRY: Nobody liked that second Darren. I didn't care for the second Darren.

LARRY: But you bought it.

JULIA: Oh my God.

JERRY: Do you understand what this is? It's iconic television here. The set's an icon. (*Indicating Michael*) He's an icon. (*Indicating Julia*) She's an icon. (*Pointing offstage in the direction of Jason's exit*) He was an icon. (*Indicating himself*) Icon. (*Indicating Larry*) No-con. There's no John, Paul, George and Larry. (Season Seven, "Seinfeld")

Despite their objections, however, in the next scene, Jerry and Julia (playing Jerry and Elaine) indulge Larry who, for a matter of a few minutes, plays George Costanza. In yet one more sense, Larry is George—but he is no "second Darren." This time around, no one is buying it. Larry quits the show (as the real Larry was wont to do in his *Seinfeld* days), Jerry restores the original ending, Jason returns to play George, and Larry's only further involvement is to watch the episode from the comfort of his own home when it airs.

In trying to play George, however, Larry makes an attempt to fill the void in *Seinfeld* Reality left by Jason's departure—and to do so in a way that, however little sense it makes in *Curb* Reality, makes perfect sense (perfect *comic* sense) for viewers in *Real* Reality. Larry's original absence from *Seinfeld* Reality—there is no Larry, and no character played by Larry, in the show—gives him the opportunity to replace Jason in *Seinfeld* Reality as George.

The situation is compounded by the fact that viewers of *Curb Your Enthusiasm* (like *Seinfeld* aficionados) know that Larry is the basis for the character of George. Reasonable people might be willing to accept that, on some important level, Larry is George Costanza. But Larry isn't Jason Alexander, and that's both Jerry's point and the problem with Larry's suggestion. In *Real* Reality, Larry David is a *Seinfeld* icon. But in *Seinfeld* Reality, Larry David is a no-con. And, as a no-con stepping into an iconic role, Larry can't help but disappoint viewers. Larry is not George.

Of course, Jason isn't George, either. Jason *plays* George. The comically frustrated triangle—Larry-George-Jason—remains intact, despite Larry's attempt to undermine it by replacing Jason. Without Jason, the *Seinfeld* Reality collapses—there's no *Seinfeld* without (Jason Alexander's) George Costanza—and Jerry, Julia, and Michael would be in the very same position Larry is in, existing in two realities (*Real* Reality and *Curb* Reality) instead of three. This wouldn't be so bad, and has been done before on *Curb*—both Jason Alexander and Julia Louis-Dreyfus appear as "themselves" in Season Two episodes—but without the *Seinfeld* Reality, Season Seven simply wouldn't be able to do what Season Seven actually does: produce a *Seinfeld* reunion show without producing a *Seinfeld* reunion show. It could set up that reunion, but it couldn't actually produce it. And that's an important difference.

Curb-Larry's suggestion that he play George threatens the structure of the plot arc of the entire season, which is ironic, given that *real* Larry is the author of that structure. And what it would mean for *Curb*-Larry actually to play George in the *Curb Seinfeld* reunion is an even bigger problem for everyone, as the real Jerry and Larry point out in an interview:

> **Jerry Seinfeld:** It's watching a plant grow, and then make a turn, and then go into the ground and start eating its own roots. And then you just see this loop, and go, what is that?
>
> **Larry David:** It was slightly unpleasant. ("A *Seinfeld* Moment on *Curb*")

Unpleasant is right. The pleasure we take in watching *Curb* is, at least in part, the pleasure we take in watching Larry try to do the things we never let ourselves do in real life—and then fail. The mysterious appeal of the "Larry David" character isn't simply the vicarious thrill of the voyeurism of watching someone play out our most curmudgeonly and anti-social fantasies.

Mixed in is also a fair bit of Schadenfreude. *Curb* helps us to take a little pleasure in the misfortunes of others—and, mostly, in the misfortunes of Larry David.

Just not the *real* Larry David.

It's Actually Happening

These distinctions—between the real Larry and the *Curb*-Larry, and between *Real* Reality, *Curb* Reality, and *Seinfeld* Reality—allow us to understand a variety of different things happening all at once in an episode of *Curb*, and especially in the episode, "Seinfeld." Larry David (*real* Larry) is playing with the relationships between reality and fiction, and between overlapping fictions—by situating a new episode of *Seinfeld* within a new episode of *Curb Your Enthusiasm*. Although the *Seinfeld* reunion is not a separately produced and independently aired television special or a new series finale, it's nevertheless a real (and the first) reunion of the *Seinfeld* characters and actors, on the real (although updated) *Seinfeld* sets, and it really was aired on television (on November 22nd, 2009, albeit on HBO rather than NBC).

Whatever else the episode is, it's a real *Seinfeld* reunion show. Just not the real *Seinfeld* reunion show inhabitants of *Curb* Reality take it to be. It's real for us—the really real viewers—in a different way than it is for the characters on *Curb*, and this difference in reality (which is also a difference in perspective) makes it possible for us to see how this episode's show-within-a-show *is* and *is not* the *Seinfeld* reunion, and in a more general way, how we can despise, care about, and laugh at Larry all at the same time—in fact, at the very same moment about the very same things.

A scene between Cheryl and Larry allows us to see all of these realities and differently real people, situations, and events operating at the same time. Larry sits down with Cheryl after she's just finished rehearsing a scene with Jason on the Monk's Diner set, and Cheryl expresses how impressed she is with Larry, seeing him in his element.

Cheryl: It's like you're the man, you know?

Larry: No big deal.

Cheryl: It's the *Seinfeld* reunion.

Larry: I know.

Cheryl: That's a big deal. It's actually happening. (Season Seven, "Seinfeld")

Cheryl's last line here—"It's actually happening"—can mean different and incommensurable things. Because, although in the context of the scene it seems that Cheryl is offering Larry a sort of compliment, her line also captures a reality beyond both *Seinfeld* and *Curb* Realities. *It's actually happening* not only for Cheryl David, but also for Cheryl Hines. The *Seinfeld* reunion show is actually happening for her—and for us—too.

Curb-Larry's intent throughout Season Seven—to use a fictional reality to have a definite impact on real reality (or what is for him "real reality," and is for us *Curb* Reality)—is precisely what the real Larry David does to us in *Real* Reality by crafting a plot arc of this complicated sort. This isn't exclusive to Season Seven—as we've seen, such reality blending occurs explicitly in *Curb Your Enthusiasm* as early as Season Two—and the layering of fictional realities over real reality is essential to the very premise of *Curb*. This layering, however, is more than an inventive and effective device for creating interesting television. *Curb Your Enthusiasm* offers viewers the opportunity to play with and in-between realities; it does this in no better or more sustained way than in the blurring of the triangle of significant (and related) personas: *Curb*-Larry David; George Costanza; and *Curb*-Jason Alexander—not to mention the *real* Larry and the *real* Jason.

With George as the hub around which Larry, *Curb*-Larry, *Curb*-Jason, and Jason spin, *Curb* forces the viewer into a kind of confusion of realities—a confusion we can only really resolve by reminding ourselves that this is all, in the end, a TV show. Something like what Larry does on/with *Curb* is only possible in fiction, but like all good fiction, it requires its audience to suspend disbelief for a while. We must believe in Larry despite the fact that we cannot believe in Larry. (Must believe . . . can't believe . . . must believe.) The only way to understand *Curb Your Enthusiasm* is to reaffirm the non-reality—the nothingness—of the character at its center, while simultaneously treating him as somehow real. We can adore and despise Larry

David at the same time because, for us as viewers of the show, Larry David both does and doesn't really exist. Larry David, it turns out, is nothing like Larry David. He is—and is not—himself.

II

What Would Larry Do?

3
Idling as a Way of Life

SIMON MUSSELL

Idleness . . . is a truly divine way of life so long as one is not bored

—SØREN KIERKEGAARD, *Either/Or*

Picture an all too familiar scene. You are at a party hosted by a friend, clasping a glass of wine in one hand, bite-sized treats in the other. Some dutifully inoffensive music plays in the background as the ebb and flow of predictable conversation between half-made acquaintances rumbles on. You're introduced to yet *another* fresh face, have to remember *another* forgettable name, and shake *another* new hand (perhaps wincing at the hygienic compromises presented by a recent "wet" sneeze, and we *have* to assume wet).

Still, things are looking up. This latest specimen is attractive, amiable and suitably "liquored up" to boot. Hopes for the impending interaction are higher than usual. But this sprig of optimism is promptly pissed on, as the predictable question prattles out of the merlot-tinged darkness of our new friend's mouth. "So, what do you do?" they ask, in the process retracing the pathways forged over centuries by generations of unimaginative party-poopers.

In servilely responding to them, we die a little inside. For no question so gravely smites the soul as this one. How quickly a seemingly innocent inquiry can dampen one's mood, turning potentially enlightening dialogue into just another rote chore. Why all the fuss about *"doing"*? Who decided that *work* is the most effective judge of a person's worth? Is that *really* the key to a meaningful existence? Surely there's more to life than mere doing, right?

Philosophers have traditionally spent a lot of time thinking about such questions. From the ancients to the moderns, *The Iliad* to iPad, people over the ages have been interested in understanding what exactly constitutes the "good life." What is it that makes life worth living? And what makes a life go well? Is it money? Is it fame? Is it pleasure? Today it's generally accepted that visions of the good life differ from person to person. But if we're searching for contemporary examples of a less fettered existence, one that recoils at the horror of stolen time, then we could do worse than look to Larry David in *Curb Your Enthusiasm*. Larry's is a life of active idling. He seldom "works" in the traditional sense of the term, but at the same time he's hardly bored or passive. Larry is always involved in *something*.

This is more admirable than it might seem. Tired from the relentless demands of having to do something measurably productive at all times (and the guilt born of not meeting these unfeasible demands), I want to, with a little help from LD, defend an idle ideology. So, please, throw that BlackBerry into the ocean, leave the Prius in the driveway, ignore all home phone calls (don't even wait for the "cut off"), put your feet up on the coffee table, and join me as I try to bring some chaos into the overly orderly world of work.

No Way Out!

Why is it that we appear to be so obsessed with what a person does? When did this become such a big deal and so pivotal for all subsequent icebreaking? The German sociologist Max Weber (1864–1920) had a pretty good idea of where our occupation preoccupation originated. In his book *The Protestant Ethic and the Spirit of Capitalism*, Weber studied the rise of the Protestant work ethic in the Western world and argued that it was conducive to the emerging capitalistic societies, most notably in the United States.

A central tenet of some forms of Protestantism (Calvinism in particular) is the doctrine of *predestination*. All human beings are sinful and irredeemably flawed, so the story goes, yet God, nice guy that He is, has mercifully decided to save a few of us from damnation. The problem is that either you're one of the chosen few or you're not, and that's that. Your fate is predetermined by God and is unchangeable.

In a similar situation, you might think "Great! I'll take some of those memorial flowers for myself, I'll illegally drive in the carpool lane, I'll let the masseuse carry on with that unconventional yet satisfying technique, I'll do whatever I want since nothing can change what will happen to my eternal soul anyway." But the American citizens at the time reacted far more prudishly and industriously.

The Puritan notion of a "calling" grew in importance and people began to work harder and longer than ever before, tirelessly pushing their bodies past the usual limits, in the hope that sheer diligence and dedication would prove their status as one of God's elect. The Catholic monastic ideal of transcending the humdrum affairs of everyday life came to be replaced by this idea of finding and excelling in one's calling, whatever it might be (shrewd acupuncturist, dog-eating bookmaker, adulterous dry cleaner, snarky shop assistant, uppity waiter, you name it). This brought religious belief and values out of the home and church, and into the workplace.

These days most of the spiritual and religious underpinnings of Protestantism have lost their influence. Yet, the work ethic mysteriously haunts us like an undetectable, persistent and annoying house sound. In Max Weber's words, "the idea of duty in one's calling prowls about in our lives like the ghost of dead religious beliefs."[1] Despite our best efforts we just can't escape it. Our society is an "iron cage," brutally rational, cold and irresistible. The Protestant ethic popped in and simply won't pop out.

You want to prove that you're somebody, that you're one of the few to enjoy future salvation? Then you better pipe down, get to work, earn your corn and show your worth. This is the underlying sentiment of the work ethic and it doesn't just impose itself on those who have to toil in order to survive, or those who conveniently head to the restroom when the check arrives. It affects *everyone,* evidently even the "follicly challenged" co-creator of *Seinfeld*.

---

[1] *The Protestant Ethic and the Spirit of Capitalism* (Routledge, 1992), p. 124.

Let's consider an episode of *Curb* in which both Cheryl and Jeff chastise Larry for not working. Leaving aside the fact that Larry quite clearly is under no financial or contractual compulsion to work, there are deeper philosophical justifications for his more workshy hesitations. We will come to some of these reasons shortly. But first recall a few of the conversations in *Curb* that openly perpetuate the engrained work ethic.

> **Cheryl:** Have you just retired, and this is what you're going to do for the rest of your life? And you're never going to work again?
>
> **Larry:** Of course I'm gonna work again.
>
> **Cheryl:** When?!
>
> **Larry:** I'm going to work . . . when something comes up that I want to do. (Season Two, Episode 1, "The Car Salesman")

Later on, when meeting with Jeff for lunch, Larry says he does not want to go back into television now, since it's, "too much work." Jeff responds with incredulity and hastily reiterates the nonsensical work ethic that Americans have long since absorbed into their collective psyche. "Too much work?" he protests. "You *have* to work. You need to work." Further into the scene, Jeff changes tack slightly, now implying that if Larry continues to refrain from working he will probably go crazy.

> **Jeff:** You need to start writing, if only for your own good, your own sanity.
>
> **Larry:** Why? I'm not insane. You think I'm insane?

Cheryl also suspects that Larry's mental capacities might be under attack when she discovers he has agreed to sell cars for a while as a harmless fulfilment of a childhood fantasy.

> **Larry:** I got a job.
>
> **Cheryl:** [*with glee*] You did? Well, that's good. Did you call Jason [Alexander]?
>
> **Larry:** [*pauses*] I'm selling cars.

Cheryl: [*with disbelief*] What? . . . What is wrong with you?! You've committed to this?

Larry: Yeah. It's only for, like, a couple of days, or however long I want to do it . . .

Cheryl: This is so stupid.

Larry: Why is it stupid?

Cheryl: It's insane!

Larry: Hey, some people run in marathons, they wanna see if they can do that. Other people . . . swim the English Channel. All I wanna do is work in a showroom for a little while, so what's the big deal? Who's more insane? (Season Two, "The Car Salesman")

When Richard Lewis ("Himmler's ghost" himself) turns up at the dealership to see for himself that, sure enough, Larry is selling cars, his reaction suggests some sort of heinous deviance from normality on LD's part.

Richard: This is a practical joke, right? . . . What are you, *fucking Willy Loman?* . . . And I thought I had dark secrets, what the hell is this all about?

Larry: It's not a "dark secret."

Richard: Larry David selling cars is not a "dark secret"? (Season Two, "The Car Salesman")

As so often happens throughout *Curb,* Larry finds himself in a minority. Once again he's an outcast, a bum, a social deviant, or, as Susie Greene would say, a "sick, four-eyed, pervert fuck" who apparently risks his sanity, wellbeing and social status. And why? Because he suspects that the idea of incessant and unnecessary labor is not all it's cracked up to be.

I Took a Risk

I think we should come to Larry's defense and compare the pains of forced work with the joys of spontaneous idling. But this takes some doing because the everyday understanding of idleness is almost exclusively pejorative. It's most often associated with laziness, inactivity, slovenliness and a general lack of ambition or get-up-and-go. The idle person, it is claimed, is content to stay in bed all day and exert as little physical and mental energy as possible. This idle life apparently leads to squalor, dependency, moral malfunction and unhappiness.

Benjamin Franklin said, "It is the working man who is the happy man. It is the idle man who is the miserable man." But this common conception of idleness is narrow and misguided. It refers to a wholly *passive* and lazy state of being, whereas in the guise of Larry David we see that idling can be a more *active* pursuit that just happens to follow a different value system.

In his alternative perspective on working and idling, Larry is touching on some fundamental questions concerning the purpose of life. And to this end he is in good company. The British philosopher Bertrand Russell (1872–1970) wrote an essay entitled *In Praise of Idleness*, in which he complains that "immense harm is caused by the belief that work is virtuous."[2] That slaving away in some job, *any* job, in a compliant and stoical manner is somehow an indicator of one's moral worth is an idea that has traditionally been used to prop up existing power structures. The myth of the inherent nobility of work lingers on and makes a suspect of anyone who dares deviate from the norm.

Russell, like Larry, if not an inventor was certainly an "improver." The philosopher cast his critical eye over the society of his day and sought to break it down and rectify it. Russell witnessed the rising "cult of efficiency" and the idiocy of overworking, and argued that "the road to happiness and prosperity lies in an organized diminution of work" (p. 12). There is no reason to fear idleness and greater freedom from work. In fact, historically leisure has been "essential to civilization" (p. 15). Many of humanity's most noble achievements are born of idle thoughts and uncoerced work. No doubt there will be the classic kneejerk response from the Cheryls and Jeffs of the world who think we would all be at a loose end were we to work only a few hours per day. But this sort of argument stands as an indictment of our limited culture and imagination.

Larry's imagination, on the contrary, is profusely fertile. With it he can comfortably fill his days with a whole host of idle

---

[2] Allen and Unwin, 1935, p. 9.

activities. Whether it's popping bubble-wrap, trying to learn a card trick from a young "magician," having leisurely lunches with friends (Jeff, Jerry Seinfeld, Richard Lewis, Steve the gay choreographer, Rosie O'Donnell) or strangers (charity car wash vendors, Haboos the hospitable Muslim, the competition winner), bowling with Ted and Mary, going to the *Playboy* mansion, visiting the cinema, playing poker, bingo, the Newlyweds game and golf, singing in the car ("Hey, Officer Krupke, krup you!"), helping a very "particular" blind man move into his new home, playing dolls with Sammy, enjoying some "vanilla bullshit latte cappa thing," and so the list goes on.

The one thing we hardly ever see Larry do is *working*. Even when we do, it is through free choice. The car salesman experiment, the performance in the Martin Scorsese film, the writing of the *Seinfeld* reunion and the role of Max Bialystock in *The Producers* are all freely undertaken. Larry works on things that chime with his unique talents, instincts, desires, abilities, and values. This is an ideal towards which we can all aspire. We'd certainly be much the happier and fulfilled for it. The decoupling of life and work is demonstrably detrimental to the hopes of enjoying our brief time on this Earth. Bringing working and living into harmony once again is a high ideal. But just redressing the balance between work and life would be a start.

The Whole Cashew-Raisin Balance Is Askew

In *Curb Your Enthusiasm: The Book*, Larry David describes the sheer stupidity of waiting in line at a restaurant. "It makes you realize the importance you're placing on what you're waiting for. And in the case of a restaurant, you sort of feel like an idiot" (p. 35). This is also true of life in general. As we count down the hours until the weekend—that supposed oasis of liberation from work—life's significance dawns on us.

When we're compelled to work at things not of our own choosing, resentment and anticipation well up inside us. There's a real sense of injustice about it, like we're being robbed of our precious time. Larry knows and appreciates the incalculable value of time and it is no doubt this deeper understanding that feeds his desire for idleness. Recall his reaction upon hearing from Auntie Rae about another robbery in the local area. Larry's concerns are not so much with the criminals, but rather with time-hogging neighbors:

> **AUNTIE RAE:** There's been another robbery in this neighborhood. I was just talking to the neighbors, it's the third one this month.
>
> **LARRY:** What are you talking to the neighbors for?
>
> **AUNTIE RAE:** They came over and let me know what's going on, Larry.
>
> **LARRY:** You don't need to talk to the neighbors, okay?
>
> **AUNTIE RAE:** Yeah, but Larry, there's been a *robbery* . . .
>
> **LARRY:** I'd rather have the thieves than the neighbors. Thieves don't impose . . . The neighbors want your time. The thieves want your things. I'd rather give them things than time. (Season Seven, "Funkhouser's Crazy Sister")

Our awareness of time's inexorable flow, and our grim terminus as mere mortal beings, is heightened when we're engaged in activities we would rather avoid. True, time does fly when you're having fun, but who cares so long as you're having fun? I'll take an enjoyable life that seemingly flies by over one that's protracted and joyless any day. It's like the classic Woody Allen joke about the two old Jewish women in conversation at a restaurant, where the first woman notes how terrible the food is, before the second adds, "I know . . . and such small portions."

To change our outlook on life often requires an incentive and they surely don't come much stronger than realizing one's impending ending. This awareness need not spring from some dramatic near-death experience, like nearly drowning in the ocean, being thrown over a balcony by a disturbed former *Looney Tunes* employee, or being bitten in the privates by an aggressive German Shepherd. As human beings, knowledge of our unavoidable demise should force us to reprioritize. For instance, most of us already spend around a third of our life just *sleeping*. Do we *really* want to give up another huge portion of it to overworking? As Lin Yutang (1895–1976) wrote, "If this earthly existence is all we have, we must try the harder to enjoy it while it lasts."[3] Time truly *is* of the essence, and control

---

[3] *The Importance of Living* (Heinemann, 1938), p. 161.

over as much as possible needs to be given back to us. The problem today is that our so-called "free time" is simply not *free enough.*

Leisure time is contaminated by its latent connection to work. Think of work and leisure as raisins and cashews. Suppose that, like Jeff and Larry, we *love* cashews but we're not so crazy about raisins. When cashews are all that we really want, we can accept a *few* raisins here and there provided they don't hinder our cashew experience. But getting the balance right and staying below the raisin threshold is like walking a tightrope. Too many raisins will actually sully our enjoyment of the cashews. What happens when the whole raisin-cashew ratio is askew, when the raisins start to become the prime ingredient in our lives, banishing the cashew to obscurity? *Such small portions!*

Once we've reached such a topsy-turvy situation in which the raisins are eradicating our most treasured cashews, we need to take a step back from our everyday routines. We must reflect on the point of life and realize that, ultimately, it's not about toil and struggle. It's about maximizing idleness, fun, and the joys of spontaneous human flourishing.

Sure, there'll be some smartasses who'll say, "Hey, quit your whining. Thanks to the advances of capitalism and technology over the past century, our lives have gotten so much easier!" But think about what we're actually comparing here. It's true that living and working conditions in previous times were terrible, and, yes, our lives are undeniably better by comparison. But, as Larry knows only too well, *"better"* doesn't mean *"good"!* Of course our lives will come off pretty well so long as we're thumbing through a book of freaks.

So let's not get complacent now that we're surrounded by such wonders of invention as high-powered hand dryers, vacuum packaging, orthotics, hybrid cars, smoke alarms, Joe Pepitone jerseys, cell phones and the like. Work still gets in the way of living, perhaps even more so than ever before. We need to follow Larry's lead and take a more leisurely approach to life, making sure to put enjoyment above the dictates of the work ethic. Life's *too* short to work *that* hard.

In fact, let's take a closer look at Larry's life. There are two great forms of idling in which he often indulges throughout *Curb.*

Idle Pleasure No. 1: Talking the Talk

We've been quite negative so far, criticizing the notion of work that's not freely chosen. But let's look at the flipside now and say something positive for idling, taking some concrete examples from *Curb Your Enthusiasm.*

Walking and talking leap out as two major themes in the show. Both of these activities when undertaken properly lend themselves to an idle life. Let's start with talking. Despite complaints from his father that he has too little "respect for speech" (Season Five, Episode 1, "The Larry David Sandwich"), Larry's way with words is exemplary. There's an unwavering attentiveness and subtlety in the way he converses with and listens to other characters. Even during the many peaks of contestation in *Curb,* Larry remains as involved as ever, hanging on the other person's every word, giving the time and effort needed to satisfy the demands of dialogue.

As well as the more rigorous requirements of genuine dialogue, there are also the more joyous elements of spontaneous conversation. Larry clearly has a musical ear as he's quick to pick up on catchy phrases like "pity points," "fanfare," "porn party," "surrogate etiquette," "omission-commission," and suchlike. When Krazee-Eyez Killa runs some lyrics by him, Larry listens very closely and at the end gives constructive feedback on the potential overuse of the word "fuck." He suggests maybe substituting "bitch" for the final "motherfucker" (Season Three, Episode 8, "Krazee-Eyez Killa").

This attention to detail is only really made possible by a *leisurely* pace of interaction. Once the "time is money" brigade has imposed its will upon us, all conversation gets reduced to pure means of efficiency. Talking becomes thoroughly standardized and streamlined. So-called "small talk" is barely more than an empty gesture, a perfunctory preamble to the more pressing task of "getting down to business." As Theodor Adorno (1903–1969) lamented, "In the form of the few sentences about the health of one's wife that prelude the business discussion over lunch, the utilitarian order has taken over and assimilated even its opposite."[4] Clearly, this state of affairs is neither ideal nor idle.

---

[4] Theodor Adorno, *Minima Moralia* (Verso, 2005), p. 41.

According to the Socratic Method in ancient philosophy, a laid back but nonetheless thoughtful dialogue is extremely effective in illuminating ideas and improving understanding. Each character in a dialogue speaks in turn, usually offering opposing or clarifying questions, in order to approach the truth of the matter. It is seen as an engaged, virtuous and communal activity. But, as anyone who's had a meaningful conversation (or dabbled in philosophy) will know, these things take time. They're not the sort of things that can be rushed. If this is the case, what point is there entering a dialogue if we know beforehand that the topic can't be properly explored? We need to be able to follow a conversation "to its completion." This is surely why Larry abhors the dreaded "stop and chat." In "The Massage" episode, he and Jeff pass a man, Rick Crane, who gleefully greets Larry and slows his gait as if to stop. Larry minimally acknowledges him and keeps walking. Jeff is confused and questions Larry's apparently antisocial act.

JEFF: Why didn't you say hello to him?

LARRY: He wanted to do a stop and chat, I didn't wanna do a stop and chat.

JEFF: "Stop and chat"? Where do you come up with these things? "Stop and chat."

LARRY: I don't know him well enough for a stop and chat.

JEFF: Just a "Hey, how are you, nice seeing you too, take care."

LARRY: No, it's more than that. For him, all I need to do is just say hello and move on.

JEFF: You know, that was kinda rude. (Season Two, Episode 10, "The Massage")

Defiant perhaps, but rude? Hardly. Larry is just expressing his disdain for enforced conversation (which isn't really conversation at all). The stop and chat, the unexpected interruption, has to be one of the least appropriate settings for a meaningful conversation, save perhaps a doctor's waiting room, karaoke bar, or mid-coitus. For what can really be communicated or shared within such a short space of time? Two people, each going in opposite directions, are suddenly thrown into a position where they must perform some ritualized exchange of outworn platitudes before they can continue with their day. It's a whole to-do!

If both parties were idle and had the requisite time and interest, then maybe it'd be worth stopping and chatting. But genuine discussion requires patience, time, openness, thought, and development. It's not helped by incessant clockwatching or hastiness. Lin Yutang claims that "conversation only exists in a society of men imbued in the spirit of leisure, with its ease, its humour, and its appreciation of light nuances. For there is an evident distinction between mere talking and conversation as such" (*The Importance of Living*, p. 217). Larry knows how to talk the talk and expects other people to as well. If we don't give enough respect to the demands of genuine dialogue, then we should probably keep our traps shut and keep walking. Which brings us to the second idle pursuit.

Idle Pleasure No. 2: Walking the Walk

One of the most rewarding forms of idling is the humble walk. Whether done alone or in the company of others, walking is a timeless pursuit that seems to stubbornly spit in the face of the insistent speed of modern life. Like the dedicated conversationalist, she who walks is in no rush. The idle stroller is observant, open, attentive, and reflexive. Through his ambulation in *Curb,* Larry clocks up some serious mileage and has numerous encounters along the way. He travels from place to place, conversing with a Funkhouser here, avoiding a house tour there, retrieving his dry cleaning one moment, sipping a coffee the next.

Larry being Larry, his more pedestrian adventures are not always plain sailing. Sometimes, even when pacing the pavement, he gets into conflicts. But in general while walking Larry appears far more relaxed than when he's driving or flying. No cries of "schmohawk!" from Larry the pedestrian. No run-ins with bitchy cabin crew when you opt for the autonomy of the sidewalk. Also, when confrontations do flare up on the street, Larry's recovery time seems a lot quicker than usual. Walking dissipates anger and annoyance far better than driving. The amble may be the oldest and one of the slowest forms of transportation but it's still surely the most satisfying.

Friedrich Nietzsche argued that music should be composed along the rhythmic elements present in the act of walking. This suggestion is put into practice in the majority of the *Curb* soundtrack. The natural left-right propulsion of Larry's gait is nearly always accompanied by uplifting and similarly forward-moving music. The tuba in Gilbert and Sullivan's "Three Little Maids from School Are We," Luciano Michelini's "Frolic," and Franco Micalizzi's "Amusement" is like a character in itself, as its notes aptly mirror and narrate Larry's locomotion.

The comfortable and comforting pace of a good stroll is suitable to an idle life. Walking can affect a change in perspective, provoking a more philosophical and discerning outlook. Never mind the stop and chat, let's walk and think! Our friend Lin Yutang points out the "philosophic contradiction between being busy and being wise." "Those who are wise won't be busy, and those who are too busy can't be wise" (p. 155). Just as the art of true conversation withers without proper appreciation and time, so the ancient art of ambling today lies in danger of being flooded by the tsunami of meetings, appointments, deadlines, timetables, get-togethers, and all the other time-taking terrors of toil.

The greatest philosophical walker was probably Aristotle (384–322 B.C.) who, as legend has it, would philosophize while walking through the Lyceum, the school that he founded after studying for twenty years at Plato's Academy. This was referred to as the "peripatetic method" of teaching. It even inspired the name for a whole movement known simply as the Peripatetic School, which comprised Aristotle's followers. Over two thousand years later, the German philosopher Walter Benjamin (1892–1940) wrote of the *flâneur* (literally: "stroller" or "idler" in French). The flâneur walks for pleasure, full of curiosity, vicariously experiencing the world through the sensorial flood of people, signs, sounds, smells, window displays, shops and cafés.

Flânerie flourished in the Parisian shopping arcades of the nineteenth century. It was a form of active idleness against the demands of work. The flâneur enjoyed a different pace of life, a walking pace. While wandering through one's environment, taking it in at close hand with an eye for every detail, thoughts begin to flow, problems seem to resolve themselves. Phrases pop into our heads. Objects and occurrences spark off endless connections in our mind. We feel a part of something larger than ourselves, even if we might be walking entirely on our own. Walking is a creative and productive activity, even (or *especially*) in its very idleness.

An idea not won by walking isn't worth much. That's what Nietzsche said. Perhaps this explains why Larry (like the flâneur) always carries around with him a trusty notebook to record his observations, musings, and storylines. Note how freaked out he gets when the notebook seems either lost or stolen (Season One, Episode 6, "The Wire").

The ideas that come up while walking cannot be preplanned, recreated, or forced. They are the result of a spontaneous confluence of circumstances. Not everything can be tightly controlled, micro-managed, neatly slotted into a convenient "window" in our overstuffed schedules. We must be able to go with the flow of life in order to fully experience it, reflect on it, appreciate it, and enjoy it. This demands an idle disposition and far more free time than is allowed by our saddling work ethic.

"Besides the noble art of getting things done, there is a nobler art of leaving things undone," said Lin Yutang (p. 167). Larry is the idle idol since he willfully leaves things undone. Not everything, but just the unnecessary bits. He does enough and no more because, simply put, life's too short to be wasted waiting in line.[5]

[5] With thanks to my fellow Davidians, Norah Mikhnevic, Sean Carroll, Nick Goulds, Guy Reder, Doug Haynes, and Chris O'Kane, all of whose humorous attentiveness and passionate idleness almost rival that of Larry.

4
People Just Don't Do That

DAVID SVOLBA and CHAD FLANDERS

It's the quintessential *Curb* moment: Larry is waiting in a doctor's examination room, and—mostly from boredom—he uses the doctor's phone to make a local phone call to Jeff, his best friend and agent. When the doctor at long last arrives, he asks Larry, "Did you use that phone?" Larry replies that, yes, he did—and what's wrong with that? The doctor's reply is a variation on the age-old appeal to rules of common sense and good manners: people don't use the phone in the examination room. *They just don't do that sort of thing; it's just not done.*

Curb Your Enthusiasm is an extended and many times uncomfortable meditation on the value of such rules as "Don't use the phone in the doctor's office." We'll call these "rules of civility." These are the rules that specify how we should and should not behave in certain social situations—weddings, funerals, parties, churches and synagogues, restaurants and theaters, doctor's offices, and so forth. They are also the rules that Larry routinely violates, usually with hilarious effects.

But more than simply making us laugh, *Curb* is *provocative* comedy, inviting us to ask: Why shouldn't we do those types of things that people just don't do? What gives rules of civility their alleged *authority*? Larry stands in a long line of philosophers—we could even say it starts with that gadfly, Socrates himself—who question the reasons why we shouldn't do what "people just don't do." And in Larry's defense, it can be hard to see why not doing what people "just don't do" is a virtue at all. When Larry uses the doctor's phone he doesn't *harm* anyone and nor does he treat anyone *unfairly*. So what's the problem?

When we look closely at rules of civility and ask about their justification, Larry appears to have a good point. Why should we go along with what everybody does, when what everybody does doesn't seem to serve any real purpose? What's the big deal with civility?

HBO's ad campaign for *Curb* once asked us to admit that we were all a little like Larry David. And of course we are, because at various points in our lives, we see the absurdity of social conventions like the ones Larry repeatedly transgresses. We get annoyed, like Larry, with having to be civil, when civility seems to have no point. It's strangely satisfying to see Larry call out and challenge these conventional rules, even if we choose to stifle our annoyance and follow them. So is it time to follow Larry's lead and shrug off the burden of rules of civility?

We don't think so. This chapter explains how *Curb*, despite the skeptical and relentless questioning of the value of civility by the show's protagonist, ultimately falls on the side of that value. Even though we often think and feel like Larry, in bristling at conventional social rules, we at the same time *aren't really like Larry at all*. We follow these rules not because we lack the guts to do otherwise, but because it really is important, most of the time, to not do the types of things that people just don't do.

A Show about What?

When friends who haven't seen *Curb* (hard to believe we have any such friends, really) ask us what the show's about, we say it's about the meaning and value of civility. "About *what*?" they typically ask, at which point we like to engage in some (usually animated) storytelling.

Take the episode where Jeff informs Larry that he's hurt by the fact that Larry didn't congratulate him on his purchase of a restored '57 Chevy ("AAMCO," Season One). "It's a car," Larry explains. "I didn't know I was supposed to congratulate you on buying a new car." Jeff responds, with total sincerity: "Yes, Larry. You were." Larry's bafflement (which seems sincere) shows that he didn't really know there was a norm of civility in play in that situation.

In that same episode Larry faults someone else for violating a norm of civility. Larry's annoyed that a dinner guest would presume to sit at the head of *his* table. But clearly, his guest didn't think that civility required that he *not* sit in that seat, especially given Larry's suggestion that guests sit anywhere they like. In both instances—Jeff and the car, Larry and the dinner guest—at least one person wonders *what* the right rule of civility is, or whether there even is a rule. This is a recurring theme in *Curb*: confusion among the characters about what it means to be civil.

Another recurring theme involves disputes in which the rules of civility are clear and the issue is about the importance of following them. These scenes make up some of the most memorable episodes of *Curb*, and, in their way, some of the most philosophically deep. Recall for example the fantastic episode in which Larry gets into an argument with Ben Stiller at Ben's birthday party about whether it's wrong of Larry to not sing "Happy Birthday." Everyone, including Larry, knows that party guests are *supposed* to sing "Happy Birthday," but what if, like Larry, one just really hates that song? Why should Larry go along with what everybody else is doing, and why should a grown man care if another grown man sings "Happy Birthday" to him?

So *Curb* raises two distinct questions about rules of civility. First, given some social situation, what (if anything) does civility require? Second, supposing we know what civility requires, why should we care? What's so important, at the end of the day, about being civil—or even just pretending to be civil—towards each other? *Curb* often shows how funny it can be when people sincerely disagree about the meaning and value of civility. It turns out that people tend to become pretty uncivil when disagreeing about civility! This is the central irony and comedic core of *Curb*. So that's what we mean when we say that *Curb* is a show about the meaning and value of civility. It's all about the conflicts, arguments, and tensions that inevitably occur when people disagree about the meaning and value of civility. It makes for great comedy—and great philosophy.

Civility *à la* Larry David

Is Larry David a civil person? Yes and no. Sometimes—well, sort of. The truth is that it's complicated.

On the one hand, it's undeniable that Larry very often violates rules of civility. There's no doubt that he can be outrageously uncivil. Whether he's being obtuse, as when he compliments a man at a pool party on his young son's massive erection, or for more deliberate or *principled* reasons, as when he stubbornly refuses to thank a woman for buying him dinner on the grounds that her husband paid for it, Larry is often shown behaving badly in social situations. He is very often doing what is just not done.

On the other hand, we shouldn't conclude from Larry's frequently uncivil behavior that he is altogether indifferent or hostile towards rules of civility. For as much as we see Larry running afoul of rules of civility we also, perhaps just as often, find him stridently *enforcing* some of these rules. Larry has strong opinions of his own about what's done and what's not done—he recognizes at least some rules of civility. And apparently he takes these rules very seriously—witness his frequent invectives against strangers who "misuse" their horns in traffic or talk in a movie theater. So Larry's just as likely to be the source as he is the target of accusations of incivility.

What explains Larry's selective adherence to rules of civility? Why do some of these rules strike Larry as valid and worthy of compliance while others strike Larry as unreasonable rules that he needn't comply with? The answer is not merely, as we might be tempted to suggest, that Larry is only aggravated by uncivil behavior when it adversely affects him. This would simply be to paint Larry as a selfish lout. And although there is certainly some truth to this, it's far from the whole story.

If Larry were simply selfish, we should expect to see him doing things that he criticizes others for doing, so long as they benefited *him*. But this is not the case. We could catalogue Larry's outrageous behavior throughout *Curb*, but still not find one instance of Larry talking in a movie theater or laying on his car horn. For if Larry thinks that something is "just not done" then it's not done by him, either. In this respect Larry holds himself to the same standards he holds others to, which is just to say his commitment to those rules of civility he accepts is not rooted in his own self-interest. It has to be deeper than that.

Here's the start of a more promising explanation of Larry's ambiguous relationship to rules of civility. For Larry, a rule of civility is valid only if it forbids a kind of behavior that he himself would criticize or resent. Basically, Larry's litmus test for valid rules of civility looks to be something like the "Golden Rule": if doing X would upset Larry, then he takes care not to do X himself. It's Larry's observance of the Golden Rule which explains why he sees nothing wrong with refusing to sing "Happy Birthday" at a birthday party but considers talking in a movie theater beyond the pale. Larry couldn't care less if others serenade *him* with a children's song (so why should anyone else?) but he would prefer not to hear someone else talking while trying to watch a movie in a public theater. This still is a little selfish on Larry's part—Larry's own likes and dislikes are still treated as the ultimate arbiter of civil and uncivil behavior—but it's at least a consistent selfishness!

Rather than characterizing Larry as a completely uncivil person it's more accurate to say that Larry follows his own "personal" code of civility. And, to be sure, sometimes Larry's personal code of civility leads him to do what really is civil; that is, his behavior matches up with conventional understandings of what it means to be polite and respectful of others. Other times, Larry's code of civility seems quite idiosyncratic, and sharply at odds with conventional rules. So the somewhat surprising truth is that Larry's a hard case. Is he, or is he not, a civil person?

There are two strikes against Larry. The first strike goes to Larry's motivations for being civil. If Larry's only being civil when and because it happens that some ways of being civil (not talking in theaters, for example) match up with his likes and dislikes, we might wonder whether he has the right *motivation* when it comes to being civil. Doesn't being civil mean being civil because you think you *ought* to be civil, and not just because you happen to *want* to? Wouldn't a truly civil person not just act in a civil way, but act civilly for the right reasons?

Actually, this is a really tough question to answer. To be sure, sometimes we want people not just to act the right way, but to do it for the right reasons. Motivation often matters. So when Larry apologizes for making a stray Hitler reference, we don't want him merely to say he's sorry, but actually to *feel* sorry. Otherwise, we might worry that his apology wasn't really an apology at all. But civility seems to work differently.

Civility is for the most part about keeping up appearances: about doing what other people expect you to do, both when you want to do that and when you don't. It's not about doing things for the right reasons. In this way, civility is a lot like acting—think of Larry playing Max Bialystock. Do we care about Larry's motivations for playing the character? Not really. We care more about whether it's a good *performance* (except for Mel Brooks, who wants it to be a bad one!) In a similar way, civility is mostly about *acting*, not about *being*. A lot of politeness involves just sucking it up.

Suppose that Larry begrudgingly goes along with some social conventions, even though he dislikes it. Suppose, for instance, that he doesn't answer the phone during sex with his wife, even though he really wants to, and doesn't see the reason why he shouldn't. Here would be an example of a triumph of civility! (Of course, Larry answers the phone.) In a funny way, civility seems like a virtue that swings free of whether we want to be civil or not. We're not more civil if we like being civil. Nor are we less civil if we really hate being civil, and *act* in a civil way anyway—which is something Larry rarely does. But he does do it *sometimes*.

The fact that Larry's occasional civility is guided by his own likes and dislikes and his own judgments about how people ought to act raises a second and deeper problem with Larry's personal code of civility (strike two). Suppose we grant that it's not so much a problem when Larry is civil; it's because he happens to like being civil in those instances. The deeper problem is that Larry is *selectively* civil: he's only civil when it suits him. Larry doesn't see "civility" *in general* as having any bearing on what he should or shouldn't do. He picks and chooses when he wants to be civil, depending on whether he happens to agree with the rules of civility in a given instance.

But a person who does this is not a civil person. A civil person recognizes that there are certain rules that have a bearing on his conduct whether or not he agrees with them, or whether or not he likes them. It's fine if a person also *likes* being civil; we might even admire such a person. But it has to be the case that at least in theory, she would act in a civil way, even if she didn't necessarily agree with this or that rule of civility or happen to enjoy having to live up to them. Larry doesn't get a pass on being uncivil just because he doesn't like certain conventions that most of us—unthinkingly—abide by. Nor does he become a civil *person* by acting civilly when it suits him (we told you it was complicated). Larry picks and chooses when he wants to be civil, and that's a mark of an uncivil person, just as much as violating rules of civility is a mark of an uncivil person.

But now another question emerges—*so what?* Maybe Larry isn't a *genuinely* civil person, but what's really so bad about *that?* Would Larry really be a better person if he just blindly sung "Happy Birthday" (or whatever) just because everybody else does? That looks a lot like uncritical obedience to social rules, or adopting the mindset that psychologists and sociologists pejoratively refer to as *groupthink*. Well, we're later going to suggest that rules of civility are not so easily dismissed. It's important to be civil. But before we make that argument let's delve deeper into the case *against* civility.

Larry David versus Civility

We've suggested that Larry's attitude towards rules of civility is ambiguous. He'll uphold some conventional rules, but only the ones that match up with his own likes and dislikes. So if following a rule of civility means that Larry's likes (and more importantly dislikes) are validated, then he's all for it. But if there's no justification beyond "People just do or don't do this" then Larry won't be on board, and indeed, he'll be aggressively skeptical and questioning. Here we'd like to explain why Larry's skepticism about rules of civility may seem well deserved.

Let's start with an example—in fact, one of our favorite scenes from *Curb* and as illustrative of the whole thematic upshot of the show as any other scene in the series. Larry has gone over to Jeff's new house to pick him up. While waiting for Jeff to get ready, Jeff's wife, Susie, invites Larry to take a tour of the new house. Larry declines Susie's invitation. He's seen houses before, after all, and thinks they all basically look the same. What's the point of a tour? Susie is livid. She tells Larry to "get the fuck out" of her house.

There are several reasons why this short scene is perfectly representative of the comedic thrust of the entire series.

- First, we have Larry violating a rule of civility on the grounds that he sees no point in it. He knows of course that guests are expected to graciously accept invitations to tour their friend's new homes, but he regards this expectation as based on a silly convention and hence ignores it.

- Second, Larry's position is understandable. *We know just what he means and just how he feels*. The rule does seem pretty arbitrary. For although most of us wouldn't think to decline the invitation under such circumstances (we aren't Larry David, after all), we recognize that there's something ridiculous about having to feign interest in a friend's new place. What do we expect to see (what do *they* expect us to see?) that we haven't seen before? This helps explain why Larry, despite his behavior, remains so likable. His behavior may be outrageous but it is also perfectly *understandable* to the viewer. We know where Larry's coming from, and we ourselves have likely been tempted to say and do what Larry actually says and does.
- Third, Susie's reaction to what she takes to be Larry's uncivil behavior is itself egregiously uncivil. This is another familiar aspect of *Curb's* comedy. Larry's response to Susie's invitation is indeed rude, but so too is Susie's response to Larry's slight, and probably even more seriously so. It is this saving grace of the series that prevents Larry from being *too* contemptible. He wins our sympathy when he is the object of uncivil behavior, even when that uncivil behavior is caused by his own incivility!

Suppose we imagine ourselves adjudicating this dispute between Larry and Susie. Larry has undeniably violated a rule of civility—the rule that says we should graciously accept invitations such as that proffered by Susie—but Larry's position is that the rule is stupid and thus not a rule he has to follow. Who's right? Well, there's much we can say on behalf of Larry. We might ask, for example, why Larry should feel compelled to feign interest in something he (not unreasonably) has no interest in? Why the charade? Wouldn't it be better if Susie simply recognized the fact that Larry may not be as interested in the layout of her new home as she is, and, more generally, that things we care about a great deal may mean little or nothing to others? For that matter, wouldn't it be more genuine and more *honest* if we just said and did what we really felt like saying and doing, rather than saying what we don't mean and doing what we don't really want to do?

Come to think of it, what, exactly, are Susie's grounds for complaint? A great many moral philosophers—philosophers who concern themselves with questions about what makes actions right or wrong—tell us that actions are wrong for one of two reasons. Either the action is *harmful* to others, causing them some injury or undermining their well-being, or the action is *unfair* to others, where this means others have a right against being treated in that way. But Larry's unwillingness to tour Susie's new home doesn't seem to have either of these wrong-making features.

In declining Susie's invitation Larry doesn't do Susie any harm. It's not like Susie is in some significant way injured or worse-off because of Larry's refusal to take the tour. She's just annoyed, and there's no ethical imperative against causing people annoyance. Moreover, Susie can't criticize Larry on grounds of fairness—it's not like Susie has a right to Larry's interest or time, as she might if she had graciously accepted similar invitations from Larry in the past, and was now deserving of the same consideration she showed him. Larry is consistent, and would never cajole someone into taking a tour of his home. So although Susie may have a point that Larry's refusal to tour her house is uncivil, Larry's behavior doesn't seem *immoral*. But then in what sense, if any, is Larry doing something *wrong*?

Susie's indignation may seem even more unwarranted when we consider that there's very little Susie can say in response to Larry. The only 'justification' Susie can muster is that "it's *just* wrong not to accept such invitations," that "people *just* don't do such things." (Of course, Susie expresses her point in more colorful language.) Susie's inability to say more in this case isn't her fault—the fact that this is the only response she can come up with is what tells us that we're dealing with a rule of civility. It's a characteristic feature of such rules that they are supposed to be *prima facie* justified—it's supposed to be just obvious that you don't do what the rule of civility proscribes your doing. But of course this hardly looks like a justification from the point of view of someone like Larry, who has thought to challenge the rule in question, or thought to ask, "Well, why shouldn't I simply decline the invitation? What's really so bad about that?" Indeed, it looks plainly circular—Larry should follow the rule because, well, it's the rule.

Not only is this kind of justification logically suspect, but isn't there also something worrisomely *conservative* about it? We don't mean "conservative" in the political sense, but rather in the sense that this kind of attitude towards conventional social rules—taking their authority for granted or at face value—seems like an obstruction to social progress. The history of our society includes many now obsolescent social rules that our society is better off for having abandoned (insert your favorite example here). But these rules might still be with us if no one had ever thought to question them. In light of this, Larry's lack of deference for the conventional social rules of his day begins to look not only warranted but *admirable*. He's the only character on the entire show who's willing at times to point out that the Emperor has no clothes, that the rules which everyone else slavishly follow are in fact groundless and without any clear justification.

Maybe we're getting carried away now, but Larry's incivility may even seem defensible as minor acts of *civil disobedience*. Larry is that stubborn individual who refuses to defer to society when its mandates conflict with his own individual reason and conscience. In our culture we often celebrate such people as "individualists" who have the "courage of their convictions," so why the pervasive hostility towards Larry?

Larry David 1, Civility 0

Wait—weren't we supposed to be *defending* the value and importance of following rules of civility? If we've been at all persuasive thus far, it should seem to the reader that we've left ourselves quite a task. (*Larry David 1, Civility 0.*) Let's try at least to even the score.

The crux of *our* position is that despite compelling arguments to the contrary, the fact that people just don't do certain things is often a good reason to not do those things ourselves. And we believe this for two reasons. The first reason is that although rules of civility are not themselves moral rules—there's nothing immoral *per se* about declining Susie's invitation to tour her new home or not singing "Happy Birthday" to Ben—uncivil behavior may be immoral in a more indirect way.

The second point is more *consequentialist* or results-based. Simply put, a social world in which rules of civility are generally followed would likely be a much better social world than one in which they're not, or one in which rules of civility don't exist at all. A world full of Larry Davids would be pretty unbearable.

Claims about what morality requires are notoriously controversial, among philosophers and non-philosophers alike. But few would deny that morality requires, minimally, that we adopt the attitude that the feelings, opinions and interests of others *matter*. They place constraints on what we're *morally* permitted to say and do. This is reflected in the fact that the person who entirely discounts the feelings, opinions and interests of others when deliberating about his speech and action is the paradigm of the immoral person, a moral monster.

We think that this uncontroversial and basic moral rule—respect the feelings, opinions, and interests of others—has important implications when it comes to understanding the authority or importance of rules of civility. For rules of civility are, at bottom, conventional vehicles for *expressing* or *communicating* the relevant attitude of *respect* for the feelings, opinions, and interests of others. When we violate such rules of civility we send others a message, the message that they don't really matter to us.

To illustrate, let's return to the dispute between Larry and Susie about whether it's wrong of Larry to refuse Susie's invitation to take a tour of her new home. No doubt Larry would be right to point out that by refusing Susie's invitation he doesn't do her any tangible harm and nor does he treat her unfairly. And Larry's just being honest when he informs Susie that he doesn't particularly *care* about seeing the new home, that it doesn't really interest him, and that he doesn't think it's that important. But Larry errs by neglecting to appreciate that, whether important to him or not, it *is* important to Susie, and as Susie's friend that ought to carry some weight with Larry. The fact that it matters to Susie ought to motivate Larry to accept Susie's invitation, since regardless of whether what matters to Susie also matters to Larry, *the fact that it matters to Susie ought to matter to Larry.*

By accepting her invitation Larry would express or communicate a message to Susie—"Your feelings and interests matter to me"—and by declining her invitation Larry expresses the opposite message. This is why Susie is so incensed by Larry's behavior. She feels *disrespected*, as though her feelings and interests count for nothing with Larry, and she understandably lashes out. Whether or not Larry really thinks that Susie's interests don't matter, communicating that message to her is itself morally suspect.

All valid rules of civility are susceptible to this same general justification. Our conventions regarding what's "just not done" are there so we don't do things (perhaps inadvertently) that communicate to others a lack of respect for their interests, opinions, and feelings. It is therefore important that we follow these conventions, for this is how we convey to others the fact that we take seriously the basic moral rule that requires us to respect their interests, opinions and feelings. These rules of civility are not justified directly by moral considerations, like prohibitions on harm or imperatives of fairness, for then rules of civility would just collapse into moral rules. Rather, rules of civility are justified more indirectly. We owe it to people to be civil because we owe them respect, and the way we express that respect is through following arbitrary and sometimes even bizarre social conventions. So in this way being civil is no more and no less than a public display of our intended compliance with that very general moral norm mandating respect for others.

Having said this, we're now in a better position to appreciate why, as we already mentioned, there is something deeply confused about Larry's reasons for following those rules of civility he does accept. Larry follows a rule of civility on the condition that *he* would want others to follow that rule as well. But although Larry's consistency is laudable, this really misses the whole point of rules of civility. The crucial point here is that rules of civility are neither justified nor unjustified by what Larry (or any of us) happens to want and like. Just the opposite, in fact: *they're a means by which we communicate to others our understanding that it's not all about what* we *happen to want or like*.

So Larry David's rules of civility are not really rules of *civility* at all. It *looks* like he cares about certain rules of civility, but

---

[1] We're much indebted to Cheshire Calhoun's insightful remarks in his article, "The Virtue of Civility," *Philosophy and Public Affairs* 29:3.

it's probably closer to the truth to say that these are not genuine rules of civility but rather more like Larry's personal policies that sometimes happen to correspond to rules of civility.

The value and importance of communicating respect for the interests, opinions and feelings of others is not the only reason why we should follow rules of civility. There's also the straightforward reason that our shared social life just goes much more smoothly when rules of civility are recognized and respected. There is less conflict and ill-will. Less indignation and resentment.

In fact, this is perhaps the great *argument* behind *Curb Your Enthusiasm*, if in fact there is one. Episode after episode, we witness a social world in which rules of civility are either opaque, ignored, or brazenly flouted, where social relationships are marked (and marred) by misunderstandings, recriminations, disputes, and so forth. It's a nice (and hilarious) world to visit, but who would want to live there?

Cue Music

Is *Curb Your Enthusiasm* a deeply philosophical show, or do we just view it this way because we're philosophers? That's a difficult question to answer. But our take on *Curb* is that it's not just a show that obliquely touches on philosophical issues—rather, the entire show is a prolonged philosophical investigation into the value and importance of civility. We're inclined to think of *Curb* as something like television's equivalent of what philosophers call a *thought experiment*—an imaginative exercise where we consider what would happen if. . .

Whether or not we're right about this, not many shows on television, and certainly not many *comedies*, provide such rich material for philosophical reflection.

III

Larry's Search for Meaning

5
What, No Good?

ANNA MUDDE and ROBERT PIERCEY

DUCKSTEIN: I feel badly for you, because life is like this (*spreads arms wide open*), and what you've done is made it like this (*puts hands close together*).

LARRY: (*pointing to Duckstein's hands*) I want to make that smaller.

DUCKSTEIN: Really?

LARRY: Yes. Shrink it. Shrink it. Put the hands together. (*Duckstein puts hands together*) That's what I want!

—Season Eight, "The Bi-Sexual"

"Maybe one day I'll get a chance to do something good for somebody." Larry says this at the beginning of "The Grand Opening" (Season Three). He and Jeff are standing outside a school, looking at a group of teenagers with shaved heads. Jeff explains that one of their classmates is undergoing chemotherapy, and the kids have shaved their heads in a show of solidarity. Larry is moved: the kids are so selfless, so considerate, so . . . *good*. He wants to be good, just like they are.

This isn't an isolated incident. A concern with being good is one of *Curb*'s major themes. The characters are very interested in right and wrong, and they put a lot of energy into discovering the right thing to do. In almost every episode, there are passionate debates about how to treat other people, animals, and the planet.

Some of these debates seem trivial: Are diners obliged to coordinate tips? If I give you a gift certificate to an expensive restaurant, do you have to invite me along? If you're at the driving range and a ball rolls toward you, are you obliged to pick it up? How long is one expected to spend moving furniture for a blind stranger? Is it okay to express concern about his decorating choices?

Other debates are darkly humorous: Are you a bad person if you commit suicide and don't leave a note? How about if you engage in vehicular fellatio? Or if you use a racial slur to get out of jury duty? These may not be the ethical questions that interested Mill or Kant, but a concern with goodness is clearly a big part of the show.

But as always on *Curb*, there's a twist. Sure, the characters *say* they want to be good. But again and again, their concern with goodness is exposed as a sham. They want others to *think* they're good, and they try hard to *look* as though they're good. But they do these things to win admiration, or to have something to hold over their friends, or to shame others into doing what they want. They don't really care about being good. They care about seeming good, because it's an effective way to manipulate others.

Consider, for instance, the episode called "The Anonymous Donor." As it begins, Larry and Cheryl arrive at the NRDC headquarters for a ceremony honoring its benefactors. Larry has paid for a new wing; his name is on the wall. Another new wing is proclaimed to be the gift of "Anonymous." It soon becomes clear that the anonymous donor is not anonymous at all. Everyone knows it's Ted Danson, because Ted has let his identity be leaked. No one but Larry thinks there's anything odd about this. On *Curb*, it goes without saying that anonymous donors will reveal their identities. They may make a big deal of being above "all the fanfare," but that's just a tactic for getting even *more* fanfare. And while Larry condemns Ted's use of this tactic, what really annoys him is that he didn't think of it first. "Nobody told me that I could be anonymous and tell people," he says to Cheryl. "I would have taken that option."

It's sometimes said that morality is what you do when no one else is looking. In *Curb*, it seems to be what you do *only* when others are looking. What's the point in donating money if no one admires you for it? Why give a kidney or help a blind man move if it doesn't win you praise? The strange part is that with the occasional exception of Larry, no one admits to feeling this way. People claim to take right and wrong seriously. But their actions reveal that they don't value goodness. They value the appearance of goodness, and they value that only because it helps them get what they want. In this respect, *Curb* depicts a world in which morality is dead, but the memory of it is powerful. It is a world in which there literally is no good.

Being Affectionate with Something German

In its treatment of goodness, *Curb* illustrates a condition called *nihilism*. Friedrich Nietzsche describes nihilism as a state in which "the highest values devalue themselves,"[1] one in which there is widespread "skepticism regarding morality" (p. 7). In a nihilistic world, people no longer take morality seriously, because they sense that nothing really matters. Nothing is truly valuable; no action is better or worse than any other; all issues are equally trivial. Nietzsche thought the Europe of his day was becoming nihilistic, thanks to the collapse of organized religion and the failures of philosophers and artists to find alternatives to it. He feared that as time passed Europeans would become more and more nihilistic, less and less attached to the values of the past. This worried him. Nietzsche had little use for Christian morality, but he also wasn't sure human beings were strong enough to face nihilism head on. He wondered where they would find the strength to live and create, once they had rejected the values their civilizations were built on.

Since Nietzsche's time, people have wondered what it would be like to live in a nihilistic world. Nietzsche himself seemed to think that the appearance of nihilism would be world-shaking. He thought people would find it agonizing to live in a world where nothing really matters. Well, maybe a few people feel this way—especially the ones who've read a lot of German philosophy. But *Curb* offers a different perspective on nihilism. In Larry's world, the disappearance of morality is humdrum and unremarkable. The characters take it as obvious that there's no right and wrong, no good and bad. It still matters to them whether someone is generous, or anti-Semitic, or open to romantic relationships with people in wheelchairs.

---

[1] *The Will to Power* (Vintage, 1968), p. 9.

But these things don't matter in the ways we might expect, or for the reasons we might expect. They matter because they affect our self-interest, and what's more, they often do so in ways that seem trivial or stupid. On *Curb*, if you play ironically at being a wife-beater (or a battered wife), the danger isn't that others might think you really abuse your spouse. The danger is that the person who sees you might refuse to be your dentist (Season Two, "The Shrimp Incident"). For the characters on *Curb*, things never seem to matter in the ways viewers expect them to.

On *Curb*, people find this sort of nihilism so ordinary that they're surprised when someone actually takes right and wrong seriously. *Of course* anonymous donors leak their identities. Deep down, we all know that charity is nothing but self-aggrandizement, so how can we blame those who are good at it? Being shocked by cynicism marks you as a rube. And *of course* Larry should apologize to Jeff's parents when they overhear him calling Cheryl "Hitler." After all, they had a gay cousin who escaped Nazi Germany. ("A gay Jew in Nazi Germany? He must have had a hard time. What a combo!"—Season One, Episode 1, "The Pants Tent"). But in the world of *Curb*, the reason Larry should apologize isn't that he's trivialized the Holocaust. It's that Jeff's parents have been nagging him about the remark. Insensitivity, spousal abuse, generosity—these things matter, but not in the ways we expect them to matter. *Nothing* matters in the ways we viewers expect it to matter.

This Isn't a Game, Larry

Imagine you get a tip: there's about to be a major terrorist attack in your city. What would you do? If you're like most people, you'd immediately cancel your plans and leave town. You'd probably warn as many people as you could, starting with your family and friends. Maybe you'd alert the media so that others could protect themselves as well. You might have some tough decisions to make. If the person who gave you the tip asked you not to tell anyone, you might be torn about whether it's okay to violate her confidence. You might even decide it's *not* okay and keep quiet. Whatever happens, you'd take the issue seriously. You'd rise above the petty annoyances of daily life, saying to yourself: *This really matters.*

Now consider what happens when the same scenario unfolds on *Curb*. Wanda tells Larry and Cheryl that she has reliable information about a terrorist attack on L.A. She also asks them not to tell anyone. What do they do? They don't leave town, or alert the media, or call their loved ones. Instead, Larry treats it as an opportunity to smooth over his tiff with Mindy Reiser, who is annoyed that he didn't speak to her in a restaurant. To Larry, this tiff is just as serious as the terrorist strike. He drives to Mindy's store and tells her the news, pleased that she can no longer be mad at him. What we'd expect to be a matter of life and death becomes part of a childish game of hurt feelings and one-upmanship. And it never occurs to Larry that it's more serious than that. Granted, he'd like to leave town, with or without Cheryl. ("It almost seems a little selfish," he tells her, "that you'd want both of us to perish"—Season Three, "The Terrorist Attack"). But it never crosses Larry's mind that he has a duty to warn everyone he knows, let alone a city full of strangers. It never occurs to him that people's lives are more important than a childish tiff. Having something to hold over Mindy means more to Larry than saving someone's life—maybe even his own.

This doesn't make Larry a bad person. But his actions are those of someone who inhabits a nihilistic world. They're the actions of someone convinced that all issues are equally trivial. This nihilism was already present in *Seinfeld*.[2] There, the abortion debate was depicted as no more weighty than a debate between Kramer and Poppie about when a pizza becomes a pizza. ("It's not a pizza until it comes out of the oven!" "It's a pizza the moment you put your fists in the dough!"—*Seinfeld*, Season Six, "The Couch").

But *Curb* pushes nihilism to unprecedented heights. It's not just that the characters take trivial issues seriously, or vice versa. Much of the time, taking an issue seriously isn't even an option. It just isn't on Larry's radar that protecting people from a terrorist attack might be more important than his game of one-upmanship with Mindy Reiser. In the same episode, it doesn't occur to Cheryl that saving their own lives might be more important than their plans to attend a benefit at the

---

[2] As pointed out by Thomas Hibbs in *Shows about Nothing: Nihilism in Popular Culture from The Exorcist to Seinfeld* (Spence, 1999), pp. 159–166.

Braudys's house. And throughout Season Five, when Richard Lewis needs a kidney, it doesn't occur to Larry that there might be things to weigh besides his own desires and fears.

We can't blame Larry for not wanting to donate a kidney. Many people in his situation would feel the same way. But most of us would feel at least a little torn about this—and more than a little guilty. These nobler considerations don't exist for Larry. It simply doesn't occur to him that giving a kidney might be a good thing to do, let alone something he's obliged to do. It's a horror to be avoided at all costs. To Larry, it goes without saying that morality is a tool to help you get what you want. When there's no upside to an action—such as giving a kidney—there's no reason to take it seriously.

Beautiful Service. Sorry for Your Loss. Where's Larry?

Situations like these tell us something important about nihilism. A world where the highest values have devalued themselves is *not* a world where people no longer care about what they should do. It's a world where nothing matters more than anything else, a world where all issues are equally weighty and equally trivial. As a result, it's a world where people have no sense of proportion—no awareness that some things are objectively more important than others. This inability to weigh the importance of things is all over *Curb*.

Consider what happens when Larry's mother dies. He's in New York at the time, shooting a movie with Martin Scorsese. His mother becomes sick, goes to the hospital, and eventually dies, all the while insisting that no one call Larry and ruin his big trip. When Larry gets home and learns not only that his mother has died, but that he's missed her funeral, he's outraged, and yells "This is insane!" (Season Three, "The Special Section"). He thinks he's the only person who gets it—the only one who understands what matters. But later in the episode, he shows the same lack of perspective, as he uses the death to talk Cheryl into sex and to convince Richard Lewis to split a mantra with him. Larry doesn't feel like a vulgar opportunist. It doesn't cross his mind that he *shouldn't* exploit his mother's death. He doesn't like being on the receiving end of this treatment, but he can't make sense of the idea that it's wrong.

On *Curb*, it's not just actions that are nihilistic. All the trappings of morality are missing as well. Real ethical debate, for example, doesn't exist. People talk endlessly about what's right and wrong, but their discussions are transparent attempts to look good and manipulate others. In a way, this is liberating. Larry can have a reasonable, earnest conversation with Krazee-Eyez Killa about avoiding repetitive lyrics by juggling profanity. Mothers can openly discuss their daughters' intimate medical conditions with male colleagues, oblivious to their discomfort. And it's no surprise to find yourself fighting with a stranger over who will get to the doctor's office first.

The downside is that as people talk, their principles are so easily discarded that real discussion never takes place. In the "Opening Night" episode, when Larry finds David Schwimmer's lost watch but quickly loses it again, there's a debate over whether or not Larry owes Schwimmer a watch: did Larry lose a watch that belonged to someone else, or was the watch for all intents and purposes *still* lost? Schwimmer wants Larry to replace the watch, while Larry thinks this is beyond the call of duty. The two seem to be arguing about a principle: do we owe our friends special moral consideration or not?

But on another occasion, Larry and Schwimmer take opposite sides in a debate over the same principle. On the flight to New York, Larry suspects that Schwimmer has tattled to a flight attendant about Larry's seat not being in the upright position. Larry expects Schwimmer to keep his mouth shut, although cutting corners on flight safety to protect a friend is probably beyond the call of duty. In this case, Larry expects Schwimmer to go the extra mile—just as Schwimmer expects Larry to go the extra mile and buy him a new watch. In the end, Larry is able to return Schwimmer's watch, after wresting it from the arm of the hotel employee who found it. But once more, resolving the dispute isn't enough for Larry. He has to know: "What did you say to that stewardess?" Larry's position in this situation is the one he takes in many of the debates on *Curb*. We might be arguing about affirmative action, or whether to remove our shoes, or where to have our next meeting. The goal is always the same: to get what we want, while claiming the high ground.

Not surprisingly, there are few role models on *Curb*. There's no one to turn to for moral guidance, no clear example of good behavior. Anonymous donors are just looking for glory. Marriage and family are dysfunctional, even at their best. Parents don't want to bother their children by dying, and spouses think adultery makes a great anniversary gift. Politicians are beneath contempt: even Barbara Boxer (D-California) admits that she steals dry cleaning.

Religion is ridiculous and is never taken seriously. When Larry criticizes Christians, it's not because they don't respect his Judaism; it's because they take religion, *all* religion, too seriously. (In "The Baptism" (Season Two), he wonders: "Why do Christians take everything so personally, with Christ? I like lobster. Do I go around pushing lobster on people? Do I say, 'You must like lobster'?") The twist is that the lack of moral authorities doesn't mean that people have stopped telling each other what to do. In a nihilistic world, everyone is as much of an authority as everyone else, so we all have the same right to judge other people's behavior.

On *Curb*, it's total strangers who care most about our ethics. That person telling you to leave your water outside the movie theater isn't an usher; she's an audience member just like you. Random passersby yell at you for being anti-Semitic, just because you've been whistling Wagner. All of this makes perfect sense. If there's no right and wrong, there are no moral authorities, and if no one's an authority, everyone is. It turns out that a nihilistic world isn't one where people don't judge. It's a world where everyone judges us all the time, and there's nothing we can say in our own defense.

Philosophers often talk about *the* good. By this they mean an impersonal standard that makes some actions better than others, some lives more worthwhile than others.

- **Plato thinks the good is what he calls a *form*: something outside time and change, an eternal standard that gives universal answers to moral questions.**
- **Aristotle thinks the good is happiness, especially the kind of happiness that comes from acting rationally and contemplating the truth.**
- **The philosophers known as utilitarians define the good as the greatest pleasure for the greatest number.**

Philosophers disagree about what the good is, but most of them agree that there is one. They agree that there's a way to distinguish right from wrong, the serious from the trivial. On *Curb*, there's nothing of the sort. There's no way to distinguish actions that are right from actions that just serve our selfish interests. There's no way to distinguish things that really matter from things that don't. But the good hasn't exactly vanished. It's been hollowed out, leaving behind an empty shell. The language of morality remains. People still talk as though there's a good, although deep down, they know there isn't. But the language still casts a spell. That's why looking like you care about morality is the surest way to get what you want. If you seem good, you can get away with being bad.

A Get-Together Guy?

Is there any way out of this predicament? Since Nietzsche's time, philosophers have tried to find one. One suggestion that has convinced many people appears in Alasdair MacIntyre's book *After Virtue*, which suggests that *community* offers a way out of nihilism. MacIntyre thinks, as *Curb Your Enthusiasm* does, that morality is a thing of the past. Our society, says MacIntyre, has "simulacra of morality, we continue to use many of the key expressions. But we have . . . lost our comprehension, both theoretical and practical, of morality."[3]

The reason, says MacIntyre, is that moral principles make sense only in a certain social setting. That setting is a community where people agree about what the goal of human life is. Ancient Greek city-states were communities of this sort. So were the religious communities of medieval Europe. When people think life has a goal, and they agree about what that goal is, moral rules make sense. These rules act as a bridge from the way we are now to the way we could be, if only we achieved our goal. Since the scientific revolution, though, we've found it harder and harder to think of life as having a goal. Not coincidentally, we've also found it harder and harder to take morality as seriously as we once did. We still have rules left over from earlier periods of history, and these rules still have us in their

[3] *After Virtue* (University of Notre Dame Press, 1984), p. 2.

grip. But we no longer have the context to make sense of these rules, and so we're haunted by the fear that they're meaningless. In particular, we no longer have a way of choosing between the incompatible principles invoked in many contemporary debates.

Take the debate over abortion. The camps in this debate are sharply opposed, but they both appeal to principles that seem compelling. One side makes plausible claims about the rights people have over their own bodies. The other makes equally plausible claims about the value of life and the importance of protecting it. We find ourselves drawn to both principles, so it's hard to see how we could determine which side is right. And this leads us to suspect that *no one* is really right: that the reason we can't find the truth in this debate is that there is no truth to find. Seen in this light, principles like "Respect individual rights" and "Value life" seem like empty talk. MacIntyre compares them to the ancient Polynesian taboos: we feel like we should care about them, but we can't remember why. We suspect they're a sham, but we can't admit it—perhaps not even to ourselves.

According to MacIntyre, there's only one way to hang on to morality: rebuild the social settings that make sense of it. We need to cultivate new communities, communities like the ones where morality originally flourished. We can't go back to ancient Greece, but we can build new communities that give content to moral life. Creating and sustaining a community is an art. It's a complex process in which people come together to achieve a common goal. To succeed, they have to act in certain ways. They need justice, courage, and other virtues. If the community is working properly, there's a perfectly good answer to the question of why I should care about doing the right thing. I should care because it's necessary to keep the community going, and my own well-being is inseparable from the community's.

Is getting together the answer? Does community offer a way out of the nihilism depicted on *Curb*?

My Days of Elevator Etiquette Are Over

Frankly, no. For MacIntyre's proposal to work, communities have to be good things—or at least, not terrible things. Living with others can't be hellish. People can't be hostile to each other all the time. They must be willing to live harmoniously, willing to work with others for the common good. That's not how community functions on *Curb*. French philosopher Jean-Paul Sartre famously has a character in his play *No Exit* say that hell is other people, but even he couldn't have imagined how bad social life is in Larry's world.

On *Curb*, other people are a constant source of misery. They're always trying get something from you: a letter of recommendation, or an introduction to Julia Louis-Dreyfus, or a new pair of glasses. When you try to be nice to them—when you let them leave an elevator before you, for example—they throw your kindness back in your face. A visit from relatives is the deepest pit in hell: they drink your liquor, and sing at all hours, and whine when you don't say goodnight. Your in-laws wake you up when you accidentally eat a cookie manger scene.

> "Larry, you ate the baby Jesus and his mother, Mary" "I thought He was a monkey" . . . "You didn't see the toasted coconut hay, the barn . . .?" "I thought it was all part of the zoo. . . . I'll make it up to you" "You can't make it up; you just swallowed our Lord and Savior" (Season Three, "Mary, Joseph, and Larry")

Even the people closest to you aren't all that great. Larry loves Cheryl, but when they renew their marriage vows, he doesn't want to promise to love her for all eternity. The rest of his life—fine. But in the afterlife, he wants to be a free agent. On *Curb*, the best you can hope for is to be shunned. When Larry injures Shaq at a Lakers game, all of L.A. treats him like a pariah. But Larry's not unhappy. It's the best thing that's ever happened to him. Delighted to be left alone, he tap dances in a Starbucks and buys drinks for the whole store.

Even the threat of anarchy doesn't make social life worth the trouble. When Auntie Rae tells Larry that there have been burglaries nearby and that he should get to know the neighbors, he says: "I'd rather have the thieves than the neighbors. The thieves don't impose" (Season Seven, "Funkhouser's Crazy Sister").

Community isn't the answer. So it looks like there's no way out. On *Curb*, morality is a sham, and our last, best hope for fixing it isn't an option. To be clear, the problem isn't that there's a right thing to do, but that people can't rise to the challenge of doing it. Nor is it that people *could* rise to the challenge but are happy to settle for an inauthentic morality. The problem is that on *Curb*, morality is taboo all the way down. It's a sham, but a powerful sham. People feel obliged to care about it—or to act like they care about it—even though deep down, they know it has no substance. *Curb* leaves us with only the worst parts of morality: the smugness, the guilt, the endless worrying about what others think of us. We want to be good, we feel like we ought to be good, but we can't, because our communities are ones where goodness is impossible. In these communities, we're haunted by the memory of something that no longer exists.

Many philosophers have claimed that *ought* implies *can*: that if we're obliged to do something, it must be possible to do it. On *Curb*, ought doesn't imply can. We can feel a crushing obligation to be good even if being good is impossible. Knowing that goodness is impossible doesn't make the guilt go away. As a result, *Curb* depicts morality as something tragic. People feel obliged to do the right thing, obliged to act as if they care about being good. They sometimes try their best to be good. But they never succeed, because the world foils them at every step. Thomas Nagel might have been talking about *Curb* when he said that "We have always known that the world is a bad place. It appears that it may be an evil place as well."[4]

Having Said That . . .

So in "The Grand Opening," when Larry yearns for the chance to do something good, it seems hopeless. We know he'll never succeed, because he lives in a world from which goodness has vanished. But has it vanished completely? Actually, there are glimmers of hope. There are rare moments in *Curb* when, against all odds, small communities form and spontaneously do something good.

The end of "The Grand Opening" is a nice example. It's opening night at the restaurant in which Larry has invested. Like all the owners, he's on edge, because their new chef has Tourette's Syndrome, and is prone to scream obscenities with-

[4] Thomas Nagel, "War and Massacre," in *Mortal Questions* (Cambridge University Press, 1979), p. 74.

out warning. The restaurant has an open kitchen, so if he does start swearing, the customers will hear. Sure enough, just when the opening seems to be going smoothly, a torrent of French-accented filth comes out of the kitchen.

Everyone freezes. But Larry thinks of the kids with the shaved heads, and remembers his wish to do something good. Seeing his chance, he unleashes a string of obscenities. Jeff follows his lead, and soon, everyone in the restaurant is swearing at the top of his and her lungs. The camera pans back and Larry smiles. Not only has he shown solidarity with the afflicted; he's created a happy little community of diners, all brought together by kindness and filth. It's not a traditional community. It's certainly not the kind of community MacIntyre would like us to cultivate. Larry's community is based on a lack of civility, a mix of obscenity and comically bad luck. But it's a community all the same. The people there are united by a common purpose, and they're happier than they would be alone. Despite all the cynicism, Larry has done a little bit of good.

That doesn't make everything better. It's hard to know how stable this new community is. Do the diners join in because they want to help, or because of a childish delight in bad words? How can we keep the community going once the swearing stops? Can Larry repeat his gesture in other settings? Would he even want to?

The whole scene is so absurd, so disconnected from the rest of life, that it offers little to build on. But if nothing else, it shows that tragedy isn't the whole story. We can always hope. And once in a while—if we're lucky—we might find ourselves being pretty, pretty good.[5]

[5] Thanks to Matt Faubert and Peter Norman for their help with this chapter.

6

Judaism, Where Are You?

KEVIN ZANELOTTI

It seems as though Larry David hates Jews. A surprising range of critics make this charge, alleging further that Larry, himself a Jew, is a "self-hating Jew." In a 2005 *Jerusalem Post* editorial, Arye Dworkin condemned *Curb Your Enthusiasm* for "teetering on the tightrope that separates humor from self-hatred."

Michael Savage, a talk radio personality who makes Glenn Beck look like Bill Moyers, even suggested that "if Hitler were alive and he hired a propagandist to create an image of the 'ugly Jew,' he couldn't do better than to hire Larry David."[1] The veneer of humor, the critics claim, conceals anti-Semitic attitudes that distort and slander Judaism while providing David with the cover of "it's just entertainment!" From the Catholic League to the Anti-Defamation League, Larry's antics have been described as tasteless and sometimes even harmful to Jews, Judaism, and religion in general. The good Jew never mixes meat and milk. Is Larry David at fault for mixing his acerbic brand of humor with Judaism?

If it's true that Larry is guilty of such a non-kosher mix, then maybe he's not the only one in the ethical hot seat—for if he's a self-hating Jew, then perhaps we're laughing where we should be scolding. Criticism of the show forces us to address an interesting philosophical question: what happens to faith when we "curbs our enthusiasm"? Is the kind of perspective on

---

[1] *Savage Nation*, Talk Radio Network, November 7th, 2009.

life represented by Larry's character in *Curb* essentially *inauthentic* when it comes to religion?

Is Larry a bad Jew? Are *we* bad people for laughing with Larry? Or, is there a philosophical perspective from which we can see Larry's take on religion as genuinely authentic and, consequently, continue to think well of ourselves as we watch and enjoy *Curb*?

The Self-Hating Jew and Baldness

As a result of the many historical diasporas ("scatterings") that flung Jews from their home in Palestine to the far reaches of Africa, Europe, and Asia, the story of the Jews is one of continual dislocation, movement, settlement, and more dislocation. Jews repeatedly found themselves as outsiders surrounded by decidedly hostile majorities. In such situations, it's common for some members of an oppressed group to begin seeing themselves as others see them. Stereotypes become internalized.

Take Larry's disgust at self-hating bald people. The bald man who hides his baldness is, for Larry, someone who has "bought into" the non-bald agenda: a self-hating baldy. "False consciousness," to borrow Karl Marx's term, can result, where the stereotypes and worldview of a dominant group are adopted by those in the minority. This process is insidious since the self-serving and arbitrary world-view of the dominant group may come to seem natural, as "just the way things are." This phenomenon is called "ideology"—not just seeing reality through a distorted "lens" that serves the interests of a dominant group, but also not realizing that the lens is there *in the first place*.

Historically, denigration and dehumanization of the Jewish minority by non-Jewish majorities was exacerbated by claims among Jews *themselves* that some sub-sets of Jews are "bad" Jews. Jews who were suspected of "assimilating" to Western cultures (dressing, acting, and speaking like non-Jews) found themselves labeled as "self-hating" Jews, betrayers of their tradition and people. The idea of Jewish self-hate emerged in these contexts as a pernicious shorthand for understanding, and often caricaturing, the complexities of Jews living among non-Jews.

Theodor Lessing, a German Jewish philosopher, helped popularize the image of the self-hating Jew in, appropriately enough, a book titled *Jewish Self-Hate* (1930), where he branded as self-hating those Jewish intellectuals who opposed Zionism (the national movement for the return of the Jewish people to their homeland). The organizational psychologist Kurt Lewin further cemented the phrase in the Western cultural vocabulary with his "Self-Hatred Among Jews." Lewin focused on Jews who, he claimed, "dislike everything specifically Jewish" and "show dislike for those Jews who are outspokenly so, and will frequently indulge in self-hatred."[2]

"Larry Jew"? (G)oy Vey!

What's the evidence that Larry David is a self-hating Jew? In "Meet the Blacks" (Season Six), Larry refers to himself as "Larry Jew" after noting the irony that a black family's last name is, in fact, "Black." While perhaps innocent in itself, this scene does reveal the ease, and potential carelessness, with which Larry makes light of all-things Jewish. In another episode (Season Two, "Trick or Treat"), while in a line at the theater Larry offends a fellow Jew and theatergoer when he carelessly whistles a Wagner melody. Hitler just couldn't get enough of Wagner, you see. Confrontation follows, with Larry screaming at the offended Jew: "Judaism, where are you?" But Larry has his revenge—he hires a string-quartet to play Wagner on the Jew's lawn. Elsewhere, Larry calls temple "a trial" (Season Two, "The Massage"), says of a Bar Mitzvah "Can you think of anything worse?" (Season Three, "The Benadryl Brownie"), argues with Susie about who has more of a "Jew face" (Season Four, "The 5 Wood"), and consistently pokes fun at Orthodox Jews (Season Five, "The Ski Lift").

Curb Your Enthusiasm has offended other religions as well, most notably when Larry infamously, though inadvertently, splashed a painting of Jesus Christ with his urine (Season Seven, "The Bare Midriff"). This did not go over well with the Christians. But to his critics the treatment of Jewish culture and themes in *Curb* is fundamentally more disturbing; after all, Larry is a Jew.

---

[2] *Resolving Social Conflicts* (Harper and Row, 1948), p. 164.

The arc of the last episodes of Season Five, which includes a storyline about Larry's reluctance to donate a kidney to the ailing Richard Lewis, seems to support the charge that Larry is a self-hating Jew. To avoid giving Lewis his kidney, Larry ingratiates himself with the head of a kidney transplant bank (a Dr. Heineman) in order to move Lewis's name to the top of the list. Heineman is an Orthodox Jew, and Larry attempts to woo him by *playing the part* of a good Jew. *This* Larry listens religiously to Jewish radio, gets worked up when talking about Israel, and would never go to a ball game on the Sabbath. Because Cheryl is a *shiksa* (a non-Jewish woman), in "The Ski Lift" episode (Season Five) Larry even has Susie play his wife, complete with *Tichel* (a head-scarf worn by Orthodox Jewish married women) and tales of how she met Larry at a Hillel function at college.

At one point Larry finds himself stranded on a broken ski-lift with Heineman's daughter. When she mutters "Hashem" as an aside, Larry has no idea what she means. (Hashem is one of the names of God in Judaism.) Later, as they remain stuck on the lift, the daughter points out that as an unmarried Jewish woman she cannot be alone with a man after sundown. When she asks Larry to do the right thing and jump, he responds: "What are you, fucking nuts?" He then calls Lewis to tell him his name won't be put at the top of the list after all—Larry's gig as a good Jew was up.

But the most troubling scenes are from the last episode of Season Five, "The End." Larry is told by a private detective—who originally was hired to get the dirt on Heineman—that he is adopted. "Larry Jew," it turns out, is a *goy*—his parents are gentiles ("Cone," *not* "Cohn"). Yet, instead of feeling loss, Larry actually seems *relieved,* as if a great Yiddish weight has been lifted from his shoulders. Rather than "*Oy vey*!," Larry's every action screams: "Yay!" In scene after scene, Larry embraces his gentile heritage with passion and uncommon cheer, a transformation in everything from dress (Larry adds a fanny pack to his wardrobe) to his very character (Larry begins attending church, and actually *enjoys it*—witness his rendition of "Go Tell It on the Mountain"). From *kvetching* Jew to kneeling in a church pew, the gentilification of Larry is complete.

But there's more.

As a gentile, Larry gets ethics. His gentile mother begins to soften his selfish resistance to helping Lewis when she advises,

"You must practice love and forgiveness. Give him the benefit of the doubt. What would Jesus do?" Larry nods, moved by her words. His transformation into a caring and selfless friend is clinched when he attends church and is deeply moved by the pastor's sermon on friendship. As a result, Larry resolves to give Lewis his kidney. As a Jew, Larry is selfish and uncharitable—as a gentile, Larry becomes a *mensch* (a good person)!

Finally and perhaps most potentially damning, when he finds out the private detective's mistake, that he is, in fact, a Jew, Larry seems *crushed*. Larry's enthusiasm seems curbed *only* when he is a Jew—as a gentile, he embraces life with zeal (Larry chugging brewskies with the boys at a sports bar?!) and compassion. A critic might point out that while Larry *does* go through with the donation of his kidney to Lewis, he does not do so willingly. In fact, Larry is told of the mistake regarding his adoption on the way to the operating room, and screams in response: "I'm not adopted. Get me the fuck out of here!" Fortunately for Lewis, Larry's effort to escape fails and the operation takes place. Unfortunately, Larry takes ill during the operation and dies. Larry ascends to heaven and meets his *real*, Jewish mother (a Jew in *heaven*? Larry's Judaism seems a bit Christianized). Bea Arthur, in her last role as the deceased Mrs. David, scolds Larry for giving his kidney to Lewis: "What kind of *schmuck* are you?" How different from Larry's gentile "mother," who lectured him on the virtues of friendship and sacrifice.

These scenes certainly do not paint a flattering picture. Larry pokes fun at Orthodox Jews, misrepresents their customs, and seems to revel in offering stereotype after stereotype of the "ugly Jew," hence Savage's comment that Larry would have done well as a Nazi propaganda minister. To borrow a line from Jeff, this certainly does *seem* to be one "big bowl of wrong." Can "Larry Jew" be redeemed?

Larry Gentile

Those who claim that Larry David is a self-hating Jew seem to assume that there is an *authentic* way of embracing faith and being a "real" or "genuine" Jew. The French philosopher Jean-Paul Sartre identified *inauthenticity* with self-deception and what he called "bad faith." Sartre was an existentialist philosopher, which means he focused on how the individual confronts her responsibility for being the sole source of meaning and value in her life.

Rather than having some fixed "human nature," we are, according to Sartre, what we make of ourselves. Human nature, were it to exist, would be common to all and would provide the parameters for what a genuine, authentic human life should be. But the idea of human nature is intelligible only if God exists as the *source* of that nature; since Sartre denies that God exists, he denies any form of human nature. That's why Sartre famously claimed we are "condemned to be free"—we have no choice but to embrace our freedom and make of ourselves what we will, even though in the absence of God there are no objective standards to guide us. In this sense, radical freedom creates absolute responsibility, and thus a perpetual anxiety in the face of choices we must make but for which we have no ultimate justification. So, for Sartre, authenticity involves embracing oneself as an ongoing project of *radical* self-creation.

Bad faith is a matter of rejecting responsibility for one's freedom and of treating oneself as a mere *thing* in the world. Mere things lack genuine possibilities. By contrast, a person, Sartre claims, is nothing but a wellspring of possibilities and choices, and a choice that brings one possibility to actuality at the same time that it closes off other possibilities.

Decisions matter! Yet, if Sartre's right we routinely try to escape the burden of that responsibility by having others decide for us, or by justifying our choices in reference to some external authority such as a religion. "I had no choice!" we often plead, but for Sartre we are *nothing but* our choices. Denying that there are many possible choices and believing that you have no choice—*that* is to treat yourself as a thing.

When Jeff succumbs, again and again, to his cheating ways, rationalizing that Susie's coldness leaves him no choice—*that* is bad faith. A person living in bad faith fails to honor what Sartre calls "facticity" and "transcendence." Facticity refers to those "facts" about ourselves that we did not choose but that limit us, concrete details such as sex, language, race, and nationality. Our ability to go beyond what we are and to embrace our creative freedom is what Sartre refers to as transcendence. I may be Italian (my facticity), but that doesn't mean I have to act like a character from the Sopranos (my transcendence is my freedom)! Bad faith would be my justifying acting like Tony Soprano by saying, "But I'm Italian!"

Bad faith may be a matter of a person denying his transcendence and identifying wholly with his facticity. For example, in "The Special Section" (Season Three) Larry's father fails to tell him of his mother's death, claiming that his mother didn't want to ruin his trip to New York. The senior David is fleeing from his responsibility, claiming that some "fact" of the situation—the mother's wish—decides for him. On the other hand, bad faith also results when someone denies their facticity and wholly identifies with their transcendence (translation: they presume that their past is unimportant and, like a God, can create from nothing). When Larry assumes that he can simply become a gentile and leave his Jewish past behind (Season Five, "The End") he seems to exhibit this form of bad faith. Immediately after learning that his biological parents are gentiles, he adopts those beliefs. He similarly dismisses them and re-adopts his Jewish beliefs when he finds that he was not adopted.

If Larry is in bad faith, then isn't there some merit to the claim that he's a bad, self-hating Jew? Since comedy is a relation between an artist and his audience, perhaps we can get a handle on the charge that Larry is a self-hating Jew by approaching the issue from *our* perspective—after all, we're "buying" what Larry is "selling." The charge against Larry necessarily implicates us as well, and leads to the more general question: Is there an ethics of laughter? The supply-demand nature of entertainment links the ethics of supplying questionable comedy with the demand that makes supply possible. So, if we can determine our status as Friends of Larry, then we may be in a better position to determine whether Larry is a friend (or enemy) of Jews.

Are You My Caucasian?

In "Krazee-Eyez Killa" (Season Three), Larry strikes up an unusual friendship with a rapper, the boyfriend of Wanda Sykes's character. When Krazee-Eyez asks, "you're my nigger, right?" we laugh at Larry's response: "Yes, I'm your nigger." Later, Larry gets more mileage out of the bit when he turns the tables, asking Krazee-Eyes, "Are you my Caucasian?" Is it wrong to laugh at such humor? Is it wrong even to call it humor?

When it comes to humor, context is everything. Consider the question: "Is it ever wrong to laugh at a joke?" One possibility is that we are using ethical language and concepts incorrectly when we apply them to humor. The idea is that just as I can't use my scale to tell me my mood, I can't use ethics to evaluate humor. Humor, so it is argued, is *meant* to be extreme, exaggerated, transgressive, and outrageous. According to this philosophical position, we check our ethical hats at the door when we enter a comedy club—or watch comedy shows such as *Curb*. Let's call this the "Just Joking" Defense, since someone challenged for making a racist or sexist joke often relies on this way of thinking when they respond: "I was just joking! Can't you take a joke?"

Ronald de Sousa, a contemporary Canadian philosopher, rejects the Just Joking Defense, which he argues in *The Rationality of Emotion* is based on a faulty assumption.[3] The error is in assuming that laughter is involuntary. Here's the idea: since generally we are only ethically accountable for acts that are voluntary, it follows that we can't really be held accountable for laughing at jokes, even offensive jokes. Laughter, like sneezing, is on this view something that simply happens *to* us.

Take the scene when Larry and Jeff bust a gut while reading the freak book during Ted Danson's birthday party, thus disturbing the festivities. If the Just Joking Defense is correct then they should not be blamed. They did not *choose* to laugh—the book's freakish photos simply made them laugh, in the same way pepper makes us sneeze. But this ignores the fact that while Larry and Jeff may react mechanically, they nevertheless *are* responsible for allowing themselves to become the kinds of people who are powerless to restrain themselves. By not practicing restraint in the past, and by not recognizing that laughing at a "freak" may be mean-spirited, they put themselves in a position where they would be helpless to laugh at the freak book. So, not everything is really a laughing matter, after all.

---

[3] Ronald De Sousa, *The Rationality of Emotion* (MIT Press, 1987).

As de Sousa further notes, the Just Joking Defense is unacceptable since it incorrectly assumes that humor is ultimately trivial—it is, if the defense is correct, not something that should be taken seriously. Humor, in other words, can be neither moral nor immoral since it is essentially *amoral*. For instance, Larry gets himself into trouble when he meets Richard Lewis' dermatologist. When he finds out that the dermatologist, a black man, has been Lewis' doctor for fifteen years, Larry jokes: "Even with the whole affirmative action thing?" (Season One, "Affirmative Action"). The doctor is understandably offended, and Larry's response that "it was just a joke" seems to indicate a kind of *amoralist* interpretation. For the amoralist, humor creates a space where right and wrong don't apply. Making a bad joke or laughing at a bad joke is *playful* rather than serious. And, so the claim goes, one may be *playing with* a concept like affirmative action without *using* that concept in the usual sense. This is the heart of the Just Joking Defense.

Perhaps Larry was attempting to poke fun at the attitudes of some whites towards affirmative action, with the joke being his "wink and nod" to the doctor, essentially saying, "I'm not one of those white people who think affirmative action is reverse discrimination—I'm okay." Philosophers who believe that the essence of humor is a feeling of superiority may find this interpretation attractive, as would those who, like Freud in *Jokes and Their Relation to the Unconscious*, see humor as a "safety-valve" that allows us to release feelings and ideas that we normally repress.

Philosophers who point to incongruity (the unexpected) as being the basis of humor may add that Larry is banking on the doctor seeing the incongruity of a progressive white man saying things that racist whites say. But what each of these perspectives misses is that the joke *is* offensive and the doctor is understandably and rightly offended. The "joke" offends since no context is provided that would allow us to see anything *but* offense. The doctor does not know Larry, so Larry cannot presume he will be "in" on the joke. There are no extenuating circumstances that would lead the doctor to be anything but offended—and we're shocked as viewers that Larry (the character) could be so clueless. Without establishing the proper context, Larry's statement is free-floating and thus offensive.

By "setting a context for humor" I mean clearly establishing some frame of reference that makes transparent—or as translucent as possible—the intentions and purpose of the humorist. This setting of context allows us to distinguish between an African-American comedian who uses the N-word and a comedian hired to entertain the crowd at a White Supremacist rally who *also* uses that word. In the latter case, the context establishes the use of that word as racist. By "putting a frame" on the event, language that in another context would be offensive may become funny; we do not take Chris Rock to be racist when he uses the N-word. When a Polish comedian tells Polish jokes, *that* can be funny—but only because the frame has been set and the possibility of free-floating interpretations (What did he *really* mean?) are diminished as far as possible.

Taking into account the "context-setting" feature of some humor can shed light on Larry's alleged bad faith. The Larry we see in "The End" (Season Five), a Larry who giddily embraces all things goyish and seems *relieved* that he's no longer a Jew, must be seen in the proper context. It certainly would be odd if we were to take the beliefs of Larry-the-happy-gentile as representing Larry David's genuine stance on Judaism! Larry-the-happy-gentile, like "Larry Jew," is a character, a caricature.

Larry's gentilification is meant, perhaps, to cast even greater light on the overarching "moral," if there is one, of the show: we all need to "curb our enthusiasm." In fact, couldn't we take Larry David (the writer) to be pointing to just the kind of "bad faith" that Sartre discusses? The difference here is that David *knows* it's bad faith and is poking fun at it by setting a humorous context, whereas his critics would take "Larry Gentile" as evidence of Jewish self-hate.

Now, I'm not claiming that Larry had Sartre in mind, or even that he knows who Sartre is! But great philosophers don't so much invent wisdom as make explicit the wisdom in life that is implicit for the rest of us. Larry David may not be influenced by Sartre, but perhaps his comic brilliance and the philosophical insights of Sartre are, in the present case at least, in the same neighborhood. They're both dealing with the human potential for self-deception, but they're doing so from different sides of the street.

If I'm correct and the bizarre transformation of "Larry Jew" into "Larry Gentile" in "The End" is recognized by Larry David as absurd and mock-worthy, then we can see the response of Larry's mother when his spirit meets her in the afterworld—"What kind of *schmuck* are you?"—in another light. Her response may refer to the giddy conversion *itself* rather than to the actual donation of Larry's kidney to Lewis. Perhaps Larry is a schmuck because his experience as a gentile reveals just how caught up he was in the "enthusiasm" of believing that you can leave your old life behind and become anything you want. This would mean that *Curb* is actually mocking the bad faith of "Larry Gentile" rather than disparaging Judaism. This would also cast light on Larry's startling reversal on the issue of donating his kidney to Lewis. Wouldn't it be absurd if finding out you were gentile would be enough to cause such a change? How silly. Larry's flirtation with the gentile world would be just another example of his tendency to forget his own "golden rule": curb your enthusiasm. In fact, isn't this Larry's problem in general?

Curb Your Judaism?

Jerry Seinfeld commented in the original HBO documentary that "This guy proves 'You are what you are.'" Larry David (the writer) seems remarkably unaffected by changes that would normally transform even the best of us. Wealth and fame, his friends claim, really have not changed him. This being the case, and given *Curb*'s contextualizing *everything* in terms of the pendulum swing from blind enthusiasm to humiliation and social disaster, it certainly is plausible to turn the table on the critics and respond that the "bad faith" that Larry allegedly exhibits is actually the butt of writer Larry David's joke. The critics mistake the gag itself for reality. "Larry Jew" becoming "Larry Gentile," and the miraculous transformation of character that ensues, is the punch line of the joke rather than any indication about the "real" Larry David's authenticity. If I'm correct, the issue of "authenticity" is a non-starter since the point of "The End" is to mock Larry's flights of enthusiasm rather than endorse them.

But this raises a further question: What value is there in the "curb your enthusiasm" ethos itself? What happens to faith when it is curbed?

Seinfeld, that *other* job Larry had back in the day, was famously a "show about nothing." Actually, that is not quite right. Seinfeld was a show about a group of people dealing with the perceived loss of purpose, meaning, and value that seems a feature of modern life. Faith in institutions—community, church, education, and government—that previously "grounded" our lives has eroded. We are, as a contemporary philosopher put it, "a community of those who have nothing in common."[4]

Optimism in the future and progress seems replaced with a deep cynicism toward the ideals and sense of belonging that, correctly or incorrectly, many identify with past generations. Everyone and every institution appears to have its own agenda, and skepticism with respect to seeking genuine accord and resolution to our problems seems pervasive. In this climate, the questions "What is of value?" and "What kind of life should I live?" seem to have as many answers as there are individuals. When faced with people who offer answers different from our own, we tend either to adopt an "agree to disagree" stance or to view the person with contempt and as an opponent in a "cultural war."

Our situation is characterized by what Friedrich Nietzsche, the German bad-boy of philosophy who declared "God is dead," called "nihilism"—a disbelief in any value whatsoever. Nihilism, he argued, was actually the result of the success of Christianity, which placed ultimate value and meaning in a world beyond this one. However, with the rise of science and other cultural changes, belief in God became less tenable. The infamous "Death of God" is the result—not the *literal* death of a divine being, but the loss of anything in our lives that could perform the God-function of providing ultimate meaning.

Let's assume that there is something to this interpretation of modern culture and, worse still, that feelings of meaninglessness may even have increased (perhaps due to further dislocations of an economic and political nature, and certainly as a result of the staggering technological advances of our times). Now, to return to *Seinfeld* from Nietzsche-land, we could say that instead of becoming dark, brooding presences, contemplating the meaninglessness of it all, the *Seinfeld* folks went to

---

[4] Alphonso Lingis, *The Community of Those Who Have Nothing in Common* (Indiana University Press, 1994).

great lengths *to create meaning* in their lives. Granted, they created ultimately trivial meanings about everything from "low talkers," "close talkers," "man-hands," "re-gifting," "double dipping," yadda yadda yadda (see what I did there?). Where meaning seems absent, we create meaning. The *Seinfeld* bunch did this to excess and with great zeal.

Something similar is going on with *Curb Your Enthusiasm*, but *Curb* approaches questions of meaningfulness from a different angle. Where *Seinfeld* was largely a show about trying to make something from nothing, creating meaning no matter how trivial, *Curb* is a show about our tendency to get carried away when we create meaning. Here is what Larry David said about the show's title during one of the "bonus features" found on the Season Seven DVD:

> We don't want to see people happy. And we want them, if they are happy, to keep it private and not subject the rest of the miserable world to it. We don't want to see it, hence: curb it!

The idea, I suppose, is that people are so enthralled by their own experiences that they feel a need to share their "enthusiasm" (or anger—it works both ways) with everyone else, as if their feelings do not exist unless they are made public. In a *Time* magazine interview, Larry pointed out that "people should keep enthusiasm curbed in their lives. Always keep it. To not is unattractive. It's unseemly."[5] Certainly, when discussion turns to politics and religion, this tendency to equate self-esteem and self-value with public displays of enthusiasm becomes more pernicious. Perhaps this is the heart of the *Curb Your Enthusiasm* ethos—a sensibility oriented by the need for restraint, especially in a culture in which a sense of meaninglessness may cause us to overvalue whatever meaning we *do* create.

In the end, we're dealing with civility, which P. M. Forni—a guru of all-things-civil—defines in *Choosing Civility* as being aware of how we affect and are affected by others. In this sense, *Curb Your Enthusiasm* could be seen as a kind of civility training manual.

---

5 Bryan Alexander, "Q&A: *Curb Your Enthusiasm*'s Larry David," *Time* (June 3rd, 2010).

In a *New York Times* interview, Larry David remarked that "Religion *should* be made fun of. It's quite ridiculous, isn't it? Think of how people spend their lives. They have no idea, yet they go around as if this is a fact. It's so insane, you know. If I really believed that stuff, I'd keep it to myself, lest somebody think I was out of my mind."[6] This, I would claim, is what happens to religion when it is curbed. Notice, David is *not* saying a person should stop believing in God, only that it seems perverse to inflict our enthusiasm on other people. To "curb" something is to restrain it, not to end or negate it. From humor directed at religious rituals (Season Two, "The Baptism") to rules of conduct—some Christian Scientists' avoidance of medicine in "The Benadryl Brownie" (Season Three), we need to keep our eyes on the context.

Larry's biting humor generally is directed either at people who "make an issue" out of religion, using it as a force of criticism or evaluation in social interaction, or, who, in Larry's opinion, take their religion too far into unreasonable territory. It's not their faith to which Larry objects, but what he takes to be "unseemly" public displays of their faith. Rather than railing against the irrationality of faith or demeaning the role of faith in personal life, Larry seems most concerned with public displays of religious affection. This comedic stance against *some* forms of religious behavior and expression is consistent with tolerance toward a more restrained, personal context for faith.

Rather than exhibiting "Jewish Self-Hate," Larry ridicules how *some* religious people (Jews included) express their faith. This context of *Curb*'s humor is crucial since what saves Larry from being a self-hating Jew is precisely a recognition that he is viewing religion through the *Curb* lens. Viewers of the show can be seen similarly, as being "in" on the joke regarding how *some* people treat their faith.

Some may object that the intentions of the creator and viewers are irrelevant—centuries of discrimination (and outright violence) situate language within a context greater than that envisioned by either artist or art-lover. This *is* an important consideration. But charges of Jewish self-hate on Larry's part and laughing at such a display on ours fail to account for the place of humor and, at times, acerbic self-criticism in Judaic history.

---

[6] "*Times* Talk," May 2006.

The Book of Jonah tells the story of a reluctant prophet (the one swallowed by a whale) whose missteps and vacillations are portrayed in riotous and instructive detail. Midrash, an important part of Jewish intellectual history focusing on the interpretation of biblical texts, is by nature contentious and rife with high-brow puns, similes, jokes, acerbic criticism and self-criticism.

Then there's Yiddish itself, which abounds with humor and play, so much so that a recent book on Jewish culture is titled *Born to Kvetch*.[7] "Kvetch" means "complain." A particularly pernicious stereotype is the cranky, complaining Jew. However, and given the proper *context*, Jews can cope with such discrimination and tell their story by appropriating what elsewhere is a term of abuse. In this regard, it may seem odd to charge Larry with Jewish self-hate rather than place him in a larger context that appreciates the place and role of humor in Jewish culture and history.

I'm not claiming Larry had this in mind when he named the show, but "curb" means "an enclosing frame" and can refer to a raised border that confines. Perhaps critics see Larry as a self-hating Jew because they fail to see the "enclosing frame" that the ethos of the show—the motto "Curb your enthusiasm"—creates for the show's humor. The critics' enthusiasm, it seemed, precluded them from connecting the words uttered by "Larry Jew" and "Larry Gentile" with the comic and philosophical perspective that give meaning and *context* to those words.

---

[7] Michael Wex, *Born to Kvetch: Yiddish Language and Culture in All Its Moods* (St. Martin's Press, 2005).

IV

The Whole Affirmative Action Thing

7
Do You Mind if My Caucasian Mentions the N-Word?

JAMES ROCHA

LARRY: Your bald lawyer says, technically, yes. And I can call you "bald." It's like black people calling each other "ni**er"—Hey, baldy!

—Season Eight, "The Divorce"

Even in twenty-first-century America, race relations can be uncomfortably difficult. Consider a fairly typical sitcom scenario, which plays out quite differently in *Curb Your Enthusiasm*, where Larry David has unknowingly switched phones with Leon Black (Season Six, "The Rat Dog").

Leon receives a call from Larry's black friend, Hal. Hal, thinking he's speaking to Larry, comes to believe that Larry is "doing a black guy character because I'm a black guy." Leon responds, "Black guy doing his thang, baby! Barack Obama, Motherfucker! Barack Obama—I'm the President of hitting that ass!" Hal responds, "Alright. That's not cool. Actually, that's kind of offensive. Stop it now."

But is it offensive? We now have a black president, and some people believe that is the sign that racial tensions have finally ended. Have we arrived at the point where a black guy can now just do his thang without judgment? What about a white guy doing a black guy character—can he just do his thang? Have we, as a society, come to a time and place where a person can hit that ass without us needing to know or care about the race of either the hitter or the ass?

Maybe. But if the feeling of unease associated with merely typing (and probably reading) the previous sentence is in any way an indication, we may still have a long way to go. In spite of the President's enhanced pigmentation, we still live in a society where race is ubiquitous, damned hard to confront, and tempting to simply ignore by placing color blinders over our eyes.

The point of this chapter is to make an unlikely observation: Larry David can sometimes serve as our guide through a complex social world fraught with the perils of intolerance. Larry doesn't earn this position by being perfect with respect to these issues. In fact, Larry is pretty, pretty, pretty, *pretty* far from perfect with respect to just about any social issues. However, we should choose Larry as our guide because he's always willing to embrace embarrassment for the sake of improved interactions with members of other races, especially with respect to those races that are historically disadvantaged and currently treated as different, usually by those people who believe they are racially sensitive just because they purport to ignore race.

Now, this may seem odd but I believe that Larry is perfectly situated to understand this implicit mistreatment that silently plagues disadvantaged groups *because Larry is bald*. Although in real life we must be careful not to compare the plight of Arab Americans post-9/11 to the plight of, say, fat men with belligerent wives, philosophically, our prejudices and sensitivities have an underlying connection that cuts across the various identity traits that define us. Kwame Anthony Appiah, a leading philosopher on identity issues, draws just such a connection when he notes that we all belong to multiple identity groups that provide us with labels, such as "Korean," "bald," or "doctor." These "L-groups," as Appiah calls them in reference to the labeling they place on us, can be socially designated, like "doctor," or seemingly naturally derived, as in race, gender, and follicle counts.

Appiah maintains that we do three things with respect to these groups: we fashion stereotypes based on our expected behavior of L's, we treat people differently because we believe those stereotypes, and we internalize the stereotypes we keep hearing about our L-groups.[1] This isn't always a bad thing;

[1] Appiah, *The Ethics of Identity* (Princeton University Press, 2005), pp. 66–69.

Appiah points out that much of this labeling is necessary. We need to stereotype doctors as professionals you go to when you're sick. We treat doctors differently by allowing them, and hopefully only them, to cut into our bodies. We also try not to call them at their homes just to chat (as Larry learns in "The Hot Towel," Season Seven). Finally, we hope doctors internalize these expectations and *want* to heal all of our ailments, caring about us even when we annoy them.

The problem occurs when we treat the natural L-groups the way we treat the social ones. We shouldn't stereotype or engage in differential treatment just because someone is Jewish, male, or bald. Perhaps that's why it seems like a good idea to ignore these differences. It would be a good idea if equal treatment came easily, but it often doesn't. The internalization of prejudices is problematic precisely because it's so natural to group, stereotype, and treat others differently because of their natural L-groups. Ignoring the problem only makes it worse: the stereotypes become ingrained in our subconscious because we aren't confronting them. Larry David, however, has the solution for bringing our prejudices to light so that we can see what we need to do to eradicate them.

Identifying My Caucasians through Labels

The Larry David Solution to Racial Difference, as I will call it, recommends that we confront each other on racial issues by asking questions, challenging assumptions, and always engaging in dialogues on race. We must do this work even when it's frighteningly awkward—perhaps especially then. Through this active engagement with people of all races, we can learn about each other, become more racially sensitive, and finally eliminate our most entrenched vestiges of prejudice.

Though we may wish we did not have racial L-groups, they do exist as social constructs. There is no natural or scientific answer to the question: how many hairs does a man have to lose before he becomes bald? Socially though, we generally know who's bald and who's not. There's also no important biological difference between Latinos and Asians, but socially we draw sharp lines across, and even within, racial groups.

For example, in "The End" (Season Five), when Larry cannot read a brochure, he exclaims, "It's all Chinese to me!"—

which then requires that he apologize to the Asian woman next to him. He then comes to believe she doesn't look Chinese at all, but appears to be of a Southeast Asian nationality. Larry has apologized for a comment about the Chinese to a woman who he now realizes isn't even Chinese. The woman confirms she is Thai, and Larry says, "I knew it!" Biologically there is no difference between us, but socially we draw these lines, and often are quite particular in maintaining the fake divisions. We need labels—at least for the purpose of knowing whom we're offending.

L-group labels can be useful in many ways. How often have you wanted to point out a stranger to a friend, but could find no good way to point him out other than his race? It's awkward but effective to say, "The tall black man with the martini." Appiah points out that races require social recognition from each other: "for recognition as an African American means social acknowledgment of that collective identity, which requires not just recognizing its existence but actually demonstrating respect for it" (p. 106). Overcoming racism requires that we not ignore racial groups, but that we recognize that all racial groups are equally worthy of our respect. The labels help us direct our respect in the right direction, which is every direction.

People might complain that this view implies that outsiders get to define other races, but Appiah would think that's an oversimplification of the facts. No racial group can exclusively define itself while the rest of the world actively stereotypes it, forming and acting on strong opinions of what it means to be a member of that group (p. 107). For a group to be able to define itself, what's needed—and this is what Larry David repeatedly exemplifies—is that all the outside groups step back and allow that group to define itself without interference.

As Larry consistently shows, this requires respecting that group's right of self-definition by asking them for their own definitions and identifications. Ignoring these issues will only lead to outsiders subconsciously defining that group. The *asking* is key to confronting the internalized views that are formed by outsiders. In one conversation Larry attempts to find out if he has a black man's permission, in this case Leon's, to use the term "brother":

Larry: If you were living in an all white neighborhood, and there was a brother . . .

LEON: I would know the brother, holla at him.

LARRY: Exactly. You don't mind me using the word 'brother', do you?

LEON: Nah, brother's cool. That's perfect.

LARRY: How's that sound coming out of my mouth?

LEON: That sounds cool, yeah.

LARRY: You didn't mind me saying it?

LEON: No, fuck that. 'Brother' sounds cool. (Season Seven, "Denise Handicap")

Larry seeks Leon's opinions on Larry's own language usage. There's something necessarily awkward about such a question, and we wouldn't all have the courage to ask it.

Larry, after all, is making the often worrisome assumption that Leon can speak for all black people in granting Larry permission to use "brother." Leon though is willing to grant permission in this fashion, but Wanda Sykes never would—she gets quite pissed at Larry when he asks these sorts of questions. Such as when Larry asks her if it's wrong to assume that black men wearing bowties are Muslims (Season Five, "The Bowtie"). Wanda responds, "Why you asking me some bullshit like that? What the fuck, Larry—I'm not your link into the black world, okay? So stop asking me shit about black people and stuff." To which, Larry responds with another question about black men and bowties.

Confronting others about race is never easy, but Larry neither presumes he can make decisions about black people without asking, nor does he try to ignore these issues. The first approach risks a presumptuous racism, while the second allows the possibility of racism fermenting in the subconscious. Only Larry's method respects the rights of other groups to define themselves.

Mentioning My "Ni**ers," but not Using Them

Instead of shrinking away from labels, Larry utilizes them in philosophically precise ways. Philosophers have drawn a distinction between *using* a word and *mentioning* that word.

When a person *uses* a word, she intends for the word to have its usual meaning. For example, Michael Richards *used* the n-word in a comedy club to offend and slur two African American hecklers. Larry David would never *use* the n-word, but he does sometimes *mention* it.

A person *mentions* a word when she doesn't intend for it to have its usual meaning, but instead intends for it to refer to the word itself or an utterance of it. We can say, "Michael Richards never should have said, 'ni**er' in that club," without using the n-word because we are talking about Richards's language. We aren't intending to refer to any people in a derogatory way as using the word would do. Grammatical accuracy requires using quotation marks when mentioning words to observe this distinction.

Recall when Larry overhears a man *using* the n-word to describe a "three-hundred-pound ni**er" who dropped his futon while helping him move (Season Six, "The N Word"). Larry repeats this man's conversation, only *mentioning* the n-word, and is overheard by a black doctor, Dr. Page—who doesn't know that Larry is merely mentioning, and not using, the word. Dr. Page, overwhelmed by rage from hearing this bald white man say the n-word, goes into surgery and shaves Jeff Greene bald—though, ironically, the man who actually *used* the n-word was the fully haired racist. The story is tragic with respect to both black and bald people.

Larry recounts this story once again to explain Dr. Page's rage to Jeff and Susie. This time, Loretta Black overhears and informs Leon and Auntie Rae. Larry attempts to explain that he was merely quoting someone (he mentioned the n-word, but never used it), to which Auntie Rae responds, "Fuck you Larry, with your monkey ass."

Maybe Auntie Rae doesn't see the delicate philosophical distinction underlying Larry's defense. Or maybe Auntie Rae understands the philosophical distinction, but disagrees with its relevance to this racially sensitive situation. We could understand her point as: only a monkey's ass would think it's acceptable to mention the n-word. Since Larry would have to accept Auntie Rae's authority as a black woman talking about the n-word, he would have to change.

By the episode's end, Larry is set to testify over the matter, and he is required to repeat the original remarks by the fully haired racist on the phone. After a black man enters the room,

Larry refuses to even repeat the quotation. He will not even *mention* the n-word. When following the Larry David Solution to Racial Difference, it's not enough to ask awkward questions about race, we must learn from others of different races and change our behavior accordingly.

Try Not to White It Up

Larry is always looking to improve on racial issues, but not by listening to white people. He learns by listening to people of color—but Larry consistently rejects white culture (and so has no need for listening to white people about their culture) and rightly doesn't allow white people to define people of color and their cultures (and so he doesn't listen to them about other cultures either). Larry has no need to listen to white people on cultural or racial issues.

While shopping for a baby shower present, Larry discovers a biracial doll, which he refers to as "mulatto" (Season Four, "The Surrogate"). Larry wonders whether the doll is specifically made for biracial children, and whether that means that they make a different doll for every possible biracial combination. He asks the white salesgirl if she understands what he's saying. She answers in the affirmative, but Larry responds, "I wonder if you do." Larry consistently questions whether those who neither live with the perils of racism nor constantly seek to understand them can really understand race as it plays out in America today.

For that reason, when Larry gives the doll as a present to a white couple (answering his own question: the biracial doll can be enjoyable and perhaps morally beneficial for a white baby as well), he refuses to listen when the white couple tells him that the correct term is "biracial," and not Larry's preferred "mulatto." He only agrees to change his terminology when Masasa, a nurse who is actually biracial herself, corrects him.

We cannot empower racial groups to define themselves while implicitly accepting the definitions that come from the dominant group. Larry thinks white people have had power for long enough, and in fact says that he doesn't think white people should have anything: "I think we should be sleeping on the street and eating crumbs, and I think it should be that way for a couple of hundred years" (Season One, "Affirmative Action").

What's important is not whether we take Larry literally here, but that Larry doesn't further empower the dominant L-group by accepting its definitions of disadvantaged L-groups. Larry only listens to how members of the disadvantaged L-groups define themselves, which requires communicating with those members to allow them to identify themselves.

Do Norwegians Yell at the Movie Screen?

Larry's interactions with people of disadvantaged racial groups are often awkward. But he fully embraces friendly relations with people in these L-groups, and his sincerity leads to good learning opportunities. None of us can forget Larry's immediate bond with Wanda's boyfriend, Krazee-Eyez Killa, as they swapped writing tips as experts from their distinct hip-hop and sitcom genres (Season Three, "Krazee-Eyez Killa"). Larry's recommendation on Krazee-Eyez's song is quite astute when he comments, "I would lose the 'motherfucka' at the end cuz you already said 'fuck' once—you don't need two 'fucks'. You already got the one 'fuck'. I would change the 'motherfucker' to 'bitch'. Because 'bitch' is a word that you would use to somebody who you disrespect. Isn't that so?" Larry is quite right—it is so, and Krazee-Eyez readily agrees.

Once Larry begins dating Loretta, he openly embraces black culture, such as when Larry and the Blacks attend the movies and yell together at the screen (Season Six, "The Bat Mitzah"). Some might think that this stereotypical attribution of a certain racialized behavior is itself racist—and there is some danger that it might be. Yet, as Appiah points out, we can't help but internalize some of our stereotypes, and so it would be disingenuous to pretend stereotypes are never accurate.

It's wrong to assume stereotypes are true for others prior to any evidence indicating that they are. It's also wrong to judge others for falling into stereotypes as if people had a responsibility not to act in stereotypical ways. Larry, as a white man, neither judges nor chastises the Blacks for acting in stereotypically black ways. Larry joins the group and embraces their choices: he not only yells at the movie screen, but he clearly relishes doing so. Larry so embraces the Blacks that Wanda jokes that she's nominated him for an NAACP award (Season Seven, "Funkhouser's Crazy Sister").

At another time, Larry is equally comfortable bonding with a Muslim woman who adorns herself in a burqa at all times (Season Four, "Blind Date"). In one pivotal scene in this episode, Larry is having lunch with this Muslim woman and a few mentally disabled men who had washed Larry's car. The group is having a raucously fun time, eating and laughing hysterically at jokes together, when two men who were attempting to produce *The Producers* with Larry and Mel Brooks enter and see the scene. The disgust of the two men is immense, and they find themselves having to walk out—this scene confirms their reasons for hating Larry. The contrast is clear: Larry bonds with others without judgment while many of us, far from being able to enter these bonds, would judge harshly those good souls who do.

Larry's open, though often awkward, embrace of other cultures is even more striking given his nearly universal condemnation and rejection of white culture. Larry is even dismissive of attempts to assert the existence of white cultures. Consider this exchange Larry has with a man he has just learned is named Sven:

> **LARRY:** Is that Swedish?
>
> **SVEN:** (*with clear irritation*) It's Norwegian. I don't look Swedish, do I? Big difference.
>
> **LARRY:** I'm sorry, what's the difference?
>
> **SVEN:** Culture, religion, clothes, food, dancing . . .
>
> **LARRY:** Okay. I'm sorry. Honest mistake . . . Are Swedes touchy if you call them Norwegians?
>
> **SVEN:** Why don't you ask a Swede?
>
> **LARRY:** I will. (Season Four, "The 5 Wood")

Larry is not openly abrasive in this situation: he apologizes and calls it an "honest mistake." But, just a bit deeper under the surface, you can feel Larry dismissing the idea that white cultures are equally needing of respect for their differences. Larry clearly doesn't feel Sven should be so concerned with protecting judgments about his ethnicity. The Norwegian culture is surely deserving of our respect, but it's not under attack by an oppressive, internalized system of racism. So Larry barely cares.

Chicken Boy's Courage

I'm not saying that Larry David is the epitome of accomplished racial sensitivity. Larry, being pretty, pretty, pretty, *pretty* far from perfect, gets things wrong all the time. But that really is the whole point. The Larry David Solution to Racial Difference is not easy. It requires that we make mistakes since we must engage in racial discussions with other races, which may at times risk severe awkwardness. Playing it safe and ignoring race won't do when racial matters are so intense and so necessary to confront.

Larry certainly makes a plethora of mistakes, but they are often made in the pursuit of navigating our racially diverse world. Larry may seem to cross a rather harsh line when he questions the courage of Yoshi's father, who is a surviving Kamikaze pilot. However, Larry never says Yoshi's father is a coward—he *asks* about the contradiction of surviving and being a Kamikaze pilot. When Kevin Nealon says, "There are a lot of Kamikaze pilots that are alive," Larry responds, "You say that, and I say they weren't really Kamikaze pilots." Larry is attempting to solve a difficult puzzle about a culture that he doesn't fully understand. Doing so may come off as brutish and insensitive—and does lead to Yoshi's suicide attempt—but that is Larry's way to learn. I never said Larry David's Solution to Racial Difference is safe and easy.

Larry, as he often does, comes around and apologizes to Yoshi, though he does it while eating pistachios. Yoshi, though, is weary of accepting an apology that comes during the eating of pistachios:

> **Yoshi:** That might be the way you do things in your family, but we don't snack and apologize.
>
> **Larry:** What? Is that a Japanese thing?
>
> **Yoshi:** No. No, that's a human thing. (Season Five, "Kamikaze Bingo")

In this conversation with Yoshi, Larry *attempts* to figure out whether the difference between them is because Yoshi is Japanese. Of course, the difference is not due to any peculiarities of Japanese culture. As Yoshi explains, his annoyance is due to Larry misunderstanding a *universal* cultural trait. Larry's rejection of white culture puts him in an even more awkward position when it comes to universal cultural traits. How could he know which cultural traits are universal when he has no culture? Because Larry sticks his neck out just by asking whether this is a "Japanese thing," he looks foolish. You have to risk embarrassment to embrace the Larry David solution.

Another good example of being willing to face awkward moments to learn about other races comes when Larry attempts to learn whether Chinese kids are naturally better with chopsticks. To find out, he asks a white couple who have adopted a Chinese baby whether she eats with chopsticks. They respond angrily:

> **JOHN FOWLER:** Do you think she is also a Kung Fu Master?
>
> **LARRY:** No. All I'm wondering is this: if you took an American kid who's never used chopsticks before and a Chinese kid who's never used chopsticks before, would the Chinese kid do better?
>
> **JOHN FOWLER:** So the American kid is the control group?
>
> **JAMIE FOWLER:** You know what, she uses a fork.
>
> **LARRY:** Do me a favor. The first time she uses chopsticks, give me a call. (Season Seven, "Denise Handicap")

Larry is inquiring about a biological view of race that many biologists and philosophers of race believe is unfounded, but *Larry* has no way of knowing that these particular behavioral characteristics aren't built into our DNA. Larry is right to wonder about this, and his questions are fair, though they're also embarrassing.

The Larry David Solution to Racial Difference isn't easy, and you may have to risk appearing to be insensitive on the road to racial sensitivity. Asking questions is the only way we learn without being presumptuous. And we can all understand why it's so important not to make assumptions about others because we all belong to some kind of L-group that needs to demand respect—and Larry David is no exception.

All I See Is Bald

Larry David understands, at least on some small level, the difficulties faced by L-groups seeking respect and recognition since, like almost everyone, he is the member of at least one L-group that is not universally respected nor considered dominant. Larry is bald. It's one of the advantages of Appiah's delineation of L-groups that we all belong to multiple L-groups. Even a rich heterosexual white male like Larry can experience some of the difficulties associated with being a member of an underprivileged L-group because of his baldness. Haired versus bald is not a recognized standard for divisive identity dichotomies, but for the bald, it's one of the dichotomies that most defines their existence. With Appiah's categorization, we need not separate the problems of the bald from that of other disadvantaged L-groups.

Larry experiences differential treatment at least minimally, which may help with being sensitive to the problems of others. Larry internalizes his bald experiences, which enables him to empathize with others who have difficulties in navigating a world that sets up so many arbitrary, but socially inescapable dichotomies (white versus black, male versus female, straight versus gay, and of course haired versus bald). As Appiah notes, it's natural to internalize L-group stereotypes and to seek solidarity from others who are going through related difficulties (p. 68).

Larry would agree with the importance of finding solidarity, as shown by him welcoming Jeff into the bald brotherhood after Dr. Page shaved Jeff in the previously described blind rage incident. In this exchange, Jeff inquires about bald solidarity:

> **JEFF:** There's like meetings?
>
> **LARRY:** There's no meetings, but when we see each other on the street, we nod. We'll give a thumbs up.
>
> **JEFF:** Yeah.
>
> **LARRY:** You know what? We love each other, me and my bald brothers. (Season Six, "The N Word")

Larry sees the importance of finding an unwritten solidarity with other bald people—a solidarity that is expressed rarely, but that connects people who travel through similar life obstacles.

It's key to the Larry David Solution to Racial Diversity that we spread this solidarity out until it includes us all. It's because Larry understands so well what it's like to be disfavored based on his baldness that he has a sense of what it means to have some arbitrary distinction (such as one based on your race, gender, sexuality, career, or how much hair you have) used against you. Larry doesn't internalize his problems and think that only bald people are discriminated against. Instead, Larry realizes that if he feels some small level of pain because of some minor discrimination against his L-group, then other L-groups must be suffering even more. The point of the Larry David Solution to Racial Diversity is that we should all use our own L-groups to learn how to see the world from each other's perspectives. That way, we're not limited to bald solidarity or black solidarity, but there is a universal solidarity where everyone is treated with respect.

Call Me "Larry Jew"

The Larry David Solution to Racial Difference works because we must see ourselves as part of a diverse society where we work together to understand and cope with the problems we separately face. None of this is meant to suggest that we ought to accept races as real or treat baldness as if it should matter.

The point is that our society has problems that cut along identity lines. We have problems with respect to the big identity issues (race, gender, sexuality, and religion)—and those problems may be our biggest, but there are others too. We don't have to believe the differences between us are either real or important to see that the problems surely are both real and important. We might think that *Curb Your Enthusiasm* uses baldness as a joke, but people who feel mistreated due to their lack of hair take it seriously. Similarly, philosophers and scientists don't believe that race is anything scientifically real, but racism is certainly quite harmful. While the distinctions we draw between us are arbitrary and often serve little positive purpose, those same distinctions can lead to great social harms, including bigotry and prejudice.

To address the problems, we must first learn about each other. Learning about each other means interacting with each other: asking questions, bonding, sharing, and growing together across our L-group differences. That may be awkward at times, but we will never be able to overcome our differences if we do not talk to each other about them, which Larry David is always willing to do.

If this solution to dealing with our differences doesn't work, there's always the one offered by Masasa, Larry's biracial nurse:

> **MASASA:** If we all keep fucking each other, we'll all be the same race one day anyway.
>
> **LARRY:** Let's pray for that! (Season Four, "The Surrogate")

8
What Kind of Men Are Larry and Jeff?

TAINE DUNCAN

LARRY: [*watching* Girls Gone Wild!] You know what a woman would do if I ever asked her to lift up her top?

JEFF: Why do you have to analyze this? Can't we just watch this?

LARRY: She would spit on me! If I ever asked a woman to lift up her top, she would kick me in the balls and spit on me!

JEFF: We've waited a long time to see this and all you're doing is yakking. Be quiet, come on!

—Season Four, "Wandering Bear"

Bosom buddies Larry and Jeff represent two extreme variations of masculinity in contemporary American society.

Jeff has an extremely successful private life, with a wife, daughter, and stable home. However, his philandering ways have created more than a few sticky situations during the course of the past eight seasons of *Curb Your Enthusiasm*.

Larry has failed at his marriage (whether or not he and Cheryl get back together), has awkward relationships with children, and has lived in several different homes over the course of the series. Meanwhile, rather than reveling in his bachelor status, Larry is nervous around other women and self-sabotages several opportunities for sexual encounters.

In psychoanalytic theory and feminist social theory, narcissistic philanderers are womanizing men who are self-absorbed with an over-inflated sense of self-worth. This is the stereotypic "man's man"—he has a trophy wife, mistresses, and a sports car, but he also crushes others to get to the top. Neurotic impotents are men who fear judgment. They are paralyzed by the fear that other men will think less of them, so they don't take risks, and they don't assert power and control. Does *Curb Your Enthusiasm* reinforce the stereotyping of American men as either narcissistic philanderers or neurotic impotents? Or, alternatively, does *Curb Your Enthusiasm* illuminate the ridiculous nature of these false alternatives by hyperbolizing the cultural extremes?

It may not stand out when we watch the show casually, but Larry and Jeff represent equally unlivable versions of American men. *Curb Your Enthusiasm* can even be thought of as promoting a measured critique of gender roles, specifically the expectations of masculine gender ideals, that follows much of contemporary feminist philosophy and psychoanalysis. The characters of Larry and Jeff act as cultural reminders that such masculine ideals are ultimately self-destructive for a complex, ethically invested, and independent version of the American man.

Are Larry and Jeff Just Overgrown Man-Children?

Ben: You are such a baby. You're a grown man-baby!

Larry: Are you saying I'm a man-child?

—Season Four, "The Blind Date"

As children, we lay the groundwork for our expectations as adults. We learn how to treat others from our families, from our societies, from our cultures, and, very basically, from our first relationship with our parents.

The need for relationships and basic recognition is so fundamental that it may be universal for all sentient creatures. As the psychoanalyst Jacques Lacan explains, "it is a necessary condition for the maturation of the gonad of the female pigeon that the pigeon should see another member of its species, regardless of its sex; this condition is so utterly sufficient that the desired effect may be obtained by merely placing the mirror's reflective field near the individual."[1] So the possibility for

1 Jacques Lacan, *Écrits: A Selection* (Norton, 2004), p. 5.

development and maturity as fully formed adult creatures—even in the bird world—depends on the potential for connecting and identifying with another. Without seeing someone else to identify with, the pigeon can't finish developing. For the human psyche, this is also true.

One of the first lessons we learn as infants is a mutual dependency on another human being. We need our mothers to supply milk, and we need our fathers holding us. As we grow older we come to understand that we need others to understand us—our needs, our desires, our wants. And to make sure they understand us, we realize that we have to understand them.

As Jessica Benjamin explains, "very early on we find that recognition between persons—understanding and being understood, being in attunement—is becoming an end itself. Recognition between persons is essentially mutual."[2] Benjamin takes this idea from the nineteenth-century German philosopher Georg Hegel, who explained that the adult subject undergoes a tension between the need for independence (being a complete subject), and the need for recognition (recognizing our dependencies on others). In other words, identifying with others as subjects is not only an ethical decision about how best to treat others, but it is also an important decision for constructing self-identity. Recognition comes to mean the mutual development of self-identity in relation to others.

This means that the abilities we cultivate as children to identify with and recognize others establish our patterns and abilities for our adult relationships. If we never grow out of the awkward stages in development, and never learn to recognize others for who they are, we can never fully realize our own self-potential. This can cause terribly maladjusted adults!

Why Is It So Hard to Get a Date?

LARRY: [*on dating women*] This is the thing that I'm the worst at in the world. This and drawing.

—Season Four, "Mel's Offer"

[2] Jessica Benjamin, *Like Subjects, Love Objects* (Yale, 1998), p. 33.

If it's so obvious that as children we develop mutual dependencies based on recognition, and as adults we are all dependent on each other, why all the fuss about explaining the theories for recognition? How do we get untenable ideals of masculinity instead? The simple answer is that we're taught to forget these things. As we grow, develop, and become adults in the contemporary world, we are taught certain ideal ways of being. Oftentimes, these ideals stand in direct contrast to our psychological, emotional, and ethical needs.

Young men are often taught to be independent and strong, with young women being taught to provide care *for* others, and not necessarily *with* others. Feminine gendered developmental theory is intimately interconnected. If you think about Susie and Cheryl's characters, for example, they seem to have developed partially in relation to their husbands. Cheryl is strong and assertive, but not aggressive. She bolsters Larry against his insecurities without adding to them. Susie, on the other hand, is forced to respond to Jeff's lack of emotional attachment and instability by being aggressive and opinionated, but not emotional. Despite their obvious personality differences, Susie and Cheryl are both conditioned to meet the needs of their husbands to adequately compensate for their limitations.

Because the idealizations of masculinity are ultimately self-destructive and actually unachievable, they manifest as psychological problems for the men on the show. Larry's character on *Curb* presents one type of this terribly maladjusted adult. He never seems to be able to identify fully with other characters on the show, and he never seems to be able to fully realize his own potential. He's a neurotic personality who feels extreme helplessness, or impotence. His best friend Jeff Greene represents the other type of poorly adjusted male adult. He also has difficulty recognizing others for who they are. He embodies a narcissistic personality, and just uses people for his own interests.

A Neurotic Impotent for the Woody Allen in All of Us

Larry: I don't tell my wife anything. I don't confide in her. I don't trust anybody.

—Season Two, "Thor"

Early in the very first season of *Curb Your Enthusiasm*, Larry establishes himself firmly as a neurotic personality. In "Porno Gil," for example, Jeff must undergo heart surgery, but before he does he asks Larry to hide his porn from Susie. In this episode Larry perfectly represents the generalized fear and anxiety that psychoanalysts refer to as "neurotic anxiety." He doesn't want to help Jeff hide his porn, not because he is morally opposed to the pornography—although he does say that he doesn't care for it—but because he's afraid of being caught, afraid of forgetting Jeff's alarm code, afraid of being unable to find Jeff's stash. He's practically overcome by his fears. Since Freud, neurotic anxiety has been characterized by the generalization of fear and anxiety. It's not fear of a particular thing (that would be phobia), nor is it the specific fear of the father (that would be castration anxiety). Instead, neurotic anxiety afflicts adults who are psychologically handicapped by the fear of libidinal impulses, the drives that make up Freud's concept of the Id (for example, desires for sex).

So what does this mean? First, castration anxiety and the Oedipal complex are interconnected: Freud explained that all little boys must go through a specific stage of development, when they fall in love with their mothers, and come to see their fathers as threatening competitors. Since the mother does not have a penis, the boy who begins to fear his father will fear that perhaps the father cut off his mother's penis, and could do the very same to him—this is castration anxiety. The process of seeing the mother as an object of affection, fearing the father (and wanting to beat him) as a sexual competitor, and eventually resolving this conflict through identification with the masculinity of the father is known all together as the Oedipal complex.

The self-control and identification processes that must be completed to resolve this stage of development demonstrate the relationship of the Id, Ego, and Superego. The Id is like the impulse center of your personality—your sex-drive especially—and must be controlled. The Superego is the part of your mind that's ideal. It aims for absolute perfections, while the Ego functions to realistically balance your desires and expectations within the limits of lived experience.

As it plays out, neurotic anxiety is a generalized fear that your Id will emerge and you will act inappropriately according to some unchecked drive. In order to compensate for this feeling of powerless self-control, anxiety emerges. According to some contemporary theories of masculinity, this neurosis can be caused by the very expectations placed on idealizations of men and masculine control and power.

As Michael S. Kimmel explains, men as a group are expected to have power and control. However, individual men often have to defer to their bosses, their families, and their more powerful friends. This disconnect between the expectation of power and control, and the feeling of a loss of control and power causes fear and anxiety. Frustration with powerlessness manifests itself as a competition among men for perceptions of power and self-control. Because men secretly feel powerless, but want to appear powerful to other men, a fear of the perceptions of other men takes hold. As Kimmel explains, "This, then, is the great secret of manhood: *We are afraid of other men*."[3]

Larry is definitely afraid of other men, of women, of pretty much the whole world around him. In "Thor" (Season Two), Larry is even afraid of the power of children! Granted, his fear is that a professional wrestler's children will nark on him to their father, but even so . . .

This episode also demonstrates how debilitating neurotic anxiety can be for sexuality. In this episode, Jeff and Susie temporarily separate. Jeff is again worried about his porn stash. This time, Jeff's worried that his wife Susie will find out about his fetishes, and will use them against him if they get a divorce. Larry confides in Jeff that he has no fetishes or unusual interests, and purposefully tries to be as "vanilla" as possible so that Cheryl won't think he has any weird sexual proclivities. But after he hails his jogging neighbor Wanda by yelling, "I'd recognize that tush anywhere," Cheryl thinks he has a butt fetish. This mortifies Larry, who has always been afraid of others' judgments.

I don't know whether Larry really is an "ass-man," but neither does Larry. Larry's generalized fear of others has made him impotent even as far as understanding his own sexual desires. His fear of acting inappropriately is so strong that he

---

[3] Michael S. Kimmel, "Masculinity as Homophobia," in *Sex, Gender, and Sexuality* (Oxford University Press, 2008), p. 65.

has cut off his own libidinal urges from himself. This frustrated sexuality and fear of women comes back to haunt Larry all through Season Six, when he's separated from Cheryl and has difficulty with dating other women.

In "The TiVo Guy" (Season Six), Larry self-sabotages a chance with Lucy Lawless. He injures his testicles by wearing the wrong kind of underwear, and then ruins his chances with Xena the Warrior Princess by being overly forthcoming about his current testicular predicament. He doesn't know how to talk about sex or sexuality partly due to his fear of being judged sexually inadequate, and partially due to a fear of saying the wrong thing at the wrong time!

This fear of being judged contributes to Larry's tendency to judge other men as well. In "The Thong" (Season Two), Larry decides to cut off a relationship with his otherwise effective therapist after seeing the therapist in a thong swimsuit at the beach. Larry is so uncomfortable with this nontraditional display of the male body that he judges his therapist unworthy of a further therapeutic relationship. His beliefs about appropriate male behavior and dress are so carefully protected that he can't even run the risk of associating with a less-than-manly man. It's as if he's afraid of associating with the atypical man for fear of being judged-by-association. This seems to fit Larry's other neurotic tendencies, and to fit Michael S. Kimmel's evaluation that our unrealistic expectations for masculinity cause men to fear and judge other men. For Larry, then, his neurotic anxiety not only hinders his own personality and sexuality, but it also causes him to unfairly judge others. This combination of neuroses and being judgmental makes having a relationship difficult for Larry—whether it be with his wife, his therapist, or a potential lover. If we're all happiest and healthiest when we relate to and appreciate mutual dependencies, then the type of isolation Larry feels from his fear, anxiety, and judgment is definitely undesirable!

Is Jeff a Lothario or Just a Philanderer?

JEFF: Who stops a whack-job?!

—Season Two, "The Massage"

Neurotic impotence obviously seems undesirable. Who wants to be immobilized by fear and made to feel sexually inadequate? But who wouldn't *want* to be a sexually promiscuous, womanizing man without fear or anxiety for the perceptions and judgments of others? Who wouldn't want to be like Jeff?

Reflecting back on the "Porno Gil" episode, it's easy to see how Jeff's unique pathology stands in direct contrast to Larry's neuroses. Jeff doesn't want to be caught with porn if he dies, but not because of any shame of his Id, or generalized fear. He's worried about preserving his reputation among his friends and colleagues. And because of his high self-regard, Jeff has no qualms asking Larry to find and hide his porn stash. It's obvious in this short exchange that he's more concerned with his own potential discomfort than with Larry's actual discomfort about taking the task.

In other episodes, Jeff is successful at engaging in multiple extramarital affairs, and is seldom caught. When he is caught, he seems to be forgiven quickly. This narcissism may appear ideal in the successful womanizing philanderer, but it also has its corollary in psychoanalytic diagnosis and contemporary critiques of masculinity.

Neurotic anxiety was caused by the internalization of fears thought to originate in the Oedipal complex, but Freudian descriptions of narcissistic development focus on the relationship of mother-infant relations. All infants have what Freud characterized as primary narcissistic tendencies—babies are unable to differentiate the world from themselves. They see their desires for food, relief from bodily functions, and affection as being the purpose of the world. They have not yet experienced the separation of the self from the world. However, as babies develop, Freudians maintain that the relationship between mother and child should encourage the separation of the baby as a subject from the objects of the world. Babies must learn that there is a wider world outside the nursery, and that this world is much more than a place for fulfilling individual desires and needs. The child must also learn to see the mother as another independent subject, in order to balance an appreciation of the connection of the self to the world and to other subjects.

After Freud, most of the more recent philosophers and psychoanalysts have focused on how the absolute nurturing role of the mother and the apparent absence of the mother's own individual identity have forced boys to separate absolutely from the mother. They're discouraged from identifying with this selfless nurturing goal, and become independent as a result. On the other hand, girls are encouraged to over-identify with the mother's nurturing, and are psychologically constrained because they are never able to fully identify as separate individuals. However, new theories of masculine development have tried to stress how this nurturing practice also has an impact on the development of boys, and can negatively encourage boys to develop secondary narcissism.

Secondary narcissism is the pathological narcissism that would contribute to the philandering masculine ideal. Narcissists of this order re-establish themselves as the center of the world, in response to the perception of the inadequacy of the mother and father as people to model themselves after, and in response to a heightened sense of expectations about their own abilities.

If little boys are supposed to identify with their fathers, they must be given strong role models in their fathers, and their mothers must encourage appropriate separation. When this does not happen, when the separation is too extreme, and when the father is not enough of an ideal model, the secondary narcissist lacks the tools for developing relationships with other subjects, and independence from objects. The boy creates new expectations for himself and the world, attempting to make himself into the role model he misses in his father. One way to think of this is having an overactive Superego: your ideal expectations are so high, and so valuable, that when they're not met, you retreat into yourself. You don't care what others think, because they seem to be even less powerful and interesting than you are, so you assert yourself as the untouchable center of the new world.

Explaining the role of detaching from mothers, Isaac D. Balbus writes: "If mothers suppress the separation and over-reward the merger of their little boys and girls, then they will grow up to be men and women who privilege connection over separation. If mothers suppress the merger and over-reward the separation of their little girls and boys, then they will grow up to become women and men who privilege separation over connection."[4]

---

[4] Isaac D. Balbus, "Masculinity and the (M)Other," in *Masculinity Studies and Feminist Theory* (Columbia University Press, 2002), p. 212.

It's the forced attempt to polarize the development of boys and girls that contributes to the development of secondary narcissism in boys. If little boys are exclusively taught that they should not be nurturing at all, then they will never learn that other individuals share and depend on the same world. This secondary narcissism is then reinforced and maintained by social masculine ideals of power, independence, and sexual prowess—the same ideals that reinforced the tension at the heart of neurotic anxiety. The philandering narcissist is already predisposed to self-centered lack of care for others; when society also says that the "cool guys" are those who "bag chicks" or who "have the most toys," then this personality type is not only reinforced, but actively promoted.

In "The Massage" (Season Two), Jeff tries to set Larry up with a "Happy Ending" massage. At first Larry doesn't realize what's going on. And by the time he does, he has already had "twelve pumps." He immediately feels guilty and stops the massage, but is too afraid to tell Cheryl what has happened and why. Instead, Cheryl's psychic tells her to beware of Larry cheating with a redheaded woman with tattoos—exactly what the masseuse looks like. Cheryl later sees the masseuse and, at the close of the episode, confronts Larry.

Throughout the episode the implication is that if Larry had only told Cheryl what had happened, he would not have been "caught." But I suggest that we go even further: if Jeff had only told Larry that the masseuse was a sexual masseuse, or had considered Larry's potential difficulties with the masseuse, the situation may not have occurred in the first place. Jeff seems to have a complete lack of awareness that his best friend Larry is pretty neurotic and might feel uncomfortable with the unexpected hand-job! Even the fact that Jeff suggests this masseuse to Larry is based on Jeff's frequent personal use of her services—further characterizing Jeff as a narcissistic philanderer.

The most extreme example of Jeff's pathological narcissism comes in "Funkhouser's Crazy Sister" (Season Seven). In this episode, Jeff sleeps with Funkhouser's sister. However, Jeff goes beyond his usual womanizing ways and the twist is that Funkhouser's sister Bam-Bam has just been released from a mental institution. Funkhouser trusts Larry and Jeff to watch Bam-Bam one afternoon. But rather than taking this task seriously, Jeff gets bored and decides to entertain himself by seducing the woman he's supposed to be babysitting.

After the fact, Jeff denies having slept with Bam-Bam, and when she tries to tell others about the experience, he uses her diagnosis to say that she is making it all up. She's just crazy! Jeff's narcissism reaches a new high in this episode. He is not only insensitive to his marriage commitments, and lies to his friends and family, but he manipulates a woman's disability to sleep with her and then deny it. He also pulls Larry into the deception, again asking Larry to help cover his butt. He does not seem to be wracked by guilt at the experience. The only reason he wants to disguise what he has done is to avoid punishment.

The pathology of narcissism may look less self-destructive than neuroses. But we really do live in a world where we're mutually dependent on others. If we alienate and manipulate those others, we isolate ourselves, which inhibits our own growth as human beings.

You Four-Eyed F@ck and You Fat Piece of Sh*t!

JEFF: You never congratulated me on my new car.

LARRY: What, are you kidding?

JEFF: No, I'm not kidding. I was pretty hurt by it.

LARRY: I never congratulated your new car?

JEFF: I was hurt by it.

—"AAMCO," Season One

If Larry's neurosis was caused by failing to meet the social pressures on men to be the *most* successful, the strongest, and the most sexually adept and experienced, then Jeff's narcissism was also caused by the illusion of *being* these things.

It doesn't matter that Larry is in fact a successful writer, has been married to a beautiful woman, and owns nice houses. In his mind, it is never enough to meet expectations, so he focuses instead on his rejected sitcom proposals, his awkwardness in first dates, and his unhappiness with power lines on his property. Similarly, despite the fact that Jeff technically works for Larry, that his wife frequently kicks him out of the house, and that he actually relies on Larry to get him out of binds, Jeff's absolute self-confidence reigns supreme. So Jeff becomes the guy who sleeps around, who always gets let back in to his house, and who supplies Larry with Lakers tickets.

In both cases, at their most pathological, Larry and Jeff become cautionary figures. They demonstrate what happens to men when boys are raised to be competitive, self-interested, and isolated. They show us what happens when men are encouraged, even as adults, to be better than other men, to make more money, to have more beautiful women, to be independent of others. For the most part, most men are neither Larry nor Jeff. Most do not end up being completely incapacitated by social fear, nor do most throw out all inhibitions in favor of being a manipulative womanizer. These are the extremes. But if these are the pressures of society, how do men possibly become otherwise?

Jeff and Larry may themselves hint at the possibility of being something else, of being men and still being connected to the world and to others, and of developing a strong sense of self in relation to that world. When push comes to shove, Larry and Jeff depend on each other. Their flawed but deeply felt friendship demonstrates a mutual dependence on each other. Despite their differences, who other than Larry would Jeff ask to hide his porn? And to whom other than Jeff would Larry tell his fears of being labeled a sexual deviant? They seem to have a love and a need for each other. And this love and need seems to be mutually beneficial—a true relationship between subjects. Larry is not afraid of Jeff's judgment as he is afraid of the rest of the world. He can tell Jeff his secrets. And Jeff values Larry's friendship, despite sometimes abusing it. He often asks for Larry's help, admitting weakness.

As friendships go, this isn't all bad. Kelly Oliver argues for love and relationships with others founded in a psychology of critical self-reflection. She thinks that a sort of self-reflecting loving eye is made possible through a re-negotiation of identity.[5] Men and women are not stuck in a pre-determined iden-

[5] Kelly Oliver, *Witnessing: Beyond Recognition* (University of Minnesota Press, 2001), p. 219.

tity based in masculine ideals, or fully constructed by our relationships to our parents. Instead, identity is fluid—we are constantly creating who we are through our actions and interactions with the world. Oliver emphasizes that we depend on others for our identities, but that both our identities and our relationships change and evolve to make us better:

> The other's potential to make me better than I am is the power of love. In this case, I fall in love with love, with the precarious process of subjectivity that connects the tissues of my sensations, affects, thoughts, and words—the tissues of my being—to the tissues of others . . . And being together is the chaotic adventure of subjectivity. (p. 224)

Larry's dependence on Jeff, and Jeff's reliance on Larry may be their saving grace. The chaos of *Curb Your Enthusiasm* ultimately works, and only becomes watchable, because of these relationships.

When Larry steals flowers from Funkhouser's mother's memorial, we laugh nervously, uncomfortably. We don't want to emulate this behavior. We want to stop it! On the other hand, by breaking these extreme behaviors with moments of tenderness between Larry and Jeff, in the moments where you can see that they really are friends, *Curb Your Enthusiasm* makes us care for these characters. We want them to make better choices. We want them to be people we would *want* to model ourselves after. So Larry and Jeff might illuminate the pitfalls of our expectations for American masculinity, but they also give us glimpses into a way out. They show us, however briefly, that by cultivating real friendships and relationships we can work towards becoming better people together.

For the most part, these glimpses are fleeting. We see Larry try very hard to be a good friend when he buys Jeff his favorite discontinued sponge cake in "The Nanny From Hell" (Season Three). Similarly, Jeff attempts to be a good friend when he gives Larry his courtside basketball tickets in "Shaq" (Season Two). In both instances, Larry and Jeff display selflessness and true friendship, overcoming their pathological limitations. But only for a short while!

The male character who arguably comes closest to living an alternative masculinity that is complex, ethically invested, *and* independent is Leon. Some may argue that Ted Danson also represents an ethically invested male character. However, I think Larry summed it up best when he said of Ted, "That's fake philanthropy and faux anonymity!" Frequently, Ted's values seem to be posturing, which may be just another form of narcissistic personality disorder.

Leon Black is by no means perfect—he has a tendency to be a bit of a Lothario himself, and is a little quick to offer physical threats—but he demonstrates a real investment in interpersonal and mutually beneficial relationships. He doesn't seem to be hung up on neurotic anxieties, and he recognizes his own limitations without being overwhelmed by them. In Seasons Six and Seven Leon didn't merely bring some of the most hilarious one-liners to *Curb*. He also brought a new model of friendship to Larry.

In one of his first scenes on the show, Leon is accused of leaving a stain on the bedspread in his room. But, Leon replies, it couldn't have been him because he "brings the ruckus to the ladies!" At first, then, it appears that Leon will just be another narcissistic philanderer. However, later in the same episode, "The Anonymous Donor" (Season Six), Leon goes out of his way to retrieve Larry's missing Joe Pepitone jersey. It ends up being a mistake, and Leon ends up threatening an innocent man out of his own jersey. But Leon's heart was in the right place. There was no self-interest involved, and Leon wasn't self-conscious about putting himself out there. He was simply trying to do a good deed for Larry.

On other occasions, Leon is a good friend to Larry by telling him truths he needs to hear, even when he might not want to. Think of the scene in "The N Word" (Season Six) when Leon is willing to confront Larry on Auntie Rae's behalf. He cares about Larry, but in a way that challenges Larry to be a better man. He can't accept Larry's accidental erections or apparent use of the "N word." But rather than simply judging Larry, writing him off, or too quickly forgiving his mistakes, Leon challenges Larry to do better.

In addition to his ability to cultivate friendships that promote growth and mutual recognition, Leon is also unafraid of asking for help when he needs it. Unlike Larry and Jeff, who are both afraid of being judged unmanly when in a position of need, Leon sees that everyone can use a little help sometimes. He offers his own help, and he expects his friends to do the same for him. A good example of this occurs in "The Rat Dog" (Season Six), when Leon goes to Larry to ask for interview advice.

So, in the end, does *Curb Your Enthusiasm* reinforce the stereotypes of men as either patriarchal and narcissistic philanderers or neurotic impotents? Or does *Curb Your Enthusiasm* illuminate the ridiculous nature of these false alternatives by hyperbolizing the cultural extremes? Maybe this is a false dichotomy. Maybe we should think that, in showing the discomfort of these extreme states of being, *Curb* does not glorify or encourage such behavior, but instead demonstrates how unproductive such behaviors really are. And by giving us glimpses into the possibility of true friendship between Larry and Jeff, and a potentially even better model through Leon, *Curb* also lets us see the possibilities for ethical, healthy, and independent American men.

V

Yelling for Society, for Everybody

9

He's Applying the Golden Rule. Are *You*?

BEKKA WILLIAMS

When you think of Larry David, strong dedication to following the rules probably isn't the first thing that comes to mind. Indeed, a repeated theme of *Curb Your Enthusiasm* is Larry's tendency to get himself into trouble by failing to do what others expect of him.

He ignores Cheryl's fear of dying in a plane crash in favor of ensuring the repair of his TiVo, he tries to trick a Christian Scientist into taking allergy medication, he picks up a prostitute in order to use the car pool lane, and he takes flowers from a roadside memorial. I could go on—as could you.

In truth, however, Larry David is a dedicated and consistent rule follower. While rather selective in the rules he accepts as legitimate, when Larry accepts a rule he goes to great lengths and physical discomfort—literally, as in "The Massage" (Season Two)—to act in accordance with it.

What's He Supposed to Do?

Larry would be the first to admit that he doesn't always follow the rules of polite society. But that doesn't mean that he isn't a good rule-follower. We can see this by doing a bit of philosophy and asking ourselves what it really *is* to be a rule-follower. This may seem a silly question. Of course, a rule-follower is just a person who follows the rules, right? But which rules? All of them, all the time? Most of them, most of the time? Surely you don't have to be *perfect* to be a good rule-follower. (There's probably a rule against exiting a car during a carwash cycle. But we wouldn't want to say that Cheryl's desperate escape from the carwash in "The Grand Opening" (Season Three) renders her a rule-flaunting renegade.)

We must also consider the source of the rules. If we were to consider Larry a rule-follower only if he followed every rule endorsed by anyone (social rules, rules of etiquette, moral rules, rules of law, and so forth) we would quickly end up with cases in which Larry would be a rule-breaker no matter what course of action he chose. All this requires is a situation in which two rules (of whatever source) make incompatible demands.

In "The Ski Lift" (Season Five), Larry finds himself stuck alone with Rachel (the daughter of the head of the kidney consortium) in a ski lift at dusk, and she jumps to the ground to avoid breaking Jewish law. Many of you probably felt, as I did, that it was rather rude of Larry not to offer to jump himself. (He was a perfect gentleman, however, in offering to share his edible panties!)

Nonetheless, there are safety-based rules in place when we ride on a ski lift: foremost amongst these, we should not jump out of it. So if Larry had jumped, he would have broken a rule (as Rachel did when she jumped). But, of course, the only other option was not to jump, thereby breaking the Jewish law. Whatever Larry did, he would be breaking a rule, and the same is true of Rachel. Thus, if we understand rule-followers simply as those who *in fact* comply with all (or even most) rules, we'll be forced to say that some people can't be good rule-followers no matter how hard they try—simply because circumstances have conspired against them.

This seems rather harsh, though. In fact, it was largely *because of* Rachel's strong dedication to the Jewish law that she violated the ski lift safety rule. It would be rather perverse to label Rachel a rule-breaker simply for violating the safety rules. So we don't want to say that Larry is a rule-follower only if he follows all the rules (all, or even most, of the time).

Another reason for rejecting the view that good rule-followers are those and only those who in fact follow the rules involves the possibility that people may break or follow rules completely by accident. Indeed, a person might follow the rules while actually *trying to break them*, as Hasidic dry cleaner Anna did when an earthquake prevented her from fulfilling

Larry's anniversary gift and cheating on her clueless husband Schlomo ("The Survivor," Season Four). We certainly shouldn't credit Anna with following the rules of marital faithfulness when she would have broken her vows but for the earthquake.

He Doesn't Subscribe to That Dry-Cleaning Law!

This leaves us with the difficult question of precisely when failing to follow a rule counts against a person's credentials as a rule-follower. There are, in fact, two quite different categories of rule-breaking:

1. **You might acknowledge the legitimacy of a rule yet break it anyway**

or

2. **You might not acknowledge the legitimacy of the rule in the first place (either because you aren't aware of the rule, or because you have considered and rejected it).**

Take Larry's agent Jeff Greene. Jeff *acknowledges* that it's wrong for him to cheat on his wife Susie, yet he repeatedly does it anyway. In this case, it is pretty clear that Jeff is not acting as a good rule-follower should. A rule-follower must at least try to follow the rules he accepts.

By contrast, consider Larry's after-hours phone calls to the Greenes and *Seinfeld's* Julia Louis-Dreyfus in "The Wire" (Season One). After much debate with Cheryl, Larry decides that the rule against late-night calls does not come into effect until 10:30 P.M. and calls at 10:20 with the thought that this is perfectly acceptable—only to be told (loudly) by Suzie that calling after 10:00 P.M. isn't allowed. Then, believing that Suzie was correct, Larry calls Julia at 9:50 and is informed that he has violated the 9:30 P.M. cut-off time. This case is significantly different from Jeff's infidelity. Larry actually *tried* to follow the rules, but he was simply mistaken about what the rules were.

In cases such as this, in which we are blamelessly unaware of the rules, it again seems unreasonable to hold our infractions against our credentials as rule-followers. But you needn't be ignorant of a rule in order to accept it. In "The Special Section" (Season Three) it's painfully clear to Larry that his mother's (re)burial in a secluded section of the cemetery was mandated by a rule against mutilating one's body (due to her youthful tattoo indiscretion), and he's outraged and insists that his mother be returned to her planned resting place not because he accepts but wishes to break the rule, but rather because he completely rejects the legitimacy of the rule in the first place. And thus, Larry isn't acting with the intention of breaking a rule. He's instead acting on the conviction that there is no legitimate rule to break.

Larry takes the same attitude toward the "unwritten law of dry cleaning." Larry's rejection of this rule is so strong that he attempts to convince Senator Barbara Boxer to have fairer dry-cleaning rules written into law: "Well it's not balancing out for me, Senator. I never get an item. And you know what? If I got it, I would return it. Because I think the whole system is flawed!" ("The Anonymous Donor," Season Six).

The larger point is that if people have good reason to reject a rule in the first place, their violation of it shouldn't count against their status as rule-followers. This suggests that a person who both accepts the legitimacy of rules and consistently acts in accordance with them meets the conditions of a good rule-follower—especially since nobody can follow all the rules all the time. What we want in a rule-follower is a person who truly accepts that there are legitimate rules and makes a real effort to follow them.

You Can't Fire a Survivor

Even if accepting the legitimacy of some rules and acting in accordance with those rules is enough to make somebody a good rule-follower, however, Larry is a rule-follower only if he actually does both of those things. To use the language favored by philosophers, you might ask whether Larry meets the necessary and jointly sufficient conditions required of a good rule-follower.

Larry does seem to satisfy the first condition: accepting the legitimacy of some rules. In "The Corpse-Sniffing Dog" (Season Three), Larry's horrified when his dinner companions, the Braudies, rudely insist upon sending back wine. He accepts that there's a rule of etiquette in play and he wants his dinner party to comply with it. And in "Trick or Treat" (Season Two), Larry emphatically endorses age and costume requirements for trick-or-treating on Halloween when he refuses to give candy to two teenage girls who are, according to his rules, ineligible for candy. Larry even picks up a prostitute in "The Car Pool Lane" (Season Four) so that he can use the faster lane without breaking the multiple passenger rule!

You might question, however, whether the above cases point to a difficulty for Larry's standing as a sincere rule-follower. In all of these cases it seems that Larry is following rules which are to his advantage. As the great philosopher Immanuel Kant noted, whenever your duty (the action required by the moral rules) coincides with what is to your own personal benefit, it's nearly impossible for outsiders (and maybe even for you!) to determine whether you have acted out of a commitment to moral duty, as opposed to mere self-interest. It's only when you follow the rules and thereby *frustrate* your own self-interest that we can clearly see that you were motivated by a concern for the rules rather than your own benefit.[1] And so, if we want to clearly demonstrate that Larry's a good rule-follower, we should also look for cases in which he endorses, and follows, rules which don't benefit him.

(Only!) Twelve Strokes

Fortunately, there are just such cases available. In both "Kamikaze Bingo" (Season Five) and "Krazee-Eyez Killa" (Season Three), Larry accepts a rule requiring spouses to share information, albeit reluctantly in the latter case. In "Kamikaze Bingo" Larry wants information from Cheryl, but in "Krazee-Eyez Killa" the reverse is true. Larry knows that Wanda's rapper fiancé Krazee-Eyez has been cheating on her. Krazee-Eyez bragged about this to Larry in confidence, and Larry is terrified that Krazee-Eyez will "put a nut in his eye" if he spills the secret. But Cheryl suspects that something is up and insists that spouses are rule-bound to share information. So Larry

---

[1] *Groundwork of the Metaphysics of Morals* (Cambridge University Press), pp. 10–11.

admits that Krazee-Eyez is cheating, even though he believes that doing so puts his safety at risk. Then, a mere three episodes later (in "The Grand Opening"), Larry accepts the personal disadvantages of rule-following when he refuses to fire the new chef at Bobo's Restaurant even though the chef's frequent outpourings of expletives threatens to destroy the restaurant. As Larry says, "You can't fire a survivor!"

And again, in "The Interior Decorator" (Season One), Larry follows the rules to his own disadvantage. This case is especially telling, as Larry follows a doctor's office rule *for which he himself is responsible* and which in the end works against him. After his chivalry (in his opinion unfairly) causes Larry to lose his scheduled appointment time, he insists that the "first-come, first served" rule be abandoned in favor of a rule according to which patients are seen in the order in which their appointments were scheduled. Clearly, Larry endorses his own improvement rather than the original rule. And when he later arrives early to his next appointment only to learn that the office has adopted his rule—with the result that Larry must *again* wait to be seen—he accepts that he must wait, as dictated by his rule.

Larry also quite consistently follows the rules in sexual matters with Cheryl. Season Four includes an arc in which Larry takes great care to figure out, and obey, these rules. While Larry *wants* to sleep with other women (as becomes especially apparent in "Mel's Offer"), he doesn't seriously consider doing so while married *except* when permitted by mutually-endorsed rules stemming from his engagement to Cheryl. As a tenth anniversary gift, Cheryl has given Larry permission to sleep (once) with another woman.

Not only does Larry put much thought into selecting a woman, but he also has a lengthy discussion with a rabbi about whether taking Cheryl up on her promise would be wrong—ultimately getting a green light on the pursuit: "She's giving you something out of generosity, and I think you should probably accept it in that same sense of generosity" ("The Survivor," Season Four). Larry is here consistent in his endorsement of, and adherence to, rules against adultery. And even more impressive is Larry's dedication to marital fidelity in "The Massage" (Season Two), when he inspires awe in his friends by calling a hasty end to his rub-down.

He Steals Forks from Restaurants

So Larry meets the first rule-follower condition with flying colors. How about the second condition? Does Larry *consistently* follow the rules he himself has accepted? Unfortunately, showing that Larry satisfies this condition will be a little more complicated. All we had to do before was find *some* examples of Larry clearly accepting the legitimacy of rules—which was easily done by pointing out a few examples. But merely finding a couple of cases in which Larry follows a rule can't convincingly make the case that Larry always, or even *usually*, follows the rules he endorses.

What we need, in addition to examples of Larry's rule-following, is a lack of cases in which Larry fails to follow the rules—or, more specifically, a lack of cases in which Larry fails to follow the rules *even though he accepts their legitimacy*. And short of detailing every choice Larry has made in eight full seasons of *Curb Your Enthusiasm*, our best strategy is to address the most obvious cases of Larry's rule-breaking and explain why these do not count against Larry's credentials as a dedicated rule-follower. (I will leave it to you to consider less obvious examples on a case-by-case basis. I've actually found this to make for a fun "game" while re-watching my favorite episodes!)

Some of the clearest cases of Larry's failure to follow rules include the following:

- **Larry insists on taking his water bottle into a movie theater, even though this is against theater rules.**
- **Larry is angered when the Loebs refuse to accept the Davids' wedding gift, claiming that there is a one-year window after which the exchange of wedding gifts is no longer permissible.**
- **Larry sneaks his mother into her planned burial plot, in contravention of Jewish Law.**
- **Larry uses a bathroom stall reserved for the disabled after attempting to leave a party early against the objections of his dinner party, in order to use his "home-base" bathroom.**

- **Larry attempts to walk through a drive-thru.**
- **Larry manipulates Jeff into letting the air out of a pro-wrestler's tires.**
- **Larry takes a fork from a restaurant.**
- **Larry steals flowers from Funkhouser's mother's memorial.**
- **Larry takes food from the Funkhousers' fridge without permission.**

At first glance, this list perhaps seems to show without a doubt that Larry David is *not* a good rule-follower. But in fact, each of the above rules falls into one of two categories, neither of which counts against Larry's rule-following credentials: rules which Larry doesn't accept as legitimate, or rules which don't apply in the circumstances as their very justification has been violated. These two categories are closely related, and by examining them in turn we can uncover the underlying pattern in Larry's rule-following.

He's Not an Inventor, He's an Improver

As we've already seen, if Larry is to qualify as a good rule-follower, he must both accept the legitimacy of (some) rules *and* consistently act in accordance with those rules. It would help Larry's case, however, if there were some principled way in which he comes to accept rules. It would count against Larry's credentials as a rule-follower if he selected just one or two insignificant rules completely arbitrarily—however consistently he followed them. In other words, Larry's credentials as a good rule-follower are much stronger if he's not just inventing the rules as he goes along.

But to Larry's credit, a careful investigation of the cases in which he appears to break the rules shows that Larry's choice of rules is far from arbitrary. Larry accepts as legitimate those rules which (at least in his view) follow from the values of fairness and reciprocity. Where a rule does not so follow, and especially when it fails to further any beneficial end whatsoever, Larry quite reasonably rejects it out of hand.

Take Larry's attitude toward leaving dinner early in "The Bowtie" (Season Five). At the Funkhousers' twenty-fifth wedding anniversary party Cheryl and Susie insist that Larry must use the public bathroom, as leaving before dessert isn't permissible. Although he ultimately gives in to Cheryl's demands, Larry makes explicit his reasoning in rejecting the rule: it serves no good purpose whatsoever: "What am I supposed to do, sit here for another four hours and be uncomfortable?" Larry would certainly want others to leave *his* party rather than be uncomfortable, so it's only fair that he be permitted to do the same.

And why should it count against Larry if he fails to follow a rule which has no good purpose? After all, if a rule serves no purpose, it is difficult to see what would justify a requirement to follow it. We may indeed have very good reason *not* to follow purposeless rules—especially in light of our earlier conclusion that circumstances sometimes conspire such that we are forced to violate at least one rule. Where two rules conflict, we should certainly follow the one which is supported by better reasons. A good rule-follower therefore doesn't just blindly follow the rules, he follows the *good* or *legitimate* rules.

Indeed, as the philosopher J.J.C. Smart has argued, following rules for no good reason, especially when following the rules leaves everyone worse off than they would otherwise have been, is the trademark of irrational "rule-worship." If a rule has no purpose, it's pure folly to insist upon following it! On this point, Smart demands:

> Is it not monstrous to suppose that if . . . we know that in this instance to break the rule will have better results than to keep it, we should nevertheless obey the rule? Is it not to erect the rule into a sort of idol if we keep it when breaking it will prevent, say, some avoidable misery? Is not this a form of superstitious rule-worship and not the rational thought of a philosopher?[2]

Then Why Are You Following It, Blindly Like That?

Like Smart, Larry repeatedly rejects purposeless rules from which no good can come. Larry is flummoxed by rules against

---

[2] "Extreme and Restricted Utilitarianism," *The Philosophical Quarterly* 6:25 (October 1956).

walking through the drive-thru in "Lewis Needs a Kidney" (Season Five) on precisely these grounds: refusing to serve walkers seems to serve no purpose. Serving walkers would benefit non-driving customers and increase restaurant profits, and it would inconvenience neither restaurant employees nor more traditional drive-thru patrons. Similarly, in "The Special Section" (Season Three), Larry's outraged that his mother's casket has been moved due to her tattoo. What good purpose is possibly served by segregating the tattooed dead?

Finally, Larry's insistence that reasons be given for a rule if he is expected to follow it is made loudly explicit in "The Hot Towel" (Season Seven) when Susie refuses to tell him who has been invited to her dinner party:

> **SUSIE:** It's a social convention that people don't ask who's going to be there at the dinner party. It's *just not done*.
>
> **LARRY:** Big deal! Why *isn't* it done?
>
> **SUSIE:** Because it isn't. I don't know the derivation of the convention.
>
> **LARRY:** Then why are you following it, blindly like that?

While it's folly to follow a rule with no good purpose, it's even crazier to follow a rule when following the rule actually frustrates the purpose it was intended to serve. Consider Larry's arrest for "stealing" a fork in "The Massage" (Season Two). General reasons for anti-theft rules seem not to apply in this situation, since Larry was going to bring the fork back. (As Larry himself notes, he was actually trying to *borrow*, rather than steal, it.) And in the particular case of restaurant flatware, anti-removal rules seem intended to maintain a stock of utensils for restaurant patrons to use in the enjoyment of their dinner. But as Larry tries to explain to the judge, his driver's enjoyment of the restaurant's food was itself frustrated by his lack of fork access.

Similarly, in "Club Soda and Salt" (Season Three), Larry objects to a one-year cut-off rule which disallows the Loebs from accepting the Davids' wedding gift. If it has any purpose at all, the rule seems to be aimed at ensuring that the bride and groom receive their gifts in a timely manner and that the gift-givers aren't inconvenienced. But in this case, by refusing the gift the Loebs fail to receive their gift at all (whether in a timely manner or not), and the Davids are insulted and inconvenienced far more than they would have been had the Loebs graciously accepted. By following the rule, the Loebs are frustrating its very justification—another case of irrational rule worship!

He's Applying the Golden Rule. Are *You*?

So what does Larry take to be good justification for a rule? We see early in the series that Larry's a fan of the Golden Rule: treat others as you yourself would like to be treated. In "The Doll" (Season Two), a theatergoer insists that Larry not bring his bottled water into the theater (as "there's no food or drink in the theater"). Larry here explicitly and emphatically defends his rule-following character, insisting that the relevant rule is the Golden Rule, which requires equal (reciprocal) consideration. Larry asks his accuser to put herself in his shoes and think about whether she would want similar consideration if their roles were reversed. After all, Larry's officially dehydrated. And what if he had a serious medical condition? Given that she would want to be allowed to have her water, it's only fair for her to allow Larry to have *his* water. In Larry's view, the most important rule in this case is a rule of fairness. And so by bringing the water into the theater, Larry is acting in accordance with the rule he accepts—and for which he has offered explicit justification.

This isn't just an isolated case. The importance Larry attaches to fair treatment is a recurring theme in *Curb Your Enthusiasm*. Larry makes this particularly clear in "Thor" (Season Two) when making meeting plans with Jason Alexander. Jason wants to meet, yet again, at his office rather than at Larry's home—on the grounds that it's more convenient for Jason. But while begrudgingly agreeing to meet at Jason's office, Larry expresses his displeasure with the unfairness (and lack of reciprocity) of the arrangement. After all, it would be more convenient for *Larry* to meet at *his* house. And if convenience counts as a reason for Jason, it should also count as a reason for Larry. They should take turns choosing a meeting place.

The importance Larry places on reciprocity again comes to the fore in "The Bowtie" (Season Five) when he catches a disabled man using the regular bathroom stall at his private investigator's office. This is the very same man who earlier chastised Larry for using the disabled stall! Larry argues that if he must wait for the regular stall, then his adversary, facing an exactly parallel choice, must wait for the disabled stall. After all, it's only fair.

Similarly, in "The Hot Towel" (Season Seven) Larry criticizes Christian Slater for violating an unwritten caviar rule. Slater, after wolfing down several large helpings of the delicacy, insists that there are no rules regarding how much caviar he can have. But Larry argues that when indulging in caviar at a party, one must be fair to others. Out of respect for fairness and reciprocity: "We're each entitled to take a certain amount, so everybody else can have a little bit too."

It's Only Fair . . .

Not only does Larry's dedication to reciprocity provide a cohesive account of the rules he does in fact accept (and an explanation of his attitude toward those he doesn't), it also gives a justification for Larry's behavior in cases where he seems to violate a rule even though he accepts it as legitimate. Larry would most likely recognize that, in general, you ought not to take flowers from a roadside memorial. But he feels that his case in "The Ida Funkhouser Roadside Memorial" (Season Six) is special: *fairness itself* justifies his exemption from the general rule.

Funkhouser has repaid a debt to Larry with a sweaty fifty-dollar bill from his sneaker—which Larry can't convince anyone else to take. And most frustratingly for Larry, he can't use it to buy some much-needed apology flowers. Because Funkhouser owes Larry and refuses to pay up (with clean money), Larry takes himself to be restoring the balance of fairness by compensating himself with flowers from Funkhouser's mother's memorial.

Larry even more obviously violates a rule which he has previously endorsed in "Funkhouser's Crazy Sister": the rule prohibiting taking food and drink from a host's fridge without asking first. Larry takes food from the Funkhousers' fridge. But that is perfectly consistent with fairness and reciprocity, as Marty Funkhouser has already explicitly deemed permissible

Dr. Schaffer's taking lemonade from Larry's fridge without permission.

And fairness and reciprocity are cited yet again in "Thor" (Season Two), when Larry (via a favor from Jeff) breaks a rule the general application of which he accepts: one ought not to sabotage others' cars. Given Larry's conviction that Thor has already broken this very rule, he feels that fairness justifies his own infraction of it. In fact, it's entirely because of Thor's infraction that Larry is motivated to seek reciprocal revenge in the first place.

Have You Ever Seen a Black Man Wearing a Bowtie Who's Not a Muslim?

When we keep in mind Larry's dedication to the justifying roles of fairness and reciprocity, we can explain why all of the suggested cases of rule-breaking noted above are, after all, consistent with characterizing Larry David as a dedicated rule-follower. But are there any exceptions? Are there any cases in which Larry breaks a rule *even though* he accepts its legitimacy, and *even though* there isn't a fairness-based exception at hand?

If there are such cases, they are what philosophers call "counterexamples." That is, they are examples which work counter to my claim that Larry is a dedicated rule-follower. Counterexamples are often useful in everyday argumentation, and Larry nicely illustrates their role in "The Bowtie" (Season Five) when he asks Wanda for a counterexample to the claim that all black men who wear bowties are Muslims: "Have you ever seen a black man wearing a bowtie who's *not* a Muslim?"

I must admit that there seems to be at least one clear counterexample to the claim that Larry always follows the rules he endorses unless there is a fairness-based exception: the jacket incident in "The Korean Bookie" (Season Five). The comical irony of this episode stems in large part from Larry's contradictory rule endorsements. The episode begins with Larry's outrage at Dr. Heineman's use of the money Larry gave him to repair the car that Larry (intentionally) damaged. Instead of repairing the car, Heineman (the head of the kidney consortium) uses the money to fund breast implants for his daughter Rachel—much to Larry's indignation. After all, Larry rages, the money was *for car repairs*, and Larry shouldn't have to pay for Rachel's new breasts. Not even the bottom portion of the left half!

But the Davids' friend Marla has recently given Larry a check to replace a jacket which she ruined. And while maintaining (and blatantly expressing) his outrage with Dr. Heineman during Marla's wedding celebration, Larry actually *wears* his soiled jacket—the very jacket which Marla stained and wrote a check to Larry to replace. Given Larry's continued insistence that reparation money must be used for its intended purpose, he clearly ought to have used the money to replace the jacket—but he used the check to pay his sports gambling debt instead. Larry attempts to justify his use of the money by insisting that it is his to do with as he pleases: "It's my money. I can do whatever I want with it, no?" But if Larry's right, then fairness demands that Dr. Heineman be permitted to do whatever *he* wants with the car repair money.

Here, there is no room to argue that Larry didn't endorse the relevant rule. He's upset with Dr. Heineman precisely because Heineman put the car-repair money to a different use. But it's equally apparent that there's no fairness-based reason for Larry to make an exception for himself in this case. So I must admit that in "The Korean Bookie," Larry's behavior is inconsistent with that of a good rule-follower.

We should keep in mind, however, that this is just *one* misstep in eight seasons of *Curb Your Enthusiasm*. For the full run of the show Larry has consistently followed the rules he finds legitimate—with only one exception. So Larry deserves the commendation of rule-followers everywhere. Say what you want about Larry: he's a bad friend; he's selfish and blasphemous; he's a bald asshole, and so on. Whatever bothers you most. But one thing none of us can deny is that he's a dedicated rule-follower!

This is as instructive as it is surprising. Although it's easy to assume that Larry's general uncooperativeness and continued questioning of others' rules renders him a rule-breaker, after careful philosophical investigation of the nature of rule-following we can now see that Larry is actually a very good rule-follower. . . . Given his careful consideration of the reasons supporting the rules he follows, he's quite likely an even better rule-follower than those who simply follow rules without considering their merit! And not only does this shed light on Larry's character, it's also helpful to those of us who wish to be good rule-followers ourselves.

Do you, like Larry, consider whether rules are legitimate before following them? If not, given our conclusions about rule-following, it looks as if Larry's quite right to ask: "Then why are you following them, blindly like that?"

10
That's a Problem, Not a Gift

ROBERT FARROW and JAMES RODWELL

> **LARRY:** I was under the impression that you were picking up the ticket, given the fact that I bought you a bottle of wine for $300.
>
> **RICKY GERVAIS:** That was a gift, the gift of wine. Thank you. Now I've given you the gift of art.
>
> **LARRY:** Whether you give me a gift or I give you a gift, it costs me money!
>
> —Season Eight, "The Hero"

At the start of Season Three of *Curb Your Enthusiasm*, Larry and Jeff go shopping for uniforms intended for the waiting staff at their swanky new bistro *Bobo's* ("Chet's Shirt"). As they browse around the mall boutique and exchange thoughts on the different garments, Larry is struck by a thought. He tells Jeff that he intends to buy a copy of his two-tone cream and black shirt as a gift for Ted Danson, introducing it as the shirt that Ted "really liked." Jeff is impressed and tells him that it would be a *really* nice thing to do. Larry says that he may also get another one for himself, and Jeff thinks that's a good idea too. So Larry buys the shirts. But when he gives Ted the present, a problem arises.

When Larry unceremoniously drops the unwrapped shirt on the table, Ted's first impression is that Larry has given him his own shirt, which he saw Larry wearing just a day or two before. Larry tells Ted that he bought it especially for him, and Ted accepts this with gratitude as he looks over the shirt more closely. But then he points out that the shirt has a hole in it by pushing his finger through it and wiggling it provocatively. The shirt is clearly defective. Ted argues that the defect in the shirt, together with Larry's insistence that Ted take it to be mended, undermines Larry's "nice gesture." Larry refuses to return it for him. He tells Ted to take it back himself.

As Larry sees it, he's made the nice gesture. It's Ted's shirt now and therefore his responsibility. They argue about what's supposed to happen in situations like this. Larry says that people who receive gifts should be grateful for what they receive, while Ted maintains that people who give gifts should make sure they are adequate. As Ted sees it, he's been given a problem, not a gift.

Like a lot of situations in *Curb*, this exchange provides an insight into the nature of social relations in Larry David's world. Partly it's an assured comic device. In *Curb,* expectations are routinely undermined for comedy's sake. But in this case there's clearly something more going on. Larry's unhappy encounter with Ted can be read as symptomatic of the poverty of relationships in the social world that the series depicts.

The characters seem to live prosperous lives, and often give presents, money, or favors to each other. But they rarely seem to get what they want or need. This is interesting because gift giving reflects both the way that people relate to each other and how they see themselves. We might think that the characters in *Curb* are well placed to give gifts. But, as we will see, genuine gift giving—as philosophers have sought to define it—is in surprisingly short supply throughout the sundrenched, moneyed, and over-refined world of *Curb*.

The Meaning of "The Gift"

The nature of gifts and gift giving has been a recurrent topic for philosophical reflection, but increasingly so in modern times. The sociologist and anthropologist Marcel Mauss (1872–1950) famously initiated an ongoing discussion in French intellectual circles with his study of gift giving in primitive societies.[1]

Mauss was interested in the role of gift giving in forming tight social bonds. He argued that gifts perform this role in

[1] *The Gift* (Lowe and Brydon, 1954).

primitive societies because they're understood to be extensions of the donor, which implicitly demand the recipient of the gift to reciprocate in kind. Gifts are seen as forming almost magical bonds between people, as each gift represents something of the original owner entering into social circulation. But this also means that there can be no "free" gifts because the power of each gift creates an obligation to give back. All gifts, in some sense, impose on the receiver.

Mauss's observations on the power of the gift to create obligations served as the inspiration for Jacques Derrida's more recent analysis of gifts.[2] For Derrida, there's a problem with the very concept of gift giving. We think that, ideally, gift giving must be free in the sense that it involves a genuine "giving away" of something on the part of the giver. When we give gifts we're not supposed to expect anything in return. That's what distinguishes them from everyday economic transactions. But it seems hard to think of a case that measures up to this ideal.

If I give money to a beggar, don't I get some kind of self-satisfaction in return for my kind act? When I give someone an unexpected present, doesn't that lead to an expectation that they will behave more generously towards me in the future? These kinds of considerations lead Derrida to conclude that, although we can have an *idea* of what a true gift would be, we can't identify a real-life example to match it. A true gift would involve no reciprocity, and ultimately this would mean that both the giver and the recipient would have to be unaware of the act of giving. But if that's right, we could never identify a true gift because nobody could acknowledge its existence. True gifts just don't show up in the world, and nothing we call a gift can live up to its own ideal.

Articles May Not Be Exchanged

Theodor Adorno takes up these worries in his reflections on gifts in the modern world. Adorno was a critical theorist who was interested in understanding why different forms of human suffering exist despite the fact that we have the technological and scientific means to mitigate, or even end them. Adorno had

---

[2] Jacques Derrida, *Given Time I: Counterfeit Money* (University of Chicago Press , 1992).

a surprising answer to his own question. We suffer, he said, because modern societies are dominated by capitalist relations of production that are divisive and alienating.[3]

We can give gifts, but doing so is becoming increasingly hard in the kind of social world that we live in (and even more so in the kind of world that Larry lives in). Adorno's problem isn't with the concept of the gift as such but with the problems that attend gift giving in modern capitalist societies. Think about when you've given or received gifts, and what made the gift fail or succeed. Adorno contends that the whole point of gift giving consists in experiencing "the joy of the receiver," not just at the moment of giving, but in preparing the gift, and imaginatively anticipating its reception.[4] The point here is that a gift is not something that is given in order to get something in return, *except for* delight at the experience of the person receiving it. So what would it mean to give a gift of this kind? Adorno thinks that, bound-up in this conception, is the idea that one thinks a great deal about the person one is to give to, and this requires that one *knows* him or her. A truly thoughtful gift shows that one has thought about the particularities of the recipient. But here we can see a tension developing. On the one hand, you want to get a present for someone that reflects his or her personality and interests. But on the other hand, you want to surprise them, so that the gift elicits unexpected delight. Getting this right can be pretty hard.

In the episode "The Surrogate" (Season Four) the Davids attend the baby shower for the Dusenberrys, who are using a surrogate mother. Larry and Cheryl are lying in bed together and Cheryl asks him to bring their gift, suggesting that he buy a doll for Betty Dusenberry. "What about the surrogate?" asks Larry, "Get her anything?" Cheryl tells him he doesn't need to worry about the surrogate. But Larry is nonplussed. He points out that the surrogate is also a person, that *she's* the one having the baby, and that she'll just be standing there without a gift to open.

---

[3] Theodor W. Adorno, *Negative Dialectics* (Routledge, 1973), sections 189–192.

[4] Theodor W. Adorno, *Minima Moralia: Reflections on a Damaged Life* (Verso, 2005), section 21.

While his concerns are as much to do with the confusing etiquette surrounding the celebration of a surrogate birth, Larry does seem to be genuinely interested in delighting the surrogate. Contrast this with the subscription to the *New York Times* that Larry intends to give to Marla's husband for Christmas. When he and Marla break up, Larry decides that he no longer has to give him the gift, heavily suggesting that this gift is given purely as a result of social mores and expectations ("The Seder," Season Five).

Returning to Adorno, you might suspect that all he cares about is what the giver thinks and whether they give the right gift. But it's also crucial that other people recognize that what the giver is doing is presenting a gift that simply aims to delight them as the receiver. If I go to all the trouble of delivering a gift (and it shouldn't feel too much like a strain if I am to be delighted by its success) and the receiver thinks that the time, money, and thought I invested was aimed at placing him in my debt, then the well-intended gift cannot help but fail. Gift giving is, therefore, a fragile activity. Things can go wrong with the giver (concerning their motivations for giving), the gift (whether it is the kind of gift that will delight) and the receiver (regarding their attitude towards the motivation for giving).

A Nice Piece of Fish!

Curb Your Enthusiasm is full of examples of failed gift-giving that touch on each of these three elements. To begin with, we might consider gifts that are given in response to an obligation, concessions to the pressures of social expectation. Sometimes these gifts are given purely to "balance the books." Consider the case of the wedding gift in "Club Soda and Salt" (Season Three). Larry and Cheryl get a frosty reception from Mel and Ed at the tennis courts. Soon after, Cheryl realizes that this is because she and Larry failed to buy them a wedding gift.

Larry complains about the absurdity of holding a grudge against someone for failing to buy a gift. But since Cheryl cannot stand the idea of repeating this awkward encounter, she suggests that they should "pick something up for them." Later, once Cheryl silently dismisses Larry's suggestion of buying them a "nice piece of fish," they settle on buying the couple a $300 dollar bottle of wine—that way "they'll know that it's a good one." It's as if the value of the gift has to change in proportion with their transgression.

This example highlights some of the features of the degraded form of gift giving that Adorno thinks is most common in our time. He writes that "private giving of presents has degenerated to a social function exercised with rational bad grace, careful adherence to the prescribed budget, sceptical appraisal of the other and the least possible effort." In this case, the social function is clear: Cheryl wants to give the gift so that they do not have to face a repetition of Mel and Ed's cold shoulder.

But the nature of the gift is also significant. The choice of gift is an easy one, and not just because there is a wine shop next door. They choose that gift, not because it's something they think Mel and Ed would really want (they've already given up on that), but because it's a gift that Mel and Ed cannot refuse as being unworthy. It's the kind of gift that any one of their social peers would have to appreciate. The cash value of the wine makes sure of that. Of course, we later find that social proprieties—which motivated buying the present and the choice of gift in the first place—also prevent Mel and Ed from accepting a gift given over a year after their wedding.

We see this point being made again and again in *Curb*. Gift giving often operates as a mere means of preserving social tranquility and to such an extent that anything like "true" giving appears absurd. Think of the shirt that Larry buys for Ben Stiller from Susie ("Ben's Birthday Party," Season Four). Here Larry buys the gift to mend *two* rifts in the social order: his failure to show the expected amount of enthusiasm for Susie's shirts, and his failure to recognize Ben's "no gifts" request as itself being an instance of socially acceptable deceit.

But again, the conclusion of this episode suggests that over-refined social observances like this undermine the giving of a good gift. What Larry fails to consider is that Ben's earlier approval of Susie's shirts was itself the appropriate lie that Larry had failed to tell! It seems comically appropriate that Michael (the blind pianist) ends up with the shirt, since he is the only one who cannot lie about what it looks like.

You Are Going to Love This

We might want to say that it really isn't a big deal if gifts sometimes serve the social function of patching things up when they go bad. But what if *Curb* shows us that things can be a lot worse than that? What if gifts are sometimes used as a kind of weapon, as a way of getting one over on the other person, or of showing them up in a social situation? If that were true, gift giving might not just be degraded. It would be deformed, and maybe even destroyed!

Just think about the "friendship" between Larry and Ted Danson for a moment. The scare quotes are there for a reason. Throughout the whole of *Curb* we are recurrently led to believe that their friendship is barely more than a masquerade. Behind the social niceties that they outwardly observe in each other's company there simmers a deep-seated rivalry. Perhaps the gifts they give each other are the most insidious manifestations of that rivalry.

We've already touched upon the case of Chet's shirt. Two more examples deserve a mention: the "freak book" and "the pie." The freak book is Larry's gift to Ted on his birthday ("The Freak Book," Season Six). But we know that it's really for Larry from the get-go. When Cheryl finds Larry guffawing over the freaks in the freak book, she reminds him, "This isn't for you." But the truth is that the freak book *is* for Larry. It most certainly is not for Ted, as we find out at the party when he receives the gift with a look of thinly disguised disapproval.

Either Larry failed to realize that this is a totally inappropriate gift for the outwardly refined Ted. Or, more likely, he knows he's bought Ted something he won't want. It's as if Larry were saying, "This is what I think of you, so little that I can't even spare a thought about what would suit you and your tastes." Larry puts it beyond doubt that the gift is really for him when he rudely snatches it from Ted so that he can share his rapturous glee with Jeff, stealing attention from Ted's gift opening ceremony.

Perhaps Ted appears the innocent victim in this episode, an unwitting participant in a contest he does not endorse. But let's think about his gift of the pie in "Denise Handicap" (Season Seven). What's really going on when Ted sends the dessert over to Larry's table? This is just the kind of gesture that is typical of a well-heeled, magnanimous member of Larry's set. But is it so different from Larry's gift of the freak book? Is this, in fact, an instance of vengeful gift giving? The fact that Larry tries to send the pie back might indicate that he sees the gesture as far from innocent. When Ted approaches to explain the gift, he says "This pie is the best pie that I have ever had in my entire life. You are going to love this."

Ted doesn't really care whether Larry will like the pie. He is reinstating his own good taste. Larry's acceptance of the pie would mean a victory for Ted's own self-conception as a man of good judgment, and would bring about a tacit agreement on Larry's part that the two of them are not oh-so-different after all. At least it seems clear that this is how Larry perceives the situation. He stands by his refusal to accept the gift, shifting between the excuse that he is too full, and the preposterous claim that he's "not eating dessert anymore." After insisting and telling him to "be a friend," Ted makes the desperate move of pointing out what everyone already knows: "You are making me look like an asshole."

What unites the gifts between Larry and Ted is that they reflect the tastes of the giver more than the personality of the receiver. Their gifts are stakes in a game where Larry and Ted try to assert their own identities over each other. They use gifts as tools to get ahead in their game, and the recipient has to outmaneuver the implicit insult that each gift conveys. This does not have to mean that the gift is always a bad one, as it clearly is in the case of the freak book.

Later, Larry will spend a fortune ($300 again!) on restaurant reservations for Ted and Mary's anniversary gift ("The Hot Towel," Season Seven). Perversely, Larry's real ambition here is to assert some sort of superiority over Ted, by forcing him to admit that Larry's gift was the cream of the crop and that, consequently, Larry is the best giver. Money well spent, we might think. But again we have a clear example of a gift that really reflects Larry's perverse interests, not Ted's.

Adorno is very critical of gifts given on the basis of one's own preferences instead of thinking about the preferences of the receiver. The cases we have been describing, however, look even more unappealing than these. Larry and Ted do think carefully about each other. But they do so with the intention of making the other person look worse, and they usually give each other what they would like for themselves. Aren't such gifts so far removed from the aim of shared joy that they represent the total annihilation of the gift? Here, gift giving is the *worst* kind of transaction. It's an exchange where what I get in return for my gift is the subordination or humiliation of the receiver.

In the last scene of "Chet's Shirt," we find Ted and Larry, having ruined two of the three identical shirts, racing to claim the last remaining one. But in a striking encapsulation of their relationship, and the role of the gift-object in that relationship, the race ends with two losers and the shirt is torn in two between them.

Forgiveness or Sex?

Okay, maybe Ted and Larry's relationship is particularly fraught, and it's not the most representative example. Let's take a look at Larry's relationship with Cheryl, his long-suffering wife. One incidence of gift giving that sums up their relationship occurs in the episode entitled "The Bracelet" (Season One). Larry's watching football on TV when Cheryl arrives after a trip away.

She expects their reunion to command his full attention, but the last minutes of the game prove to be too distracting to Larry, and Cheryl is offended. Larry should be happier to see her. As they lie in bed, Larry tries to assess the damage he has done, acknowledging the strength of Cheryl's feelings by saying that he can expect either forgiveness *or* sex, but not both. It's clear that, in Larry's mind, there's a kind of economy to their relationship where bad behavior deducts from the balance sheet and good behavior puts you back in the black.

Larry's credit isn't good. He gets neither forgiveness nor sex. In the morning, he asks his secretary for advice. Appalled at his behavior, she tells him that only a gift can make it right: "You gotta give her a gift," she says. "You can't come home empty handed—absolutely not!"

Larry decides to buy Cheryl a platinum and diamond bracelet that they had seen previously. Clearly, this gift functions as a kind of penance intended to absolve Larry's sins. However, before Larry has a chance to buy it, he is banned from the pretentious *23rd Street Shoppe* because he looks too much like a homeless person. He asks Richard Lewis to buy it on his behalf, but the store is closed by the time they return from lunch. Larry settles for roses as an alternative reparation, and this transactional gift is successful. "Boy!" he says to Richard on the telephone, "it's amazing how these work." But when Cheryl comes home, she says that she still wants the bracelet, and Larry is forced to confess that he told Richard that he could buy it for his own girlfriend. "So," says an outraged Cheryl, "I don't want the bracelet because we made up?"

Gifts between the Davids delight neither the giver nor the recipient, nor do they fulfill any particular social obligation. Rather, the gifts they give each other merely acknowledge the ebb and flow of power in their relationship.

There are many occasions where the relationship between the Davids breaks down into an exchange of goods and services, particularly of gifts for sex. In "The Ida Funkhouser Roadside Memorial" (Season Six) Larry and Jeff are in the ice cream store and Larry explains that he's going to buy some ice cream for Cheryl as part of his strategy to get sex. "On the days when I want sex," he ponders, "I'm a lot nicer. Then, after we've had sex, I'll just go back to being the way I am." When Larry returns and hasn't bought ice cream for everyone, the Blacks are disappointed. But Larry protests that he's not used to thinking about people other than Cheryl, and he even makes a valiant effort to justify his failure as a sin of omission (something he forgot to do), rather than a sin of commission (something he did)—in Larry's mind there's a morally relevant difference.

Later on, after stealing flowers from the memorial and giving them to the school dean he had offended earlier, Larry repeats the trick, this time giving the bouquets to Cheryl and Loretta. It's interesting that he expects equal affection from them afterwards, exclaiming (perhaps inappropriately) that they are his "two favorite girls" and that they should "give it up!" Larry's party is cut short by the arrival of Funkhouser, who recognizes the stolen flowers and gets Larry sent back to the doghouse. Rather than re-thinking his behavior, Larry decides that he needs a better gift! Cheryl, wise to how this game works, suggests the fragrance *Belle-Fille* as a gift of sufficient worth. (Of course, Larry also ends up stealing the perfume from Funkhouser's dead mother.) All this reveals quite a lot about the Davids' understanding of marriage, with Cheryl being completely complicit in the portrayal of wedlock as economic exchange.

Despicable Parody

Larry gives us his point of view on their marriage in Season Four, during "Mel's Offer." Mel's secretary is talking to Larry and tells him that she and her partner are adopting a baby. Larry responds, "you got yourself a partner! I got a wife. Not exactly a partner. More like a rival."

At dinner Cheryl mentions their upcoming tenth anniversary, and she tells Larry what gift she wants: to renew their vows. Larry tells her that his own present was agreed upon before their marriage—Cheryl told him he could sleep with someone else if they made it to their ten-year anniversary. Larry clearly sees this as something he is still owed rather than just a sweetener added at the time but never really meant. Cheryl obviously accepts the idea that sex with another person might be a suitable "reward" for ten years of marriage.

We might think of this as a selfless act on her part, as if she were putting Larry's pleasure above her own. But she only entertains the idea of honoring the agreement because she doesn't think Larry can pull it off. Cheryl is very clear about the insult that accompanies her permission: Larry is free to try to get laid, but Cheryl seems to consider herself the only woman willing to stoop that low. Her gift not only fails, but reveals misalignments in their understanding of marriage, and of each other.

Even after they break up, Larry tries to win Cheryl's favor by getting her a major role on the Seinfeld reunion show, as if it were an offering that could return their balance sheet to equilibrium ("The Reunion," Season Seven). We see Larry and Cheryl acting in mutual interest a lot in the show, and especially in the context of choosing and giving gifts.

Adorno thinks that the ideal of marriage simply cannot be realized in the world as it is. In *Minima Moralia*, he describes modern marriage as a "despicable parody" in which co-conspirators act towards self-preservation. As a community of mutual interest, he says, marriage "inexorably signifies the degradation of the interested parties, and what is perfidious [treacherous] about the existing state of affairs." We could be forgiven for thinking that this is a view of marriage that would be endorsed by the Davids in a rare moment of candor.

We Have to See This Video

We've been assuming that Cheryl is the person closest to Larry, and so reveals most to us about the most intimate relationships in *Curb Your Enthusiasm.* But, in many ways, Larry's manager Jeff is even closer to Larry than Cheryl is. Jeff is Larry's regular partner-in-crime, and the two make a habit of lying for each other, particularly to their wives. There's usually something in it for at least one of them, whether it's Larry retrieving Jeff's porn stash in case he dies in surgery, conspiring to get their hands on the "College Girls Gone Wild" video, having Larry dress in women's underwear, or deflating a wrestler's tires.

But these are all really favors, which don't qualify as gifts in Adorno's sense because they are the result of a *request*. They are not given with the intent of surprising and delighting the receiver. In fact, Larry and Jeff don't get each other gifts at all. However loyal they are, their relationship is primarily one of business. (Larry's relationships with both Cheryl and Jeff—the two people he seems closest to—have a legal and contractual basis.)

Nonetheless, although Cheryl is the one with a ring on her finger, it's tempting to think that Jeff is the one Larry is "really" married to, at least in Adorno's sense of marriage as a cohort for self-preservation.

I'll Give You Ten Dollars for a Verbal Response

At this point you might be thinking that it's just Larry and the people around him who can't give authentic gifts. But these kinds of interactions aren't limited to Larry's immediate circle, and there are lots of other examples of failed personal gifts in *Curb Your Enthusiasm*.

Larry buys his housekeeper a bra as a way of telling her that she dresses inappropriately. The eponymous "Krazee Eyes Killa" gives Larry a jacket as a way of telling him that they're friends, but he takes it back as soon as they have a falling out, revealing that the gift was just a kind of collateral and didn't really mean anything. Larry "gives" Richard Lewis his meditation mantra and then immediately wants it back, appealing to the fact that his mother had just died. When Larry offers to pay for Andy's nephew's college tuition, Andy thinks that this also means he will pay for his wife to attend cosmetology school—as if the gift is impersonal and transferable.

The weight of expectation extends to impersonal gifts, too. Anyone who watches the show will be familiar with the way Larry's views on tipping frequently cause him problems. From Adorno's point of view, there are two things to note. Firstly, any gift of money is infinitely fungible (transferable or mutable) since it can be replaced by any other money. It retains nothing personal to the giver. (The same is true of vouchers and tokens.) Secondly—and this is often Larry's argument—tipping is the fulfillment of an obligation which only *resembles* a gift. Tipping is technically discretionary, but in practice it is an expectation rather than an invitation.

What people get in return for their behavior is one of the central themes of the show. For example, Mocha Joe, the studio coffee vendor who is offended by Larry's failure to tip, cannot even conceive of the idea that a favor might be something that one does for the other person without expecting an identifiable return. This idea that nothing comes for free—which may well be implicit in the social interactions of characters in *Curb*—is disturbingly close to the surface in his character. However, everyone apart from Larry thinks Mocha Joe is in the right.

I Gotta Choose Healthier Friends

We'll turn now to the case for the defense. Is there an example of genuine gift-giving in *Curb Your Enthusiasm*? Perhaps the most generous thing Larry does for another person is to donate a kidney to Richard Lewis ("The End," Season Five). It's certainly a personal and non-transferable gift. At the time, Larry is in the midst of his temporary conversion to Christianity, and seems to give in to the spirit of generosity. He attends a sermon on the value of friendship, loyalty, compassion, and generosity of spirit, and realizes that he could be a better friend to Richard. Larry now believes that God saved him from dying in order for him to donate the organ, and Richard is grateful.

Such an act of personal generosity might well be thought of as pure and uncorrupted. However, when he tells Richard that he intends to donate his kidney he still can't resist using his newfound good grace to make a play for Richard's putter. Richard remains grateful, but only until he finds out that Larry had been complaining about his lack of reciprocity to the hospital orderlies.

Larry's fraternal attitude towards the donation is entirely fleeting. Before finding God, Larry mawkishly visits Lewis Lewis, Richard's comatose cousin (and a potential donor). When reflecting on Richard's needs to Cheryl he says "I'm not even really that friendly with him. Yeah, I've known him forty-four years, but we're not really close friends. He's more of an acquaintance. Who gives a kidney to an acquaintance?"

As soon as Larry finds out that he isn't, in fact, adopted, these former attitudes return and he tries to escape on the way to surgery, screaming as they wheel him in. On his "deathbed" after the operation he tells his visitors that, "this is what you get when you do good deeds." (Of course, they're really there to fight over his estate the very instant he expires.)

The kidney donation fails as a gift because it's predicated on Larry's false sense of self. Even if we overlook his attempt to get his hands on Richard's putter, we can't really accept that Larry's motivations are entirely well-meaning. He is simply playing the part of the "good person" he thinks he would be in a parallel universe, and his gift is not based on any compassion for Richard's medical needs.

Maybe One Day I'll Get a Chance to Do Something Good for Somebody

A more plausible example of genuine gift giving can be found in the episode where Larry's restaurant finally opens (Season Three, "The Grand Opening"). Guy Bernier, the last-minute replacement chef provided by embittered food critic Andy Portico, is prone to involuntary outbursts of the most outrageous profanity as a result of Tourette's syndrome. (Larry won't fire him because he mistakenly believes him to be an Auschwitz survivor.)

The restaurateurs are understandably nervous. The uncomfortable moment erupts when the chef yells "Fuckhead!

Shitface! Cocksucker! Asshole-son-of-a-bitch!" from the open kitchen. All the distinguished diners fall silent. Opening night appears to be a disaster.

Suddenly, Larry recalls an earlier incident, when he and Jeff saw a bald teen at Sammy's school. At the time Larry imagined that the youngster was undergoing chemotherapy, until Jeff explained that he's actually one of a number of students who had shaved their heads in solidarity with a classmate who has cancer. Larry was touched. In the restaurant he seizes his chance to make an equivalent gesture, yelling "scum-sucking motherfucking whore!" in apparent solidarity with Guy Bernier.

This might not seem like much of a gift: can this really be intended to delight? After all, Larry does have a commercial interest here. But the school flashback suggests that Larry's motivations are genuine and that his gesture is a gift, given solely to accommodate another's needs. Let people think he has Tourette's! Where's the shame? The other diners cotton on, with Jeff yelling "Cock! Cock! Jism! Grandma! Cock!" while Michael York stumbles through "Bum! Fuck, turd, fart . . . cunt, piss, shit, bugger . . . and balls!" Within a few minutes everyone and their grandma is turning the air blue. The resulting revelry is one of the surest examples of an enjoyable communal event in the whole show. Pretty good, Larry!

But there's one loose end. From Larry's point of view, this seems to be a successful gift. But we don't know what Guy Bernier is left thinking. Does he appreciate Larry's gesture? Could he even understand such an occurrence as a gift? Does he resent having attention drawn to his condition? He certainly never seems bothered by the effect of his interjections when they occur earlier in the episode. The cameras and Larry focus on the diners as the evening turns from failure to success. We never find out what Guy thinks, and so we are left wondering whether this gift was successful.

But this particular episode does tell us something important about the gift and its place in the kind of world that Larry lives in. One might easily wonder what the importance of gift giving really is in a world where material need is absent. After all, gift-giving can appear old-fashioned in a consumer society. Adorno makes precisely this point when he asks whether concern over "the decline of present-giving might seem immaterial" against "the greater abundance of goods."[5] Isn't it just sentimental to mourn the loss of gift giving if, like Larry, we have all of our material needs taken care of?

It may seem surprising to find out that Adorno and Larry are in deep accord in their answer to this question. Adorno suggests that the question misses the point. There is a deep *need to give*, and the growing possibility that any opportunity for satisfying that need might disappear is unfortunate. Larry confirms this point when he sees the bald teens. He says: "That's really something, you know maybe one day I'll get a chance to do something good for somebody like that."

There's not a hint of sarcasm in Larry's tone. His reflection registers an absence in his life: a need that he had not previously recognized, but which now shows up as unfilled. The world that he lives in is one that systematically thwarts the fulfillment of a need to give gifts to others. So, even if we decide that the most promising example of an authentic gift in *Curb* ultimately falls short, we might at least recognize that the world we live in curbs our enthusiasm in ways we can both laugh over and lament.

5 *Minima Moralia*, section 21.

VI

Is Larry a Good Apple?

11
How to Philosophize with a 5 Wood

SEAN PETRANOVICH

At first glance, some might feel that Larry David's character on *Curb Your Enthusiasm* is highly neurotic, that his behavior is that of someone who fails to fit in with society's norms and customs, or that he's just being difficult for difficulty's sake. If asked to provide a description of Larry, it wouldn't be a stretch to reach for words like 'anxious', 'anguished', or 'despairing'.

Doctor or Pharmacist?

There's lots of anxiety in *Curb Your Enthusiasm*. Think of the times when Larry hunts down a persistently annoying smoke detector, when he unleashes a lion-like roar as he tries to open the packaging on his new GPS, or when he has some sort of run-in with a bathroom or a toilet or a bathroom monitor. These are real moments of anxiety in our everyday use of the term. But existentialist philosophers have given this word an extra meaning, when they talk about *existential anxiety*.

Existential anxiety is the mood we arrive at when we realize that we are what we make of ourselves. We don't receive our identities. We create them. In *Curb*, *we* find this type of anxiety when Larry has to make a decision, any decision. It's rare that the weight of his deliberations is proportional to what we would consider their actual importance. Even the most seemingly trivial decisions are grave concerns for Larry: "Doctor? . . . Pharmacist? . . . DOCTOR? . . . PHARMACIST? . . ." The existentialist philosopher Martin Heidegger says that "anxiety can arise in the most innocuous situations."[1]

In moments of anxiety, Larry realizes the extent of his freedom as a human being. The entire weight of the world, and the way that we're immersed within it, bears down upon him. As he agonizes over his choices, Larry shows us that we're forced to make a decision regarding the way we ought to live. True anxiety shows us just how alone we are when we have to make decisions.

The existentialist philosopher Jean-Paul Sartre uses the term "anguish" to refer to those situations. Why should seemingly minor decisions arouse "anguish" or "existential anxiety"? According to Sartre, we experience anguish when it dawns on us that we have the entire responsibility for our choices, and that in making these choices we're saying that other people ought to be making similar choices.

Sartre says that when I act in a particular way, I am necessarily showing other people that I take that act to be of value to me. If we realized this before every decision we made, the decision's importance would multiply. Anguish, then, is a mood that takes place along with this realization, and the pain it brings is the pain of knowing just how important our choices are. In the world of *Curb*, anxiety creeps in at these moments because Larry does not appeal to anyone else. He makes the choices by himself, and tends to take responsibility for them. As the exchange between Larry and the mother of Richard Lewis' girlfriend goes:

> **DEBORAH'S MOTHER:** We're all responsible for our own lives.
>
> **LARRY:** I think there's some truth to that. (Season Three, "The Benadryl Brownie")

Although we may suspect that Larry doesn't believe Deborah's mother actually thinks this, it's still true that his recognition of our individual responsibility is present in most of his own decisions, and shows itself in his existential anxiety.

We define ourselves by the types of actions we choose to perform and the extent to which we accept responsibility for the

---

[1] *Being and Time* (Harper and Row), p. 234.

choices in our lives. This is why we can say that Larry philosophizes with a 5 wood. In making the choice to take the golf club out of the casket, Larry's action proclaims an image of right and wrong that he thinks everyone ought to find acceptable. He understands that it's completely unacceptable in our society to steal from a dead person. To make this decision, then, Larry must decide for himself what he's going to do. He must make a decision about what type of person he thinks everyone should be, and he confronts his dilemma with an argument. We can see his reasoning in this scene:

LARRY: That club's irreplaceable. It's ten years old. They don't make it anymore.

JEFF: I'm so sorry. I'm sorry man . . .

LARRY: Why should this guy be buried in eternity with *my* club? That's not fair. (Season Four, "The 5 Wood")

If there were a fixed essence for human beings, LD could appeal to it. Knowing the essential nature of humans could help him figure out what to do in this situation. If the existentialists are correct, however, there isn't any fixed model of humanity to guide us. Larry assigns value to this action, and makes the decision all alone in the face of ordinary funeral etiquette. While Jeff's apology demonstrates that he expects Larry to just leave the club behind, or shows that that is what he would do, Larry tackles this as a decision head-on.

According to Heidegger, real anxiety is not the type of feeling we have when we are being chased by an angry mob (when, for example, we have stolen a Joe Pepitone jersey from someone). That feeling is caused by something very specific. Anxiety is more general. As Heidegger once put this point, while fear has an object, anxiety concerns itself with "Nothing." In the tradition of existentialism, anxiety is not the kind of emotion that leads one to scream out or pound one's fists on a table. Rather, "a peculiar calm pervades it."[2] Existential anxiety involves coming face-to-face with the realization that we're in charge of deciding what will be done with our lives. It's when we confront

---

[2] "What Is Metaphysics?" in *Pathmarks* (Cambridge University Press), p. 88.

the immense responsibilities inherent to the human condition that we are truly anxious.

While in the car with Loretta in Season Seven, Larry goes out of his way to make himself seem like a bad person. As viewers, we know that his motive is to encourage Loretta to break up with him. At this moment, though, Larry offers up a surprisingly candid description of himself that cuts to one of the core aspects of both existentialism and the show as a whole:

> **LARRY:** Some people are nothing even with health. I fall into that category sometimes. A nothing—a big nothing—and I have health. (Season Seven, "Vehicular Fellatio")

If there's something more to this claim than his desire for Loretta to break up with him, existentialism provides us with one of the clearest ways of interpreting it. Sartre claims that, "If man, as the existentialist conceives him, is indefinable, it is because at first he is nothing. Only afterward will he be something, and he himself will have made what he will be."[3] We are not born as nothing in the sense that we have no bodies, or that we arise from situations that are culturally and politically neutral. We are originally "nothing" in that the way we make sense of ourselves and go about our decision-making processes will be entirely up to us as free individuals. We are "nothing" because we have to make ourselves into the people we want to be through our own volition.

If our individual actions are what define us, then it's against the background of those actions that an existentialist philosopher would claim we should judge others. Larry's critiques of others follow this same logic. He doesn't merely take jabs at people for being of a certain race, sex, or religion. He usually makes fun of people for the choices they make, for the way they choose to think of themselves, and for the values they espouse, which are often arbitrary or self-contradictory. He gets angry with Andy for choosing to order crispy onions, harasses Richard's girlfriend for not giving him enough space to maneuver in the theater, and is sickened by Jeff's sexual fantasies because they involve Cheryl. When people make decisions that Larry dislikes, he tends to be honest with them about his disdain.

---

3 Sartre, *Existentialism and Human Emotions* (Kensington), p. 15.

There are, however, instances when Larry goes out of his way to lie to people. When conversing with a friend in a wheelchair, he says that he doesn't enjoy playing golf, and that he really just enjoys sitting around all day. When Cheryl asks him to dance with her in the company of a widow, he says that he can't, so that he doesn't remind the woman that her husband isn't there to dance with her. In these instances, Larry is very aware of the presence of others, and he acts accordingly. He acts the way he wants to be perceived. While some of his lies are simply self-serving, he often tells lies because he doesn't want to draw attention to other people's limitations as long they are beyond the person's control, as disabilities and tragedies are.

Facing the charge of having proclaimed a philosophy that could only account for one individual human being apart from the society that person lives in, Sartre replies by saying:

> When we say that man chooses his own self, we mean that every one of us does likewise; but we also mean by that in making this choice he also chooses for all men. In fact, in creating the man that we want to be, there is not a single one of our acts which does not at the same time create an image of man as we think he ought to be. (p. 17)

Larry thinks we all ought to be like him, that we ought to live our lives and act in accord with his values. While existentialism doesn't tell us to follow the specific rules that Larry chooses to defend (I don't know of any report that Heidegger or Sartre commented on the proper amount of caviar to consume at a party), it does provide a philosophical foundation for his behavior.

Existentialism for Schmohawks

Existentialism often gets a bad rap. Existentialists are usually portrayed as wearing all black, sitting in dark cafes, drinking copious amounts of espresso, and contemplating the nature of death from behind bloodshot eyes. While this is a misleading caricature, there's some truth to the idea that existentialism concentrates on very serious issues, as we often hear people refer to "existential crises" when their life projects have been halted or called into question.

In its shortest formulation, existentialism can be expressed by saying that for human beings, "existence comes before essence," meaning that we must first act in a particular way before we can be defined (p. 13).

To see what this means, consider a designer who's drawing up plans for a tool such as a screwdriver. When we look at a screwdriver it's clear that it was produced for a specific purpose. There is an essence of what it is to be a screwdriver, and this involves being capable of turning screws well. Once the designer has made the specifications so it can be manufactured, the essence of the screwdriver is already in place. The essence is in the specifications before the screwdriver is actually produced. When the screwdriver is finally completed, its essence will be the same as it was when it was still an idea in the designer's head. The screwdriver's essence is fixed and the screwdriver doesn't get any say in the matter.

Now consider parents who are attempting to map out the life of a soon-to-be-born child. They might think they can take the same approach as the screwdriver designer, laying out plans on paper, and sketching out the intermediate steps needed in order for the child to become, say, a doctor or a lawyer. If the child were the same type of thing as the screwdriver, there'd be no problem. Problems arise, however, because the child will have drives and desires of her own, and will be capable of choosing a different life for herself if being a doctor or a lawyer is not what she wants. Think of the time when Larry tries to convince his nephew that he's not really a magician. As much as Larry wants to be able to dictate his nephew's identity, the matter is out of his hands. The nephew makes the choice to disregard Larry.

Sartre's claim is that human beings are very different from things like screwdrivers. For human beings, the type of creatures we are will only be defined by the way we *act*. We will be defined by the type of existence we *freely choose* to lead. Each individual, each and every person capable of saying "I," is the starting point for the person they are and who they will become. When it's time to make a decision, we can ask for the opinions of others to aid in our decision-making process, but at the end of the day we have to make choices for ourselves.

Existentialists claim that each individual's personal identity is actively determined by the sum of all of their actions. If this is true, there is no fixed human nature we could appeal to in describing ourselves. When a couple of "survivors" get into a fight and spill gravy on Larry at a dinner party, Cheryl's mom suggests that someone should grab him a sponge to clean up the mess. In a classic existentialist manner, Larry replies, "I don't understand. . . . Why don't *you* get a sponge?" Each of us is put in such a position that we must choose who we are going to be, and *make* ourselves through the actions we perform. Feeling or thinking that something ought to be done doesn't cut it.

This means that we're given a huge responsibility in deciding who we are and how we ought to live. Someone might say, "Existentialism can't be right. This isn't how most people live their lives." But philosophers like Heidegger and Sartre would agree. They would concede that it's rare that we take the time to fully reflect on each and every decision we need to make in our lives. However, there is still a sense in which we *could* live like this, if we were being completely honest with ourselves all of the time, and we weren't making excuses for our failures.

When we're completely honest, there really are *no excuses*, as Sartre puts it. We can always make different choices, even if those choices are only about the attitudes we adopt toward circumstances beyond our control. Living honestly means living authentically, and to live authentically means to completely own-up to *all* aspects of our lives within our control. Existentialism is an extremely demanding philosophy. The responsibility we have placed upon us due to our freedom is what leads us to the feeling of existential anxiety, and Larry is a prime example of its sway.

How to Be Genuinely Bald

If Sartre's right, then we don't need to be paralyzed or saddened by the freedom he claims we have. Sartre thinks we should *enthusiastically* embrace his philosophy. It's not just the big issues in our lives that require us to make large decisions. Even the smallest of choices demands our careful attention. Larry takes up the same approach on *Curb*. For him, there is no meaningful difference between religion and lobster, or between a doctor's diagnosis of cancer and a discussion about the benefits of keeping fish as pets. And there seems to be no greater value than those expressed in the complex economy of golf tips.

This shouldn't surprise us anymore. If our lives are defined by the choices we make, then even the most mundane aspects of our lives become the subject of intense contemplation. *Each and every* choice we make calls us to assert ourselves through our own free will, since the existentialists claim there are no values apart from the ones we adopt in our decision-making.

Some people say that existentialism is too pessimistic, that it highlights only the ugliest portions of human existence (such as anxiety or despair), and that it ignores the things that allow us to experience happiness. A common reproach aimed at individuals who are seen to be anxious or despairing is the imperative to "Just be happy!" or to "Quit over-thinking things!" Larry is often in situations that might lead people to offer the same advice. We might want him to relax, and not call every tiny aspect of his daily routine into question. Is it true, though, that Larry merely finds the bad in everything? Is he too pessimistic?

Maybe the opposite is true. Maybe Larry is actually *quite the optimist!* If there's no given purpose for human beings, we can use our own free actions to provide the world with value, or to show that some of society's rules shouldn't be followed. To find faults within society in the Larry David fashion requires commitment. We have to be committed to changing the world, even just little parts of it, instead of merely passing them by and accepting the status quo. A pessimist would see things in the world that need to change, but wouldn't consider herself capable of changing them. If she thought a particular practice was etched in stone according to a fixed human nature, she wouldn't even *try* to change it. As Larry says to a receptionist,

> **LARRY:** Things like this interest me. I'm not an inventor, but I'm an improver. I improve things that are broken. This is broken. This system is broken; I would like to improve it. (Season Six, "The Bat Mitzvah")

In this case, most people would either not even notice a minor inconvenience related to the bureaucratic tendencies of a proctologist, or notice them but say nothing at all (why draw more attention to ourselves when at a proctologist's?). Larry, however, commits himself to changing the way the waiting room operates, demonstrating that he's optimistic enough about the things he's capable of affecting. He's optimistic about the extent of his freedom. If he doesn't say anything, who will?

In response to some of his critics Sartre claimed: "When all is said and done, what we are accused of, at bottom, is not our pessimism, but an optimistic toughness" (p. 33). It's not that the existentialists are accused of being too sullen or angry, but that they are often disliked for reminding us that we have more responsibility than we thought. The angry reactions Larry tends to get from people usually aren't directed toward some definitive flaw in Larry's revelation, but toward the toughness associated with his rocking the boat. An object at rest tends to stay at rest. People would rather not think about what they're doing or thinking. They'd prefer to just do it or just go on thinking it. But nothing is that easy with Larry. He doesn't take anything for granted.

For both Heidegger and Sartre, we usually flee from the most important aspects of our existence and take refuge in the tranquility of what's easy and familiar. Heidegger called this our everydayness, the way we exist when we're living the lives that everyone else thinks we should. We avoid confronting the issue of our freedom. We deceive ourselves. Sartre referred to this aspect of our lives as our living in "bad faith." We trick ourselves into the belief that we are incapable of making all of the choices dictating the course of our lives. To live in "bad faith" means allowing ourselves to go about our day while avoiding taking responsibility for everything that we can.

Larry calls people out when he suspects that bad faith is operative. For example, when he tries to get Susie's brownie recipe, he's confronted with her reluctance to hand it over. She repeatedly claims that she can't, that the matter is out of her hands and she is unable to act otherwise.

LARRY: I would love if you could give me the recipe.

SUSIE: The brownie recipe? I can't do that, darling. I can't.

LARRY: No, no. What do you mean? Of course you can. (Season Three, "The Benadryl Brownie")

Larry gets angry when he hears this, because he thinks Susie is deceiving herself. Of course she *can* give him the recipe. What she *can't* do is simultaneously respect her grandmother's wishes that the recipe remain a secret and give it to Larry. As long as Susie says that she *cannot* give Larry her recipe, she's fleeing from the responsibility of owning up to her commitment. She's avoiding the freedom existentialism tells her she has. The role of dispelling people of bad faith and pushing others to take responsibility for their lives is one that Larry plays often on *Curb*.

In existentialism, the concept of bad faith is closely related to the concept of authenticity, which is another topic that occurs again and again on *Curb*. Consider Larry's attitude toward his own baldness, and the standards to which he holds other bald people. Larry's baldness is an attribute that he is very proud to display. He doesn't attempt to hide his baldness with hair plugs, toupees, or hats. His approach to his own baldness exhibits authenticity in the existentialist sense, because it involves being honest with himself and owning up to certain facts about his body and appearance. This doesn't mean that there aren't authentic toupee-wearers or authentic hair-pluggers. Someone could alter his follicular situation and remain authentic so long as he openly identified with his choices in an honest way.

The issue of inauthenticity and baldness, however, is exhibited clearly in Season Three when Larry meets a potential chef, Phil Dunlap, for the restaurant he is investing in. While Larry interviews Phil, he is extremely pleased to find out that he is also bald, and that he shares his views regarding bald men who try to hide their baldness.

> **LARRY:** Toupée?
>
> **PHIL:** No. Oh, no. Absolutely not.
>
> **LARRY:** Those guys. They should kill those guys.
>
> **PHIL:** Exactly.
>
> **LARRY:** I'm surprised Hitler didn't round up the toupée people. (Season Three, "The Grand Opening")

As the scene proceeds, Larry continues to express his disdain for people who attempt to cover up their baldness, and Phil agrees with him the entire time. Later in the episode, when Larry discovers that Phil actually *does* wear a toupée, he fires him on the spot. Phil was inauthentic because he was hiding who he was. We're not responsible for the genetic makeup we're given, but the existentialists claim that we are responsible for our attitude and honesty regarding what we find ourselves with. As Sartre says,

> Man is condemned to be free. Condemned, because he did not create himself, yet, in other respects is free; because, once thrown into the world, he is responsible for everything he does. (p. 23)

At a minimum, Phil should have defended toupées during his interview. If it's our actions that define who we are, and not merely the private thoughts we keep in our heads, Phil had a responsibility to own up to his choices.

The Stare

Sartre asks his readers to imagine a voyeur who is peeping through the keyhole of a closed door. While watching, the voyeur's consciousness is completely directed to whatever's taking place on the other side of the door. But, Sartre says, imagine what happens to the voyeur the moment he thinks he hears someone behind him. The sound brings him away from what he has been viewing, and makes him aware of himself as an object that can also be viewed. Sartre's example shows just how profoundly our consciousness is at the whim of how we think others might be gazing at us.

Existentialism's philosophy of society is demonstrated on *Curb* through the "Larry David Stare." The investigative stare that Larry subjects his interlocutors to is an attempt to glean the truth somehow in the eyes of the other. It usually takes place when one person (usually, though not always, Larry) suspects another person of telling a lie. As the scenes play out, aided by frolicking horns, Larry maintains eye contact while tilting his head one way and the other, attempting to find the magic perspective that will allow access to the thoughts of the other. After about ten seconds, we inevitably find that Larry retires with an unconvinced and still suspicious "Okay . . ." In these moments, we see Larry trying to *know everything* about another individual, but then running up against the impenetrable boundaries inherent to another person's private thoughts.

We may have our suspicions about behaviors others have exhibited in the past, questionable actions, or other motivations ("There's something about that weatherman I don't trust.

I don't like that weatherman. He's a very slick weatherman."), but what Larry shows us is that at the end of the day we must relinquish our attempts at complete mastery and recognize those things we actually have control over. Coming to realize that we cannot know all of someone else's thoughts or that we cannot completely control how others view us, both Sartre and Larry David claim that we must continue to act in such a way that we assert our values. We must act in ways that demonstrate how we think all human beings ought to live.

Sartre finds "The Look" of the other to play a huge role in our subjectivity, and the "Larry David Stare" plays an equally potent part in the constitution of many of the characters. While being stared down, the victim of the stare often looks quite nervous, knowing that he has been called out and put on the spot. In the face of the other, we realize that we're not the only ones experiencing the world, and that we're essentially sharing the world. For Sartre, "it appears that the world has a kind of drain hole in the middle of its being and that it is perpetually flowing off through this hole."[4] As the "Larry David Stare" theme music plays, any attempt to retreat into a solitary existence is removed, and the "drain hole" of Larry's squinting eyes aid in the constitution of his victim's personal identity. While under Larry's gaze, something fundamental about his victim's consciousness is altered. They're reminded that they are always potentially being watched.

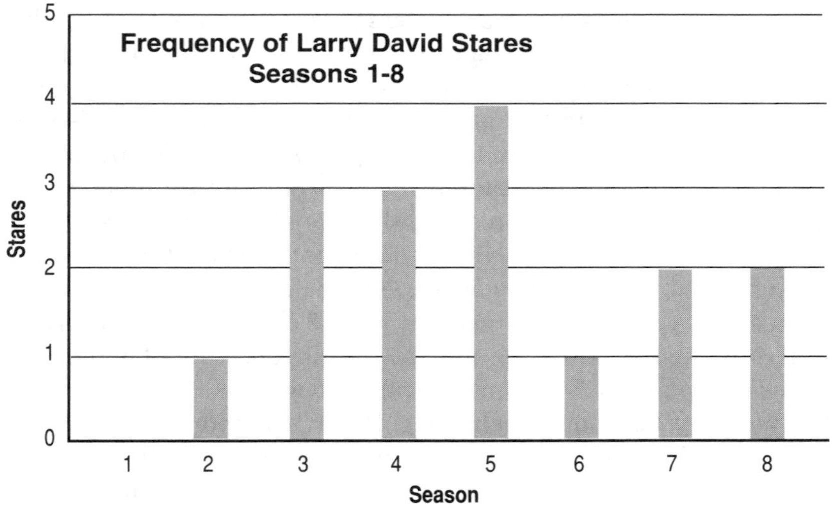

Curb Episodes Featuring the "Larry David Stare"

Season	Episode	Direction	Suspicion
2	"The Acupuncturist"	From Larry to his acupuncturist	Whether orchids are a customary Japanese gift from a man
3	"Mary, Joseph, and Larry"	From Larry to the waiter at the club	Whether he tipped the waiter twice
	——	From Larry to his landscaper	Whether he told the housekeeper about differing gratuity sizes
	——	From Larry to his housekeeper	Whether she was bad-talking him in Spanish
4	"The Weatherman"	From Larry to Susie	Whether she told Ted Danson that Larry shouldn't watch his dog
4	"The 5 Wood"	From Larry to Norm	Whether he told the golf club about Larry's dirty locker
4	"Opening Night"	From Larry to the hotel doorman	Whether he received his portion of a tip from another employee
5	"The Larry David Sandwich"	From Larry to his father	Whether he was adopted
5	"The Bowtie"	From Larry to Marty	Whether he invited Rosie O'Donnell to a party
5	"The Seder"	From Larry to his neighbor, the plastic surgeon	Whether he stole the newspaper
5	"The Korean Bookie"	From Larry to his bookie	Whether he knew about the disappearance of a dog
6	"The Lefty Call"	From Larry to the restaurant waiter	Whether he tampered with the leftovers
7	"The Black Swan"	From Mr. Takahashi to Larry	Whether Larry killed the black swan
7	"Seinfeld"	From Jerry Seinfeld to Larry	Whether Larry has ulterior motives for changing the script
8	"The Hero"	From Larry to Ricky Gervais	Whether he was dating Larry's ex
8	"Larry vs. Michael J. Fox"	From Larry to Michael J. Fox	Whether the noise he was making was an effect of Parkinson's disease, or if he was pissed at Larry

The stare represents an attempt to treat human consciousness as something that could be viewed empirically and catalogued in the same way a scientist would observe forces and material substances. It's no surprise, then, that there never seems to be any success to the Larry David Stare. If Sartre is correct that our subjectivity exists only for the private view of the individual in question, then it could never be the case that a stare could cut to the subjective truth of someone else, no matter how much one squinted. Because human beings are completely free, and thus always more than whatever they are at a given moment, there is nothing in or about them to be looked at that could completely capture their consciousness.

Larry isn't always on the sending side of the Stare, especially in the context of existentialism. After he kills the swan that belonged to the country club owner, Mr. Takahashi stares down Larry to attempt to force a confession. When Larry starts making changes to the *Seinfeld* reunion show script, Jerry Seinfeld performs the Stare on Larry to make sure Larry isn't withholding any information from him. This shows us that he too is aware of being subjected to the gaze of another person, and that this is one of the fundamental aspects of our lives as human beings.

While we might think that being preoccupied with what other people think of us is overly vain, Sartre is suggesting that it's an unavoidable part of our existence. Think of the predicament Larry finds himself in when he complains about the New-York-Yankee-hating stonemason who is, unbeknownst to Larry, standing right across from him. While he's venting to Marty about the stonemason's unforgivable hatred of Derek Jeter, his worldview is arranged in a somewhat harmonious way. He is merely having a conversation with a friend. However, when he discovers that the villain of his narrative is standing in the same conversation circle, the harmony is disrupted. While nothing seems to have changed materially, the recognition of the stonemason's presence in the conversation immediately changes Larry's situation. He gets embarrassed. For Sartre, this type of feeling is entirely inevitable in society. As he says,

> Thus suddenly an object has appeared which has stolen the world from me. Everything is in place; everything still exists for me; but everything is traversed by an invisible flight and fixed in the direction

> of a new object. The appearance of the Other in the world corresponds therefore to a fixed sliding of the whole universe, to a decentralization of the world which undermines the centralization which I am simultaneously effecting. (*Being and Nothingness*, p. 231)

While some of Sartre's language can be disorienting, the takeaway point is that we are made to feel very strange in the presence of others. This happens merely by our recognition that someone is watching.

Is Choosing Worth the Schlep?

What, then, have we learned about Larry David? If there is something like a Larry David essence, what we glean is not the product of one man instilled with a particular set of unchanging traits. What we have is an individual who perpetually chooses to live a life that exhibits what he holds to be valuable. This is done even though it repeatedly leads to existential anxiety, and must be done while being subjected to society's stares. There isn't a Larry David essence in the sense the philosophical tradition has given it, but a particular existence or style of existing based on the actions of a man who experiences genuine anxiety in the face of most choices.

The imperative put forth by the series title to *Curb Your Enthusiasm* ought not to be understood as a call to be unhappy, or to only find the bad things in our lives. We should not merely reduce the level of our enthusiasm. It's better understood under the optimistic conditions that existentialism provides us with, meaning that we can take responsibility for what we enjoy, and that we do this by authentically connecting with the things that matter to us. By curb-ing, we're invited to lead lives in which we authentically choose what is worth being enthusiastic about, and what is merely given to us by society as something that ought to be enjoyed.

It's unfortunate that existentialism gets a bad rap, but by carving off the excess of our inauthentic enjoyment, what we're left with is an optimistic and enthusiastic existence that will be continually renewed in the face of anxiety through our actions. Larry David: existentialist, anxious, and optimistic. The only question we're left with, then, is "Why don't *you* grab a sponge?"

12
Maybe Authenticity Isn't for Everyone

NATALIE FLETCHER

Every *Curb* enthusiast among us has been there: watching the screen with jittery anticipation, hands slowly covering eyes, a whisper pleading "Larry, don't, please, don't!" as our favorite klutz propels himself into a situation so awkward it merits a timeout from the TV set. How, we wonder, can someone genuinely be so socially inept, so self-serving, so *twisted*?

The routine cringe-fests that pepper Larry David's life may leave us queasy and questioning, but they're also what make his oddball character so endearing for some of us. We assume he can't help himself, that his idiosyncrasies are a testament to his true self, the *real* LD. And we value this authenticity because we think social interactions work best when people are their real selves rather than mere veneers. If given the choice, most of us would prefer to deal with individuals who are genuine, upfront, and honest about their identities than contend with spin doctors who toy with appearances to mask their true characters. But what happens if one's truly authentic self is actually morally repugnant, à la Larry David?

In everyday terms, authenticity is understood as a capacity, attitude or state where being true to ourselves is considered desirable, even morally beneficial. For philosophers interested in ethics, authenticity is often seen as a crucial part of identity-building, one that appeals to freedom, choice and commitment to create a genuine sense of self. Authenticity can be equated to a kind of transparency, where the authentic individual is open and forthright about their whole character rather than selective and calculated. It's a path away from the lemming mentality and towards the formation of a personal code of behavior. In Larry lingo, for the real individualist, it's pretty, pretty, pretty, pretty good.

Yet one of authenticity's limitations is the very fact that it's vague: if it can't be reduced to a set of standards or principles, its criteria are hard to pinpoint. As a result, for some, authenticity is really nothing more than an excuse for egoism: to be authentic is to think that your way is the only way, that you are a self-made creature, that you should and can decide the outcome of your life without external interference.

Left to its own devices, this pop species of authenticity has spawned all kinds of deviations, including our darling Larry David, whose take on authenticity is hardly socially constructive. By adopting a take-it-or-leave-it approach to his identity, Larry portrays a seemingly genuine (albeit buffoon-like) persona, alienating acquaintances and audiences alike with his absurdly awkward self-endorsements.

Sincerity Tests and Petty Rules

Though authenticity has always figured in one way or another throughout history—as a way to describe our place in the cosmos, our faith in God, our commitment to rationality—it took center stage in the late eighteenth century during the Romantic era. In a total backlash against the Enlightenment's insistence on objectivity, reason and science, Romantic thinkers stressed emotions, individuality and imagination, lauding the artist as quintessentially authentic for his ability to express and connect with inner truths and meaning. Rooted in the ideas of philosopher Jean-Jacques Rousseau, notably his concept of *amour de soi*—our original drive towards self-preservation—authenticity was increasingly perceived as something we attained by escaping overly constraining social rules and finding our own voice through candid self-expression.

At first blush, Larry seems to embody this authentic Romantic artist, striving to defy social scripts in favor of reclusive independence and a personal sense of ethics. Yet as any *Curb* buff knows, Larry clings to the most morally insignificant types of "oughts," advancing petty rules of etiquette with the assurance of a high priest, only to find himself repeatedly knocked off his pedestal, often by his own doing.

Case in point: the sign-in sheet at his doctor's clinic ("The Interior Decorator," Season One). What, pray tell, does a waiting room protocol have to do with virtue? For Larry, it's a symbol of righteous human conduct that separates the morally inconsiderate (tardy, chit-chatting patients) from the morally exemplary (um . . . him). It's quite simple, really: unless the policy benefits him, it's evil, pure evil. Not exactly what Romantic thinkers had in mind when they envisaged an authentic artist in pursuit of moral truth through introspection and soul-searching in the deep woods.

Though Larry surrounds himself with people who support his antics—from the tolerant Cheryl who tries to make him understand that, "Not everyone knows your rules" ("Trick or Treat," Season Two), to the ever goading Seinfeld who over-inflates Larry's confidence for his own amusement, "That's Larry 'How-Can-I-Help?' David" ("The Bare Midriff," Season Seven)—their loyalty does not satiate his need to officiate the world's trivialities with his preposterous commandments:

- **Chicken should never be served on skewers at a cocktail party.**
- **Everyone should bring his or her own jacket to the beach.**
- **Hired help should never be coerced into wearing bowties.**
- **The waiting-until-after-dessert rule should never be enforced.**
- **Wedding vows should never incorporate an "eternity" clause.**

Look out, Emily Post, there's a new Queen Bee of decorum in town.

But seriously, why the urge to reinvent the ethical wheel with such trifles? According to Charles Guignon in *On Being Authentic*, the problem started when otherwise promising Romantic ideals got distorted by pop psychology theories. By the twentieth century, ideas of a higher power were increasingly losing clout in the Western world: authenticity no longer had to involve something transcendent—whether a form of divinity or an absolute concept—but could be entirely self-referential. Through psychologization—or the "tendency to psychologize the issues of living"—we've done away with any useful sense of civility by describing all matters that lie beyond our individual pursuit of welfare as inauthentic social demands.

Rather than help us understand our behavior and shape it to better engage with others, pop psychology has promoted a "concentration, persistent, if not feverish, upon one's thoughts, feelings, wishes, worries—bordering on, if not embracing, solipsism."[1] We've been led to believe that we can and ought to prioritize our own interests even when that makes us unable or completely unwilling to respond to the outside world's generally agreed-upon standards of action and mutual concern. In other words, we are encouraged to think that egoism is an expression of our real, unadulterated authenticity.

Guignon is especially critical of the self-help movement that lures us into expensive, expertly branded programming meant to connect us with our authentic voice by effectively conforming to set maxims about instant gratification and band-aid solutions. He thinks these self-proclaimed gurus have cherry-picked past ideas about the authentic ideal, plucking them from the contexts that gave them meaning, only to reframe them in a contemporary conception that offers little significance beyond "me-me-me" thinking. These approaches produce highly self-absorbed individuals who take it upon themselves to judge the moral merits of their peers, convinced their feelings have a special authority.

True to form, Larry doesn't convey emotions—he vomits them. The man relishes in calling people on their failed social graces, insisting on the last word even as we, his spectators, cringe behind our couch cushions. Even in those split-seconds when we can't help but believe in his good will and concede that his opponent-of-the-moment is being ridiculous, he inevitably finds a way to shatter our illusions.

Sure, his lawyer shouldn't charge him her hourly fee to read his script. Certainly he meant well when he agreed to help a nit-picky blind man unpack his apartment. Granted, the "Happy Birthday" song can grate on the nerves. But does the aftermath of such triteness deserve a full dose of LD fury? Are

---

[1] Charles Guignon, *On Being Authentic* (Routledge, 2004), p. 93.

second chances out of the question in Larry's world? As he readily confesses, it only took one botched attempt at being a Good Samaritan to turn him off kindness altogether: he once hollered a concerned "Watch out!" to a woman about to get hit by a car only to be told off for his heroic feat—"I got out of the nice business at that point" ("The Wire," Season One). So adamant is our arbiter of rightfulness, he'll risk getting kicked out of heaven over a misplaced DVD cover.

Fueled by intense paranoia, Larry's motto may as well be "Trust No One." From hotel lobbies to the golf course, he obsessively seeks truth, using his signature sincerity test—the multi-angled stare—to assess his rivals' game. Like a card pro reading poker faces, he meticulously sniffs out signs of inner demons, doling out his version of moral reprimands as he sees fit. Damn the lying weatherman! A pox on thieving dry cleaners! When the suspected culprits bite back, as do his cast mates Ben Stiller and David Schwimmer during rehearsals for *The Producers*, sparks really fly. Although co-operation would best serve their interests as colleagues, they prefer to butt heads and scapegoat each other than find a common ground.

It's a fairly safe bet that if someone dares cross Larry, he'll find exactly how to get under their skin and stay there, rubbing them the wrong way until they erupt. Poor Wanda falls for this ruse every time, getting herself worked up over his bogus racist statements as he delights in playing the social piranha. One strike and you're out in this forgiveness-free zone: just ask the bald chef who gets fired for donning a misleading toupée. Not only is this crime against the hairless proof of gross vanity, in Larry's books it warrants analogies to Nazi persecution: "I'm surprised Hitler didn't round up the toupée people," he declares. "I mean, if I'm gonna be a sick megalomaniac and round up people who I hated, they would be on my list. I would say: 'Get the toupée people!' I'd have my henchmen going around, tugging at people's hair!" ("The Grand Opening," Season Three).

Seem extreme? Not for Larry. Anything less would betray the LD moral code that seeks to universalize untenable principles for complete banalities. On the plus side, as an ethicist-in-training, he understands that moral norms work best when they can apply to as many people and situations as possible. He even seems to grasp the difference between intention and action—those elusive twin concepts so often used by philosophers to evaluate moral character based on what we aim to do versus what we end up doing. What he's missing, however, is the criterion of worthwhile relevance.

What's the *point* of his petty rules and sincerity tests? What's their *value*? Clearly your common-sense radar is a bit off course when you think moral integrity correlates directly to the number of cashews you'd put in a bag of mixed nuts.

Bad Faith and the Scheming Egoist

An avid critic of those who exaggerate their moral worth, existentialist Jean-Paul Sartre would have loved *Curb* for its mishmash of inauthentic characters, fitting Larry snugly in his "angels of inauthenticity" bin. The French philosopher was especially fond of authenticity for its capacity to quell our blind conformity to the particular roles and maxims that define our social engagements—the very rules that govern Larry's neurotic existence.

In *Being and Nothingness*, Sartre argues against the idea that life is predetermined, describing humans as self-creators who have the freedom to be whomever they please at any given moment. Since life is a creative process, the responsible—and authentic—individuals take ownership of that process, using their own capacities and judgments as well as personally endorsed social values to create meaningful existences, in the same way that a painter might create a work of art drawing from both his own imagination and his perceptions of the world.

Given this vast freedom, the resulting responsibility is massive, often intimidating, and a sure source of anguish, especially for those of us who would rather have a grab bag of pretexts on which to base (or excuse) our chosen existential paths. But there's no sense of providence, godliness, or luck in Sartre's world—we must freely define our existences by our actions: "Man is nothing other than his own project. He exists only to the extent that he realizes himself."[2]

Sartre's most provocative example of anguish emerges in his vertigo scenario: standing by a cliff, the vertiginous man

[2] Jean-Paul Sartre, *Existentialism Is a Humanism* (Yale University Press, 1997), p. 34.

realizes that he's free either to take a flying leap off the precipice or to remain at its edge—to die or to live—and this sense of radical freedom completely overwhelms him. (In Larry's case, the precipice is the brink of a dysfunctional ski lift and the decision is whether to jump off out of respect for Orthodox Jewish law or stay safe and sound, but to each their own, right?) According to Sartre, on a regular basis, we all experience feelings of anguish where we confront a form of death, from losing a loved-one to getting fired from a job. These moments force us to choose between a challenging but authentic approach to life or a more self-deceptive, inauthentic alternative. While some of us may rise to the challenge, others will cave under pressure.

One common instance of caving is what Sartre dubs "bad faith," an inauthentic tactic through which we seek comfort in partial truths about ourselves, equating our identity either exclusively with random facts about who we are (our "facticity") or with our future possibilities (our "transcendence"). In Sartre's view, bad faith is an inappropriate response to freedom since it encourages people to be cowards by nurturing a victim complex and taking refuge in fanciful excuses. On the flip side, it can also breed egoistic "bastards" who try to cope with existential anguish by convincing themselves they have a very special role to play in the world—that their lives are somehow more significant than ours. In Larry, we find a disturbing though hilarious bad faith gumbo: the cowardly bastard, the bastardly coward.

So what's at the root of this doublethink? Some existentialist scholars point to the techniques used in advertising, public relations, and political propaganda, highlighting how they construct misleading statements (rather than flat-out lies) to deceive their audiences, using omissions, emphasis, vagueness and ambiguity to fabricate pretenses that are more appealing than the truth. In a similar way, sufferers of bad faith condition themselves to diligently avert their gaze from the undesirable facets of reality and concentrate on the advantageous aspects, thus sidestepping accountability and persuading themselves to live in denial. When they crave a way out of changing their fate, they simply deny their transcendence ("I can't help it; that's just the way I am."); when they seek absolution for their bad deeds, they just deny their facticity ("The evil creep who did that—that's not really me; I'm a church-goer, I give to charities").[3] Sound familiar?

Larry David seems like a true threat to the authentic ideal because he manages to persevere unfettered amidst widespread disapproval, designing a life that suits his whims, however morally distasteful the ensuing strategies. Here's a guy who'll feign concern over a sick dog to gain sympathy, exaggerate his Jewishness to get special treatment from the head of an organ donor consortium and claim to be a "people person" to placate his nettlesome mother-in-law. With a façade for every circumstance, Larry fakes friendship, sympathy, race, and religion to safeguard his lifestyle, manipulating others' impressions of him for the pure sake of convenience, even if it means overusing his mother's death to dodge social functions.

In reality, though, Larry's guilty of bad faith: he deceives himself into believing his version of the truth by obscuring the possible consequences of his actions and focusing squarely on his main ambition—himself. He may fervently defend his faux personas—"I'm an honest person!" "I love everybody!" "I'm a good apple!"—but he remains indifferent to the responsibilities inherent in authenticity. The proof lies in his great fear of being uncovered for the scheming egoist that he is, preferring to keep his lousy assistant Antoinette on payroll than risk her divulging his lies and deceit.

In thinking that he matters more than others, Larry makes choices that affirm the value of extreme self-interest, yet this value cannot be generalized to all humankind as it would negatively impact social cohesion. As Sartre writes in *Existentialism is a Humanism*, "Certainly, many believe that their actions involve no one but themselves, and were we to ask them, 'But what if everyone acted that way?' they would shrug their shoulders and reply, 'But everyone does not act that way.' In truth, however, one should always ask oneself, 'What would happen if everyone did what I am doing?'" (p. 25). Clearly, Larry cannot make a convincing case that his "way" has universal value so by maintaining his stance, he continues to live a lie. Within his own mind games, he becomes both the deceiver and the deceived, aware of the sham but purposely deaf to it.

---

[3] David Detmer, *Sartre Explained: From Bad Faith to Authenticity* (Open Court, 2008), pp. 78–79.

So how can we hold the Larry Davids of the world accountable? Sartre proposes banishing them all to the netherworld to duke it out amongst themselves. For him, nothing spells eternal damnation like endless judgment from a bunch of intolerable strangers. In his play *No Exit*, Sartre's trio of antiheroes learn quite quickly that "Hell is other people"—no need for fiery pits or evil spirits, the image of ourselves reflected by others is punishment enough, even for sins as gruesome as torture and murder.

Caught in a hell of his own making, Larry desperately tries to control how others see him yet constantly bungles his efforts to save face. He can't make a charitable donation without an ulterior motive—his name in lights—both coveting and resenting the accolades that Ted Danson receives for keeping his own gift (more or less) secret: "This is false philanthropy and faux anonymity!" he exclaims, incensed at being morally one-upped once again ("The Anonymous Donor," Season Six).

Larry refuses to see his freedom as tied up with the existence of others so he can't respect them. He may enlist Jeff as his fellow conspirator but only because he perceives him as a useful instrument in his schemes. Mel Brooks was right on target when he described Larry as a walking disaster that damns everything he touches ("Opening Night," Season Four). But as Sartre insists, "No matter what circle of hell we are living in, we are free to break out of it. And if people do not break out, they are staying there of their own free will."[4]

Moral Relativism and Justified Self-Interest

Though Larry's twisted moral code may suggest otherwise, our sense of ethics is supposed to help guide our interactions with others to ensure we can all get along. Many philosophers gravitate towards authenticity because it can provide this moral guide without commanding the array of dizzying rules and regulations that turns the *Curb* world on its head. Authenticity is more about style than content: figure out what you value, express it and you're set—no protocol to follow, no herd of sheep to join. It forms the basis of our ideas about individualism that compels us to choose our own paths, take initiative and follow our dreams.

---

[4] *Sartre Explained*, p. 200.

Yet if authenticity means "Anything goes" then it can apply just as well to morally unsavory actions as it can to righteous ones, revealing the dangers of a certain bespectacled baldy left unrestrained to run amok. By emphasizing the potentially disastrous outcomes of a freely chosen self, Larry demonstrates that authenticity may do more harm than good considering the human tendency towards egomania. Here the notion of an "authentic" type of egoism begins to take shape: a kind of justified self-interest that reflects the true motivations of individuals in a way that is deemed natural, rational and even moral.

For egoists like Larry, the focus remains on rights rather than responsibilities, on benefits rather than investments, resulting in a "me-against-the-world" attitude that pits them against an unnamed "other" who is trying to force them into a social mould. Crudely put, the objective becomes less about finding their inner voice than quenching everyone else's. However repugnant to the morally inclined, Larry-types encapsulate ethicists' worst fears: individualism gone awry, relativism given free reign, and authenticity stripped of its moral brawn.

This is exactly what concerns Charles Taylor in his book *The Ethics of Authenticity*. He laments the contemporary tendency towards self-absorption that makes an individual's life choices worthy of esteem simply by virtue of being chosen. In his view, because today's individualism upholds that "each of us has an original way of being human," it's impossible for us to challenge another's values without being considered disrespectful of them, even if their way seems morally questionable at best. As a result, we encourage moral relativism, a "my-way-or-the-highway" approach to ethics that motivates people to care only about their own position on things and feel entitled to disregard everyone else's.

The upshot? While humanity continues to evolve in many spheres, its ethical potential is biting the dust. Because moral relativism focuses on personal fulfillment, it tends to excuse indifference to social issues, meaning we detach ourselves from our community involvements to simply enjoy our cushy circumstances. As Taylor notes, "the dark side of individualism is a centering on the self, which both flattens and narrows our lives, makes them poorer in meaning, and less concerned with others or society."[5] And this self-centeredness can tick people off: consider the judge who sentences our fallen hero to wearing an "I-steal-forks-from-restaurants" sign in a fruitless attempt to deflate his ego.

Curb-Larry epitomizes the kind of moral relativist that Taylor fears, one who is devious, insensitive and opportunistic, unapologetically opting for a life of double-transgression theories, even if they do amount, as Jeff puts it, to a "big bowl of wrong" ("The Smoking Jacket," Season 5, Episode 6). There is something almost commendable about the way Larry justifies his cause by creating loopholes in the concept of authenticity: he is weaselly, petty, spiteful, tactless and thoroughly self-interested . . . but in the most authentic-seeming way possible.

What's worse, he's got some pretty outspoken scholars on his side. Take Ayn Rand, who's notorious for defending the virtue of selfishness, arguing that we should always be the beneficiaries of our own good deeds—that it's a-okay to put ourselves first, in fact, it's *irrational* if we don't.[6] For her, the ideal individual is a "self-sufficient ego" who snubs convention and perseveres in spite of constant opposition and adversity. No compromise, no compassion. Strong but cavalier, and not about to succumb to silly talk about altruism and turning the other cheek.

In *Why It's Hard to Be Good*, Al Gini associates this kind of egoism with the "narcissistic" personality, a clinical term that designates people who are "self-absorbed, exaggerate their own worth, show no empathy, feel entitled, seek attention, can't take criticism, love flattery, expect special treatment, try to control God, exempt themselves from rules, manipulate others and lack gratitude." Taken together, these ego-driven symptoms reveal a lack of security in dealing with the far-reaching effects of self-definition. As Gini observes, they hinder social success by distancing individuals from their relationships with others and fostering a deceptive sense of personal value: "Narcissists create for themselves a self-defined, self-contained, self-serving worldview, which rationalizes anything done on their behalf and which does not require justification on any grounds outside themselves."[7]

---

[5] *The Ethics of Authenticity* (Harvard, 1991), p. 4.

[6] *The Virtue of Selfishness* (Signet, 1964), p. ix.

[7] *Why It's Hard to Be Good* (Routledge, 2008), p. 36.

The thing is, though defining ourselves authentically does involve a sizable helping of autonomy and self-cultivation, it also draws on what Taylor calls "pre-existing horizons of significance"—the ideas, discoveries, traditions, values and knowledge bases that have culminated from centuries of diverse human evolution. Although egoists may claim to be acting authentically when they do as they please, they fail to connect themselves to this rich, vibrant background: "I can define my identity only against the background of things that matter. But to bracket out history, nature, society, the demands of solidarity, everything but what I find in myself, would be to eliminate all candidates for what matters" (pp. 40–41).

Our sense of self relies on a social context to give it meaning and direction—an idea that Susie communicates with her typical vulgarity whenever Larry flexes his egoist muscle. With surprising perceptiveness, she sees right through his half-baked ploys, labeling him a "heartless piece of shit" who doesn't care about anyone but himself and never seems to benefit from his loved-ones' pearls of wisdom. When he survives a near-drowning incident in the ocean, Susie offers a stern wake-up call: "I think this happened for a reason. Maybe now you'll respect people more, start treating them a little better" ("The Larry David Sandwich," Season Five).

But, as always, the lesson doesn't stick. When Larry does come face to face with his conscience in the mirror after a freak encounter with a hooker's stash of weed, the conversation turns trivial pretty quickly ("The Car Pool Lane," Season Four). For all his quirky charm, Larry just can't accept that his identity is embedded in—and embellished by—his dialogue with others and, more figuratively, with the world at large. Despite a fleeting experience with something akin to authentic living when he learns he is adopted, the "good person" chapter of his life is over before it gains any momentum, and his "What Would Jesus Do?" angle quickly morphs back into his "What Can Larry Get Away With?" slant ("The End," Season Five). When push comes to shove, the concept of authenticity can't seem to redeem the likes of Larry David.

Lost Causes or Staying Power?

Authenticity is a relational concept, one that enables self-fulfillment while also embracing social responsibility. It embodies the African ethical concept of *ubuntu* which views humanity as interconnected—"I am what I am because of who we all are." Far from demanding altruism, authenticity encourages us to treat others as valuable in their own right, proving that we can engage in our own projects without precluding care by viewing others' welfare as part of our personal agendas. We can "be" ourselves while also "getting over" ourselves.

Easier said than done for LD. By purporting that his are the only worthwhile points of reference, Larry falls prey to inauthenticity and reveals his severe lack of empathy, especially when his loved-ones suffer. Even on his death bed, when given a final opportunity to express gratitude, he can't see beyond his own nose. This profound self-regard sits uncomfortably with many of us because we think it threatens human dignity. Though we may not articulate our distaste in philosophical terms, we feel repulsed by Larry's duplicitous commitments as they amount to a sort of social betrayal. We see through the masquerade and wonder, "How can he let us down like this?"

The problem is, authenticity is tough stuff. In a world focused more and more on the individual, it's hard to remember there's more to life's journey than trying to fly solo in a carpool lane. Plus, with constant temptations to lie, begrudge and reproach, it may be that an ongoing, uninterrupted state of authenticity is impossibly unrealistic.

Perhaps our darling Larry doesn't have the ethical fortitude to pull it off. Maybe placing the lion's share of the blame on everyone else is far too satisfying to consider owning up to his wrongdoings. He'd rather get the last word, even if it means losing the things he holds dearest: his wife, his reputation, his ticket to a celestial golf course. Sure the authentic route may be more ethical. But doing things his own twisted way? Simply irresistible.

VII

Having Said That . . .

13
Should We Curb Our Enthusiasm?

ROBERT R. CLEWIS

CHERYL: I don't really like this, this new Larry.

LARRY: What's the matter?

CHERYL: It's just too enthusiastic, and I miss the old Larry.

—"Shaq," Season Two

Not many television shows tell us we have to do something. *Curb Your Enthusiasm* gives us a command in its very title. Or, as Larry David might have said, "Enthusiasm is good. *Having said that*, we should curb it." Even if the title was merely intended to be ironic, it still raises an interesting question: should we follow this command?

Curb Your Enthusiasm's title may be puzzling at first or require some explanation. An article in *The New Yorker* describes the title of the one-hour special *Larry David: Curb Your Enthusiasm* (1999) as "an ironic, almost superstitious reference to David's low profile" and also "a billboard for the vastly less famous *Seinfeld* co-creator."[1] *Curb's* title dropped Larry's name, and according to one opinion can be interpreted as Larry's wanting to lower expectations of success after *Seinfeld*: "The show's title can be taken as a clever way of lowering audience expectations."[2] However, Larry describes the origin of *Curb*'s title quite differently:

---

[1] James Kaplan, "Angry Middle-Aged Man: Is Larry David Funnier than Everyone Else, or Just More Annoying?" *The New Yorker* (January 19th, 2004).

[2] Adam Bryant, "A Sage for Our Time," *New York Times* (March 23rd, 2008).

> I was in kind of title-mode. I had to come up with a title for the show . . . I was sort of in that mindset, and then . . . I remember being struck by those three words ["Curb Your Enthusiasm"] because they said so much to me, you know. "Not in front of me" . . . is really what it meant. I think there was something to the title. The title actually said some things, which I liked, and it was funny.[3]

Some of us like to watch Larry because he does things that normal people only dream of doing. In that sense he's over-enthused and unrestrained. He breaks social norms and is unbound by them. Tim Gibbons, executive producer in the HBO Season Six Promo, says that the character Larry "just doesn't know when to stop, and he always pushes it farther than any of us in real life would do it." Larry Charles, the former supervising producer at *Seinfeld* and a director of *Curb Your Enthusiasm*, states in the same promo, "He is willing to explore regions of subject matter that are generally taboo." If this is right, in many cases Larry is actually too wound up, not unenthusiastic, as *Curb*'s title would lead us to believe.

Larry was asked to explain how he's similar to the fictional character he plays. (In fact, this is the most common question he gets asked, and even the most popular question people ask *Curb* cast members.) His response was simple: "That's the guy that I *wish* I was. I love that guy. This is the guy I cannot stand [points to self]. *That* guy [he kisses hand in approval]. I can't get enough of that guy. That guy does the things I wish I could do. He behaves the way I *want* to behave." *Curb*-Larry specializes in doing or saying out loud what most of us, including Larry, would only think of doing or saying. The fact that *Curb*-Larry actually does those things is, after all, what makes him a "social assassin" ("Palestinian Chicken," Season Eight). At the same time, Larry often lacks enthusiasm. For example, he doesn't want to pick up his relatives from the airport, go to religious services, roast marshmallows, or bike around France.

Sex and Religion, and Other Reasons to Be Enthusiastic

Larry tells his wife Cheryl he would love to go scuba diving, travel, and bicycling around Europe with her. He confesses this

[3] "*Times* Talks" interview of Larry David by Bill Carter, 2006.

to his therapist, who responds, "Be enthusiastic, but don't make any specific promises that you can't fulfill" ("The Therapists," Season Six). Is the shrink's advice about enthusiasm any good? (Let's leave out the part about the promises.)

Although Larry is often annoyed by other people's enthusiasm, at times he himself is very enthusiastic. In fact, sometimes he is enthusiastically opposed to other people's enthusiasm. Examples of Larry 's enthusiasm fall under different categories, so let's have a look at them.

In English vernacular, "enthusiasm" today means intense excitement for, interest in, or approval of something. The word can be used to describe the mental state of fans of sports clubs or connoisseurs of fine wines. In this sense, we're enthusiastic about a hobby or pastime such as watching *Curb*. We can be enthusiastically involved in or committed to some activity, organization, or cause.

This general sense of "enthusiasm" in which we're devoted or committed can be broken down further. Let's look at sex, religion, and breaking social norms.

If we understand enthusiasm in terms of sexuality, then there's an obvious and basic sense in which Larry gets excited. We get an idea of this kind of enthusiasm, so ripe for comedy, in Season One's very first scene, the opening of *Curb's* first episode. Larry's pitching a tent, seeming to have a constant erection in "The Pants Tent," is perhaps a vivid example of enthusiasm if there ever was one.

This is a recurring theme throughout the show's first eight seasons. Examples range from what Susie believes she sees Larry "do" with her dog Oscar, to the water bottle in the bathroom that the girl thinks she feels: "Mommy, Mommy, that bald man is in the bathroom and there's something hard in his pants" ("The Doll," Season Two). Likewise, Larry becomes excited after hugging Auntie Rae for a time that goes over his personal limit—which, he confesses, is five Mississippi-seconds ("The N Word," Season Six). Larry fails to be aroused when he's alone with Dr. Flomm—but that's because he's taking estrogen. This theme is a prevalent one.

Religious enthusiasm, or fanaticism, is the belief or conviction that we have a private revelation from or communication with a divine being. It's thinking you have insight into a supernatural realm, when no one else can confirm that you have such insight. You *might* have it, but no one else can tell.

When it comes to religion, Larry is mostly under-enthused. He's not a religious fanatic. It's true that Larry thinks he experiences an act of divine intervention when he is saved from drowning, and that he interprets this as a message from God ("The Larry David Sandwich," Season Five). But for the most part Larry is downright sacrilegious, not a religious enthusiast. For instance, when he goes to religious services, he cleans his glasses with his yarmulke and is eventually kicked out for buying scalped tickets.

Finally, there is the sense of enthusiasm as breaking social norms that the rest of us follow quite naturally and easily. We usually tip an appropriate amount, tip-toe at night, and greet someone with a "stop and chat." Larry goes overboard in such cases. He breaks the social norms by being too aggressive, too committed.

Larry tends to put his foot in his mouth. In his visit with the AAMCO owner, Larry speaks first, only to reveal information that leads to problems, as the mechanic himself only wanted to apologize to Larry for taking his place at the dinner table (Season One). Similarly, in order to resolve his troubles with Paul Reiser's wife, Larry breaks a promise to Alanis Morrisette and tells Mrs. Reiser a secret about the content of one of Morrisette's songs ("The Terrorist Attack," Season Three). But doing so only leads to further difficulties.

Larry often acts first with good intentions, merely to generate more problems. He tries to fold clothes in the store even though the employee clearly does not want Larry's help ("Krazee-Eyez Killa," Season Three). He gets too much into playing dodge ball and breaks the thumbs of a restaurant reviewer Andy Portico ("The Grand Opening," Season Three). In his visit to him to apologize, Larry ends up feeding him spaghetti with marinara sauce despite Portico's pleas. Most of us would have just apologized and let the man be. In the freeze frame at the end of "Lewis Needs a Kidney" (Season Five), Larry is delighted because Richard Lewis's cousin Louis Lewis was shot and is in a coma, not likely to survive. Larry was ecstatic since that meant (or so he thought) that he did not have to give his kidney to his friend Richard.

The fact that his enthusiasm leads Larry to break social norms raises a question: what are these norms? The characters in the show actually do a bit of philosophizing here. A social norm is an "unwritten policy" about what ordinary members of the society can or should do, or even not do ("The Table Read," Season Seven). Everybody knows that no uninvited people are allowed to attend a show's read-through. It's an unwritten rule of etiquette ("Seinfeld," Season Seven). Larry is a "social assassin" in that he breaks these rules frequently and has "honesty Tourrette's."[4] Sometimes Larry lacks knowledge of the rules altogether. But often he has a misunderstanding of which rules are relevant in a given situation, of how to *apply* the correct rule, which he knows.

Larry invites Rick-the-sex-offender over for Seder ("The Seder," Season Five). He applies the rules that we should be friendly to new neighbors and that, as Larry says in the show, we should invite to our house people who do not have a place to go for occasions like Seder. However, his friends at the dinner party apparently thought that Larry should have applied the rule that says one does not invite sex offenders to parties where there are young children playing about.

In similar fashion, Larry does not shake Ben Stiller's hand after Stiller sneezes on it. For Larry, the rule to be followed was: "Don't shake people's hands if they have just sneezed on them." But Stiller was offended, as many of us might be. Likewise, Larry declines to go on a "house tour" of Jeff and Susie's new home. For most of us, the rule is: "Take the house tour even if you don't want to do so, in order to be kind or at least appear to be." In general, Larry fails to respect typical twenty-first-century American social norms. Even Larry's friends point this out: Marty Funkhouser complains to Larry after the latter fails to introduce Marty to a stranger ("The Black Swan," Season Seven). Marty is following the generally accepted rule: "Introduce people in a social gathering to each other if they are not yet acquainted." Larry is following a different rule: we don't have to introduce people if those people are never going to see each other again. Marty reject's Larry's response. After all, we can't predict if new acquaintances will meet again in the future.

---

[4] Lloyd Braun, a friend of Larry David and a former ABC executive, used this term to describe the actor.

Similarly, Larry gets overly delighted when he learns that Marty's daughter Jodi is not going out with women anymore ("The Bowtie," Season Five). He was overjoyed when he learned she was dating a man. He "celebrated" it even though at the same time he had claimed to be lesbians' "biggest supporter." Similarly, he shouts, "You cunt" at an effeminate married man ("The Shrimp Incident," Season Two). In "Kamikaze Bingo" (Season Five), Larry untiringly asks Japanese art dealer Yoshi why his father, a Kamikaze pilot, did not die in World War II and why his plane merely grazed an American battleship. By then ordering chicken terriaki, Larry unintentionally puts the courage of Yoshi's father into doubt, leading him to attempt to commit suicide because he lost face. Finally, Larry suggests that Marty's wife travel to London with Marty, but the latter does not want his wife to go. In this case, it apparently turned out for the best, since it encouraged Marty to get a divorce, a desire of his all along ("The Divorce," Season Eight).

The cover of the third season's DVD box shows Larry looking at a glass. He seems to be deciding if it is half full or half empty. But we could also see this image in another light: Larry deciding to be enthusiastic or not. Many times Larry chooses to rein it in.

Should We Have More Enthusiasm?

There's a flip side to Larry's enthusiasm, for he often has too little enthusiasm (in the ordinary sense) or lacks it altogether. Consider this exchange by the campfire on the beach:

> **Friend:** It's a fun grill.
>
> **Larry:** I don't want to spoil your fun. You're having a good time. You know. I'm just saying, it's idiotic what you're doing [roasting marshmallows].

Larry doesn't understand the pleasure people get from roasting marshmallows by a fire ("The Korean Bookie," Season Five). And he doesn't celebrate when his friends announce their engagement a few minutes later. Everyone else does. There are scores of examples of this kind, too.

When it comes to religion, Larry is mainly under-enthused, as we've seen. This may reflect the real Larry David as well. In the interview with *The New York Times*, Larry David the writer said:

> Religion *should* be made fun of. It's quite ridiculous, isn't it? Think of how people spend their lives. They have no idea, yet they go around as if this [religious doctrine] is a fact. It's so insane, you know. If I really believed that stuff, I'd keep it to myself, lest somebody think I was out of my mind. (Interview, 2006)

And in the show, the Jewish father of a girl who vandalized his house shouts at Larry, "You're a lousy Jew!" ("Trick or Treat," Season Two). What does Larry do in response? On the man's front lawn, Larry retaliates by conducting the orchestral music of anti-Semitic composer Richard Wagner. Finally, Larry thinks saying a prayer at the dinner table is downright silly ("Palestinian Chicken," Season Eight).

Larry is sacrilegious when it comes to other religions, too. In "The Christ Nail" (Season Five), Larry claims that worshipping Jesus would be more acceptable to him if Jesus were a beautiful woman. It would be less "gay," he says. He uses the "Christ" nail from *Passion of Christ* to hang a mezuzah. (The nail eventually saves him from his handyman Jesus, who is chasing him, for it ends up piercing Jesus's foot.) He's annoyed when the AAMCO mechanic says grace. He makes fun of Richard Lewis's Christian Scientist girlfriend, asking why she just doesn't say a prayer to fix the television rather than calling the cable guy.

Larry *lacks* enthusiasm in ways that go against social norms, too. He often hesitates to do something for other people. Sometimes this includes good friends such as Richard Lewis, and at times it involves mere acquaintances such as the guy with Clark Kent glasses ("Shaq," Season Two). Larry's lack of enthusiasm sometimes concerns important actions like donating a kidney. At other times it has to do with less significant acts such as writing a "page" for someone's birthday or a letter of recommendation for "Clark Kent." When Larry doesn't get splashed on by a car while a person standing next to him does, when Cheryl's parents cut short their visit, when Shaq's diagnosis is to be out for only a week rather than two months after Larry injures him, when a doctor tells him a growth on his skin is merely benign, and when Larry learns he doesn't have to write the letter of recommendation and the gift-page, Larry becomes ecstatic. He's so excited he doesn't have to do these things that he buys coffee and pastries for everyone in the café. Larry became elated precisely because he did not have to do something. In this case, his lack of enthusiasm made him enthusiastic.

He fails to quickly offer his kidney to Richard Lewis. Instead, he tries to find a way to get out of it, even if he does eventually donate his kidney ("Lewis Needs a Kidney," Season Five). In fact, Larry doesn't even seem to enjoy his friends, as one sees in his relationship with Lewis. At the same time, and perhaps with a bit of self-deception, Larry tells a date, the one with the anus that tickles when she sits, that he stays with friends to the very end. He thinks of himself as a guy who stays by a friend's side for life, even if he doesn't enjoy being with them ("The Bat Mitzvah" Season Six).

Larry doesn't like sentimentality or too much display of positive emotion. He cuts off Jeff and Susie's daughter Sammy when she's singing the family "present" to Ted Danson for his birthday. And Larry doesn't give a "hands in" when he, Marty, and Jeff decide to go to a club to see Lewis's girlfriend, the burlesque dancer. "We don't need that," he states matter-of-factly, as if to curb everyone's enthusiasm ("The Safe House," Season Eight).

Larry derides fake enthusiasm. He perceives this in Ted Danson's character ("Ted and Mary," Season One), pointing out with disdain, "Everything is heaven with him." Larry doesn't like Ted's enthusiasm because he thinks it is inauthentic.

Nevertheless, Larry himself sometimes displays inauthenticity. Whereas most of us think that an apology should be sincere, Larry aims to give an apology that strikes the balance between being begrudging and sincere ("The Reunion," Season Seven). It's difficult for him to be authentic plain and simple, and in the end Larry has to apologize for giving an insincere apology.

All of this helps us see why Larry is so offended by enthusiasm. Partly it's because he hates inauthenticity, even in himself. He deplores enthusiasm when it's inauthentic, such as when a person tries to impress others through their enthusiasm. Here the problem is with the contemptible *object*: fake enthusiasm.

A second reason has to do with Larry himself, the *subject*. Larry is annoyed by enthusiasm in part because of his temperament, which tends toward *Schadenfreude* and melancholy. In general, he's the kind of person who dislikes excessive emotion, especially emotions that (i) are intense and (ii) have a positive tinge to them. He dislikes highly aroused and upbeat emotions. Larry's disgusted by a happy couple. On the ski lift, Larry says to an acquaintance's daughter, Rachel: "What do people have against whistlers? I think it's because they don't like to see people happy. And who can blame them? It's like a happy couple. Is there anything more disgusting than that?" Larry wants others to be calm and neutral, not intense and happy. This is rooted in the character's rather pessimistic outlook on life. To use the traditional language of the theory of humors, Larry is a melancholic.

We might think the reason Larry's easily annoyed is that he has led a hard, rough life, and thus is resentful of others. But that isn't his experience. Larry is a multi-millionaire, the successful co-writer of *Seinfeld* who lives in a big house, plays golf, and leads a semi-retired life. He has little to be angry at, so we cannot chalk up his being annoyed by other people's enthusiasm to envy and resentment. Rather, his annoyance is caused by his melancholic temperament and the object of his ridicule, inauthenticity.

What Philosophers Say about Enthusiasm

Plato thinks of enthusiasm as a kind of inspiration. He thinks that enthusiasm is required for a poet to create poems.[5] Such enthusiasm is passed from the poet to the spectator or observer, and then from the latter to other listeners. A muse, Plato says, inspires epic poets such as Homer, who then transmit their enthusiasm to others. The poets utter admirable poems because they are enchanted and possessed.

Like prophets and givers of oracles, the poets do not compose by using their skills for art or by heeding wisdom, but by inspiration by the muse or god. The muse or god is in them, as it were. Plato is critical of the poets because, while they come up with sublime and fine verses, they don't understand them:

[5] Plato, *Apology* lines 22b–c and *Ion* line 533e.

they cannot give a rational account of what they are saying. The poet simply goes into a divine frenzy or madness.

In the early Christian era, there were also religious enthusiasts. The Messalians, or the "praying folk," were a Syrian heretical sect that formed around 360 C.E. and lasted until the ninth century. They were called Enthusiasts because they thought they were inspired or possessed (*enthous*) by the Christian Holy Spirit.

Several offshoots of Christianity in the sixteenth and seventeenth centuries were called enthusiastic. The epithet was used as a term of condemnation and was applied to Quietists, Quakers, Jansenists, Congregationalists, Presbyterians, Anabaptists, Camisards, and Methodists.

John Wesley, the founder of Methodism, wrote a sermon defending his views from the charge of enthusiasm. "The Nature of Enthusiasm" begins by citing *Acts* 26:24: "And Festus said with a loud voice, Paul, thou art beside thyself." The enthusiastic man is one who, like St. Paul, is beside himself, Wesley implies. The religious leader defends his own "religion of the heart," from charges of enthusiasm by drawing similarities between his views and Paul's. This is enthusiasm in what Wesley called the *good* sense: "Some take it in a good sense, for a divine impulse or impression, superior to all the natural faculties, and suspending, for the time, either in whole or in part, both the reason and the outward senses."[6]

However, it's difficult for a person to know for sure if he has a good and *divine* impulse, much less prove to others that he has received a message from God. How does he know if his perceptions are real rather than falsely imagined, whether it is the good instead of the bad kind of "communication"? Enthusiasm, Wesley continued, also has a *neutral* sense, poetic inspiration: "Vigor of thought, a peculiar fervor of spirit, a vivacity and strength not to be found in common men; elevating the soul to greater and higher things than cool reason could have attained." This is close to the Platonic sense of enthusiasm.

Finally, Wesley says there's a morally undesirable kind of enthusiasm: "It is, undoubtedly a disorder of the mind; and such a disorder as greatly hinders the exercise of reason. Nay,

[6] <new.gbgm-umc.org/umhistory/wesley/sermons/37>.

sometimes it wholly sets it aside: it not only dims but shuts the eyes of the understanding. It may, therefore, well be accounted a species of madness. . . . Enthusiasm in general may then be described in some such manner as this: a religious madness arising from some falsely imagined influence or inspiration of God." We might call this fanaticism today. Insofar as he pokes fun at religion and religious pietism, Larry would be bothered by this religious form of enthusiasm.

Some philosophers, like Wesley, distinguished good kinds of enthusiasm from unacceptable kinds. Shaftesbury, or Anthony Ashley Cooper, third Earl of Shaftesbury, in *A Letter concerning Enthusiasm* and *The Moralists,* defends what he calls natural religion. The essence of religion is a feeling of expansive love for the universe as a whole. The truly religious frame of mind is one of *reasonable* enthusiasm. Shaftesbury takes pains to distinguish this kind of enthusiasm from false, non-rational enthusiasm. This undesirable kind of enthusiasm can lead to superstition, zealotry, fanaticism, and sectarian violence.

John Locke and David Hume use the term 'enthusiasm' much as we would use 'fanaticism'. The enthusiast is someone to be feared, even satirized or ridiculed. In typical Enlightenment fashion, Locke and Hume thought that the enthusiast overstepped the bounds of reason and claimed to know something that he could not justifiably know.

Larry makes fun of this kind of enthusiasm. Larry is primarily bothered by the excessive display of intense, positive excitement. Enthusiasm in its ordinary sense of excitement is an emotion in which we are devoted or committed to a cause, activity, organization, or hobby. The emotion has a positive tinge and a high level of arousal. It's transmissible or contagious in a good sense. A coach can ignite her players to overcome some obstacle. A teacher can stimulate his students to have a passion for a subject matter. But this ordinary sense of enthusiasm has not been very prevalent throughout the history of philosophy, and given its widespread meaning today, this is somewhat surprising.

Immanuel Kant also rejects the undesirable kind of enthusiasm we would call fanaticism. But in the mid-1760s Kant wrote about a more acceptable kind of enthusiasm, though it had its shortcomings, too. He said that enthusiasts of friendship, religion, and patriotism can achieve something great, although they misapply a principle that is good. Kant defined this enthusiasm as "the state of mind which is inflamed beyond the appropriate degree by some principle, whether it be by the maxim of patriotic virtue, or of friendship, or of religion, without involving the illusion of a supernatural community."[7]

These enthusiasts take too far a principle that is good in itself, such as a principle to be a good friend, patriot, or religious devotee. For Kant, we need to have the right principles, but we also need to know how to apply them using our judgment. This enthusiasm is thus ambiguous. The principles or rules are good, but the application misfires. Kant partly endorsed and accepted such enthusiasm because it led to great, significant, or desirable outcomes and acts. Yet even this kind of enthusiasm, as a strong sensible affect or intense emotion, involves the momentary loss of reason. And since according to Kant, reason should always be in control and never give itself over to sensibility, such enthusiasm was ambiguous.

Larry lacks this type of enthusiasm, for he is hardly an enthusiastic friend. He doesn't even seem to like his friends, as we have seen. We would probably fault Larry for *lacking* enthusiasm in friendship. We wouldn't blame him for having too much of the kind of enthusiasm that Kant criticized.

There is one last kind of enthusiasm that should be mentioned: aesthetic enthusiasm. Larry experiences it one time in *Curb*. In a publication of 1790, Kant conceives of aesthetic enthusiasm as our emotional response to some representation or idea of the morally good. Kant called it "the idea of good with affect."[8] Kant is one of only a few philosophers to write about enthusiasm as a sublime aesthetic feeling. To call it *aesthetic* feeling is to say that an onlooker or spectator, not a person trying to execute some goal, is being moved or affected. The aesthetic enthusiast is not immediately acting. He or she is witnessing or observing something morally good, such as a noble act or moral sacrifice. This kind of emotion has the structure of the sublime.

---

[7] Immanuel Kant, *Observations on the Feeling of the Beautiful and Sublime* (Cambridge University Press), p. 58.

[8] Immanuel Kant, *Critique of the Power of Judgment* (Cambridge University Press), p. 154.

The sublime has been a central aesthetic concept in aesthetic theory ever since the late seventeenth and early eighteenth-centuries. This aesthetic category refers to our intense, highly aroused emotion of uplift and elevation. Current researchers in positive psychology and peak performance refer to it as "awe," "profound beauty," and "elevation." Imagine or recall the feeling of stepping into Saint Peter's Basilica in Rome or seeing the Rocky Mountains or Grand Canyon for the first time. It is pleasant overall, but it can also involve a kind of shock that is partly disorienting. We tend to lose our sense of space or time—momentarily at least, for we can later recover it. Kant thinks the sublime is valuable in part because it shows or reveals that our actions and thoughts are free, that is, not always determined by natural causes.

Aesthetic enthusiasm appears in *Curb*, but we must look carefully for it. Larry's religious experience of being saved when drowned would not count as an example, since it lacks the necessary *moral* element. Aesthetic enthusiasm needs to be a response to a morally good thing or idea.

Larry sees his drowning experience as a direct communication from God. The experience acquires a moral component only when Larry decides to use his God-given time to donate his kidney to Lewis, that is, when he thinks he was saved for a good reason. The one moment when Larry feels aesthetic enthusiasm is related to the kidney episode: it occurs when Larry is listening to the Christian preacher with his alleged "parents" in Arizona. This calls forth moral ideas in him, makes him aware that he can do the right thing, and encourages him to be a better man. He immediately gets on an airplane to LA and does the morally right thing, what a genuine friend would do without hesitation. He donates his kidney.

Should Larry Curb His Enthusiasm?

Larry's merely a character in a fictional television series. He does ridiculous things and breaks social norms mostly to make us laugh. The creators of *Curb* did not intend the show to be moral philosophy. First and foremost, they wanted it to be funny. Nevertheless, the show does raise some interesting questions about whether Larry is worth emulating.

The cover of the Season Five DVD box displays an image of a crowd of people who all have Larry's face, as if to say: we are all Larry. But *should* we all be like him? This seems doubtful, and for the same reasons Larry the man is not like *Curb*-Larry. The writer, fortunately, does not resemble the character in this respect.

Larry plays by the social rules in real life. We're usually too polite to tell people what we really think, and so is Larry the actor and writer. He explains how he writes:

> Good is not funny. It's just not funny. But the bad thoughts are funny because they're not expressed. . . . I'm kind of letting these thoughts that go unexpressed that we all have all the time. . . . It's being able to get that bad side, that funny bad side, out, and that's why people really can relate to it . . . and I think that's why people like it. (Interview, 2006)

On religious enthusiasm: Larry, in good Enlightenment fashion, is right to reject any pretense to have exclusive insight into a supernatural realm. However, Larry is not an outright atheist, or at least does not appear to be one, especially given the drowning episode. It's just that he's not a fanatic either.

As for Larry's enthusiastically breaking social norms: such behavior mostly needs to be curbed in real life. Consider Kant's point about having both a principle and the know-how to apply it in particular cases. Larry often fails both in lacking the general principle and misapplying it when he's got it. He does not have the right social norms or "unwritten laws" or "rules" ("The Hot Towel," Season Seven), and he often misuses the social norms he possesses. That's why Larry's always apologizing. As his mother told him, that's what makes Larry "special." Other people are not like him.

All the same, there may be a redeeming aspect to Larry's norm-breaking. In small doses it can be a good thing for society as a whole. People who speak their minds move things forward because they force a dialogue and make us reconsider our views. Perhaps a society with too many Larrys would be hell, but a society with no Larrys at all might fail to realize some basic truths. Like the comedic "fool" who tells it how it is, or a Socrates who questions our basic assumptions, individuals like Larry can be a good thing for a society to have, at least in small numbers.

What J.B. Smoove (Jerry Brooks) says about the character he plays, Leon Black, applies to Larry, too. "If he thinks something, he's going to say it. It's like he's got controlled Tourette's. In life, you need somebody like that."[9] Leon in some ways resembles the character Larry David, who identifies with the Blacks when he first meets them: "That's like if my last name was Jew . . . Like Larry Jew" ("Meet the Blacks," Season Six). And they're both able to screw up each other's business in similar ways when they mistakenly swap cell phones ("The Rat Dog," Season Six).

The Platonic sense of inspiration, which Wesley calls a "neutral" sense, is innocent and desirable enough, especially for writers such as Larry and *Curb*-Larry. After all, it's good for a writer to be inspired, especially in ways that can point out certain truths about our lives. But if it led to fanaticism, Larry would be annoyed by it.

There's little reason to curb aesthetic enthusiasm because it is largely good. It may be undesirable to be a spectator too much or to overindulge in aesthetic experiences, but then again it's undesirable to do just about *anything* too much. And aesthetic enthusiasm can have the benefit of indirectly making us better people by leading us to reflect on morally good things and helping us think that we are free. It helped Larry be a better man. In leading us to believe in our power to choose, or not always being determined by natural causes, aesthetic enthusiasm can encourage us to take control of our lives and be better people.

Ordinary enthusiasm, excitement, is sometimes necessary to achieve great things, for it helps us to take risks. Yet such enthusiasm, a core American quality, can sometimes lead to bubbles in real estate and other markets, as we witnessed in the global financial crisis of the end of the last decade. Still, I don't see anything wrong with a fan's devotion to a team, or a member's commitment to an activity or organization, at least in moderation. (Hooliganism would be another matter.) As a kind of resoluteness, ordinary enthusiasm is desirable.

By contrast, *inauthentic* enthusiasm seems undesirable for the most part and should thus be largely curbed. But even here

---

[9] Dave Itzkoff, "He Tells It Like It Is, Even to Larry David," *New York Times* (January 27th, 2008).

there is an exception. Inauthentic enthusiasm, fakeness, can be a great social lubricant, since it can lead to important innovations and other advances.[10] Here there are cross-cultural differences at work. Many Europeans are less fake in this respect in comparison with most Americans, for whom a higher degree of fakeness is acceptable, even normal. The social norms put pressure on us to be a bit inauthentic, forcing us to be cheery when we are not ("Always wear a smile," "Never let them see you down") or giving us false hopes ("You can do anything you put your mind to").

From the US perspective, Europeans and other non-Americans can seem skeptical, even cynical. Consider those Scandinavian, Swiss, or Japanese attitudes that can strike many Americans as too Stoic. Compare them with the American social norms such as the "stop and chat" that *Curb* lampoons so incisively. Consider American meet-and-greet sessions in which we discuss minutia and trifles with strangers: where we come from, what we do for fun, and other senseless stuff. A lot of BS flies around in such cases; a great deal of bubbly fakeness clouds up convention center lobbies. This is precisely the sort of meaningless activity that Larry fails horribly at. Why, after all, *do* we have to stop and chat?

Having said that, the fact that Americans engage in such activities, and have this degree of superficiality or fakeness, reflects a great willingness to share and collaborate, to make oneself vulnerable. Sometimes inauthentic enthusiasm can actually be a good thing.

Americans seem to be excellent innovators partly because of this openness to collaboration and risk-taking. But in American social gatherings that same openness can expand and swell into the sort of silliness that *Curb* so delightfully ridicules in ways that make us cringe and wiggle in our chairs. And not because our anus tickles.

---

[10] I'm grateful to Matthew Burns for his suggestions and this point in particular.

VIII

The Special Section

Curbology
A Glossary of Curb-isms

ANDREA LEHN and MARK RALKOWSKI

A Bad Maniac: Pyro.

> **LARRY:** In retrospect it would have been a lot better had he been a kleptomaniac or another kind of maniac rather than pyro, because that's—
> **JEFF:** Pyro's a bad maniac.
> **LARRY:** If you're going to be a maniac, pyro is a bad maniac.
>
> —"The Wire" (Season One, Episode 6)

Able-Bodied: The politically correct way to describe a person who does not have any disabilities or handicaps.

> **LARRY:** Really! First of all, we don't like to be referred to as "normal." We're "able-bodied." Able-bodied, not normal—that's like from the Eighties. Who doesn't know that?
>
> —"The Bowtie" (Season Five, Episode 2)

Acting Without Acting: The title of a book Jason Alexander has written about acting (in the world of *Curb Your Enthusiasm*), and the concept of acting without showing any effort. The logical coherence of this expression is under dispute.

> **JERRY:** But you're still acting.
> **JASON ALEXANDER:** Yeah, of course you're acting.
> **JERRY:** Right, so it could be acting *with* acting. That could be a title, too. Having said that, I think this is a terrific title.
>
> —"Seinfeld" (Season Seven, Episode 10)

Allotment: The socially acceptable amount of hors d'oeuvres to take for yourself at a dinner party.

> **LARRY:** I think you're going over your allotment by a little bit, no?
> **CHRISTIAN SLATER:** My allotment?
> **LARRY:** You know, we're each entitled to take a certain amount, so everybody else can have a little bit, too. Feels like you're going over.
>
> —"The Hot Towel" (Season Seven, Episode 4)

Anonymous: A term people give to their charitable donations when they want to maximize the praise they receive from others.

> LARRY: Next time I give money to anybody, it will be anonymous. . . . And I'm going to tell everybody.
>
> —"Anonymous Donor" (Season Six, Episode 2)

Applesauce: A very underrated side dish.

> LARRY: We should consider it for the menu, encourage people even. . . . It's a very underrated side dish. That's my point. It's an underrated side dish.
>
> —"The Nanny From Hell" (Season Three, Episode 4)

Asker or Toucher: A question about who is entitled or obligated to pay the check at a restaurant.

> ROSIE: I had first dibs. I touched it first, Larry.
> LARRY: I asked, though. I think that gets priority. What gets priority on a check, asker or toucher?
>
> —"The Freak Book" (Season Six, Episode 5)

Ass Lever: The ass used as a lever to enhance a snuggling experience by bringing the other person closer.

> LARRY: I'm using the ass as a lever to draw you in. That's all. And it gets the snuggle tighter.
>
> —"Lewis Needs a Kidney" (Season Five, Episode 5)

Ass Man: A man who is unusually fond of women's asses.

> WANDA: This man—you have an ass fetish. Larry, you are an ass man.
> LARRY: I am not an ass man.
> WANDA: You are an ass man.
>
> —"Thor" (Season Two, Episode 2)

Bald Brothers: All bald men in the world. They love each other and live according to their own unique unwritten code, the bald code.

> LARRY: There's no meetings, but, you know, we see each other on the street, nod—we'll give a thumbs up . . . You know, we love each other, me and my bald brothers.
>
> —"The N Word" (Season Six, Episode 8)

Bald Code: A set of unwritten rules governing (i) how bald brothers are supposed to treat each other (e.g., they can call each other "baldy," but should never be involved in lawsuits against each other), (ii) how they are supposed to behave in public (e.g., they are not supposed to hide their baldness with toupees or hair plugs), and (iii) what they are supposed to value (e.g., they are supposed to be proud of their baldness).

Larry: (*referring to Cheryl's divorce lawyer*) Hey, you hired a bald man, huh?

Cheryl: That was a coincidence. I didn't really go after a bald man.

Larry: (*speaking to Cheryl's lawyer*) You know, you should have recused yourself. We can't go up against each other. It's a code. It's in the bald code.

—"The Divorce" (Season Eight, Episode 1)

Bald Community: A proud grouping of bald brothers, and supporters of bald brothers, united by a common culture, especially a bald code.

Larry: Yeah, he's a bald guy, too. It's very bad for the bald community.

Neighbor: Larry, what's very bad for the community is that he's a sex offender.

Larry: I know, but as long as he's going to be a sex offender, I wish he had a full head of hair, that's all.

—"The Seder" (Season Five, Episode 7)

Bar Misfit: According to "Danny Duberstein," it is something a Jewish male does every thirteen years to "recharge the mitzvah" and keep it at "mitzvah capacity."

Larry: Say that again.

Leon: Bar misfit.

Larry: It's not "bar misfit." Bar mitz*vah*!

Leon: Bar misfit!

Larry: *Vah*! . . . If we're going to do this thing you better learn how to pronounce it!

—"The Table Read" (Season Seven, Episode 9)

Bathroom Monitor: Someone who pays attention to how often you use the bathroom, how long you use it for, what you do while you use it, and then reports this information to other people.

Larry: It's like having a bathroom monitor. I have a bathroom monitor. . . . Her office is right across from the bathroom. Every time I go to the bathroom I have to have this stop and chat with her both before I go and after I go. It's too much.

Lewis: She means well. By the way, she tells me you go to the bathroom like ten to fourteen times a day. You move your bowels; you piss. Are you all right?

Larry: I don't want her monitoring my bathroom habits, okay?!!!

—"The Lefty Call" (Season Six, Episode 4)

Bathroom Trick: A ploy used to avoid paying the check at a restaurant.

Larry: I know what you do.

Stu Braudy: What?

Larry: Every time the check comes, how you run off to the bathroom. . . . You don't think I see that?

Susan Braudy: Fuck you!

Larry: You don't think I know about that bathroom trick? I invented that bathroom trick!

—"The Terrorist Attack" (Season Three, Episode 5)

Bats, Balls, and Gloves: A metaphor for understanding human sexuality, as well as the basic concepts in Leon's argument against Larry's theory of the lesbian advantage.

Larry: The woman is on this earth to catch balls. Interesting theory. Too bad I don't have a daughter. I would like to impart that knowledge to her.

—"The Bi-Sexual" (Season Eight, Episode 7)

Benadryl-Brownie: A brownie laced with Benadryl, which one might give to a Christian Scientist who refuses to take any drugs to clear up her allergic reaction to nuts. The ethical justification for doing so is twofold: (i) it doesn't hurt anyone, and (ii) it could strengthen her faith.

Larry: What, the Benadryl-brownie?

Lewis: First of all, she will never know.

Larry: Even if she got better, they would think it was because of prayer.

—"The Benadryl-Brownie" (Season Three, Episode 2)

Better: An ambiguous description of one's health. It means either (i) that one's health has improved relative to what it had been, which is compatible with still being sick or injured, or (ii) that one's health has improved completely.

Larry: Yeah, she asked me how I was feeling. I said, "Better." Better than before, not one hundred percent better, not all better. But better . . . In English, "better" doesn't mean completely better . . . "Better" is not all better. It's better . . .

Acupuncturist: Better is better. You said you were better.

—"The Acupuncturist" (Season Two, Episode 6)

A Big, Expansive Man: Something you can call yourself when you feel morally superior to your friend.

Lewis: At least it's an admission of guilt.

Larry: It's not an admission of guilt. How's that an admission of guilt? I was the man. I'm a big man. I'm a big, expansive man.

—"The Baptism" (Season Two, Episode 9)

Big Vagina: A vagina so large that it makes most penises seem small.

Jeff: I'll tell you what, I bet you there's a ton of guys out there who've been labeled with "small penis"—I bet you fifty percent—and it's the big vagina.

Larry: Think of it biologically: why shouldn't there be as many big vaginas as there are small penises? Right?

Jeff: These big vagina ladies are getting away with murder.

—"The Ski Lift" (Season Five, Episode 8)

Bisexual: Someone who is too selfish to be sexually attracted to just one gender.

Rosie: Pick a side already, right? Can't you make up your mind?

Larry: Absolutely! What is it, they have to have sex with everyone? Half the population isn't enough for them? They want everybody, they're so selfish?

—"The Bisexual" (Season Eight, Episode 7)

Bitch: A disrespectful word that can be used to add variety to the diction in rap lyrics.

Larry: I would lose the "muthafucka" at the end, because you already said "fuck" once. You don't need two "fucks." You already got the one "fuck." I would change the "muthafucka" to "bitch," because "bitch" is a word that you would use for somebody you disrespect.

—"Krazee-Eyez Killa" (Season Three, Episode 8)

Bow-Sorry: The way you feel when you are so sorry that a bow is called for.

Jane: Are you really sorry?

Larry: Yes!

Jane: Okay, then give me a bow.

Larry: I don't know if I am bow-sorry.

Jane: No, I need bow-sorry or I am not forgiving you.

—"The Bi-Sexual" (Season Eight, Episode 7)

Breast Intervention: The attempt to persuade a woman not to have her breasts enlarged.

Lewis: But the problem is, she's an actor, she's a singer, she's talented. But she wants to get her breasts enlarged, and it's going to drive Kenny crazy.

Larry: He doesn't know about it?

Lewis: No. I need you to help to talk her out of it. Just like a breast intervention.

—"Ben's Birthday Party" (Season Four, Episode 2)

Breast Vision: An unusually acute sensitivity to naked breasts, and the ability to see them well even from a long distance.

Larry: By the way, I did notice in the show that there's a small mole on the underside of your right breast that you might want to get checked out.

Burlesque dancer: Are you being serious? There's a mole?

Lewis: How did you see a small mole from where you were sitting?

Larry: Well, I have breast vision.

—"The Safe House" (Season Eight, Episode 2)

Bring the Ruckus: To have a sex life satisfying enough to obviate the need or desire to masturbate.

LARRY: I just spoke to my wife, and she said she was putting some flowers in your room. And she found a stain on your blanket. . . .

LEON: Well, it couldn't have been mine. Know why? 'Cause I gets mine, Larry. I brings the ruckus to the ladies!

—"The Anonymous Donor" (Season Six, Episode 2)

Cashew-Raisin Balance: The cashew-raisin ratio in a package of "cashew-raisins."

LARRY: There's only four cashews in here. Look, they're all the same. This one's got four, three.

GAY CHOREOGRAPHER: That's probably a mistake.

LARRY: The whole cashew-raisin balance is askew.

—"The 5 Wood" (Season Four, Episode 5)

Caucasian: A name a black man might call himself when asked to describe his friendship with a white man.

LARRY: Are you my Caucasian?

KRAZEE-EYEZ: I'm your fucking Caucasian!

—"Krazee-Eyez Killa" (Season Three, Episode 8)

Chat and Cut: A ploy used to cut in line without being noticed. If you don't want to wait in a long line, and you see a friend (or even just an acquaintance you vaguely know) near the front, you can cut surreptitiously by chatting with your friend or acquaintance. As long as you're there chatting, you might as well buy your ticket or get your dinner at the buffet! At that point you will have cut by chatting. You will have "chat and cut."

LARRY: She's doing a chat and cut.

JEFF: Chat and cut, really?

LARRY: She's feigning familiarity with someone she vaguely knows for the sole purpose of cutting in line.

JEFF: You're sure?

LARRY: Positive. She'll be picking up a plate any second, watch. There she goes.

—"Vow of Silence" (Season Eight, Episode 5)

Cheek-to-Cheek Contact: Evidence that a hug between men has been sub-optimal.

LARRY: Your cheek just touched mine on that hug.

STU: Ya, I hugged you.

LARRY: But still, cheek to cheek contact between men, that's unacceptable.

—"The Smiley Face" (Season Eight, Episode 4)

Coachy: A cultural identity possessed by the people who sit in the coach section on airplanes, and by some people who sit in first class.

WOMAN IN COACH: You get on first, you get free drinks, you get a hot towel . . .

LARRY: No, no, just because I'm sitting up there you're making a generalization about me, but I'm not like a first class person. I'm coachy.

WOMAN IN COACH: Maybe it's just that you're not acting coachy.

—"The Hero" (Season Eight, Episode 6)

Cool-De-La: A state of brotherly love between friends. It seems to be something you appreciate most when you lose it.

KRAZEE-EYEZ: I thought we were cool-de-la, man.

LARRY: I'm cool-de-la.

KRAZEE-EYEZ: We ain't cool-de-la?

LARRY: No, we are cool-de-la.[1]

—"Krazee-Eyez Killa" (Season Three, Episode 8)

Criminal: Paying the host at a restaurant to let you cut in line and get a table before it's your turn.

CHERYL: I'm extremely attracted to you right now.

LARRY: That's because it's criminal. Women are attracted to criminals.

—"Affirmative Action" (Season 1, Episode 9)

The Cut-Off: The point at which it is no longer socially acceptable to (i) make a phone call at night ("The Wire," Season One, Episode 6), (ii) have a birthday party ("Ben's Birthday Party," Season Four, Episode 2), (iii) accept a wedding gift ("Club Soda and Salt," Season Three, Episode 3), (v) call an opposite sex platonic friend at night ("Mary, Joseph, and Larry," Season Three, Episode 9), or (vi) go trick-or-treating ("Trick or Treat," Season Two, Episode 3).[2]

CHERYL: Ten o'clock is the cut off time. You don't call people after ten.

LARRY: No, no, no, the cut off time is ten-thirty.

—"The Wire" (Season One, Episode 6)

---

[1] "Cool-de-la" may be restricted to friendships between men, since Monina rejects it as a description of her relationship with Larry: "What is this cool-de-la shit?" ("The Carpool Lane," Season Four, Episode 6). On the other hand, Monina seems to object most to Larry's failure to pay his bill and attempt to be hip.

[2] In "The Car Salesman" (Season Two, Episode 1), Larry qualifies the cut-off rule with respect to making phone calls at night: "You get like an hour dispensation for good news!"

Date: "An experience you have with another person that makes you appreciate being alone"

—"Palestinian Chicken" (Season Eight, Episode 3)

Daytime Sex: Sex that is especially enjoyable because it is had during the day.

LARRY: Daytime sex? I love daytime sex. You can just go on with the rest of the day as if nothing happened.

—"The Korean Bookie" (Season Five, Episode 9)

Dick-World: The world seen from the perspective of a man who only or mostly thinks about sex.

LEON: Thank God he didn't hand you his dick. You know what I mean? He could have been shaking that dick up, hand you the dick, and the dick shot sperm in your face.
LARRY: Yeah, but why would he hand me a dick?
LEON: I mean it's an example.
LARRY: What kind of example is that?
LEON: I'm just comparing it to other things you could shake up . . . with Parkinson's, right?
LARRY: You just live in a total dick world, don't you?

—"Larry vs. Michael J. Fox" (Season Eight, Episode 10)

Dinner Party: A mysterious social practice often observed among normal adult humans.

LARRY: Why do you do this with these dinner parties? What is this compulsion to have people over to your house and serve them food and talk to them? What a strange thing.

—"AAMCO" (Season One, Episode 7)

Divorce: An event that we should celebrate as if it were a wedding.

LEON: You know what you should do? You should ride around and bomp the horn and shit, like motherfucker's getting married, you know what I mean?
LARRY: What a great idea! Put cans on your car, honk the horn.
FUNKHOUSER: Just divorced!

—"The Divorce" (Season Eight, Episode 1)

Domino Effect: The consequences of one person parking outside of the lines in a parking lot: either everybody is forced to park outside the lines as well, or you park poorly because the guy next to you did, but then he leaves before you do and you get blamed for being a pig-parker.

FUNKHOUSER: Why did you have to take up two parking spaces? You made *me* take two parking spaces, okay?
LARRY: Yes, I can understand that you're upset. I, too, was upset when I saw the red Volvo to my left also taking up two spaces. He created a domino effect.

Funkhouser: There's no Volvo out there.
Larry: There was when I parked, okay?

—"Vow of Silence" (Season Eight, Episode 5)

Double-Goodbye: Saying goodbye at a dinner party for a second time because you had to re-enter to retrieve something you forgot, such as a watch.

Larry: I don't want to do a "double-goodbye." I've already said "goodbye" under the worst possible circumstances. Now you want me to go in and do the double-goodbye?

—"Porno Gil" (Season One, Episode 3)

Double-Transgression Theory: The idea that you're free to do whatever you want when you're in trouble, since you're already being punished. If you're a dog and you've been sent to your doghouse for peeing on the carpet, you might as well grab a steak off the dining room table on your way out the door.

Jeff: Come on, man, you're already in the doghouse. You can't get in any more trouble. You might as well get your money's worth.
Larry: Yeah, I might as well do something else wrong.
Jeff: It's a double-transgression theory.
Larry: What an interesting theory.

—"The Smoking Jacket" (Season Five, Episode 6)

Dubious: How some people feel when you promise to tip them on another occasion.

Larry: I don't have anything for you right now. I only got, like, twenties. Sorry, I'll get you tomorrow. Don't be dubious. Don't be dubious!
Bellboy: No!
Larry: You're dubious. I'm going to get you tomorrow.

—"Opening Night" (Season Four, Episode 10)

E-jac-a-lit: Semen.

Larry: Ejaculate.

Leon: E-jac-a-lit?

Larry: Not "e-jac-a-lit," ejaculate.

Leon: E-jac-a-lit.

—"Meet the Blacks" (Season Six, Episode 1)

Elevator Etiquette: Holding the doors open for people who would otherwise have to wait for the next elevator. The upside to this etiquette is under dispute.

Larry: Let me tell you something, my days of elevator etiquette are over. Over! I'm not holding doors anymore. I'm not letting women out first anymore. That's done!

—"Interior Decorator" (Season One, Episode 5)

Encroachment: When someone uses space that you are entitled to on a plane.

DONNA: Are you really pushing my drink back?
LARRY: Encroachment.
DONNA: Encroachment?
LARRY: Yes, you're encroaching.[3]

—"The Hero" (Season Eight, Episode 6)

Fake Philanthropy/Faux Anonymity: What a person does when he or she pretends to make an anonymous charitable donation, while in fact telling other people about it.

LARRY: Nobody told me that I could be anonymous and tell people. I would have taken that option, okay? You can't have it halfway. You're either anonymous or you're not. What is it?
CHERYL: Look, people are pointing and going, "Oh, there's Larry David's wing."
LARRY: Oh, yeah, there's Larry David, the guy who has to have his name up on the wall, as opposed to Mr. Anonymous *but was really Ted.*
CHERYL: I'm proud of you . . .
LARRY: Anonymous . . . It's fake philanthropy, and it's faux anonymity. What do you think about that?

—"The Anonymous Donor" (Season Six, Episode 2)

Favor: The meaning of this term is disputed. According to Larry, a favor is something you do without expecting anything in return. According to Jerry, it's something you do expecting to be paid.

LARRY: I asked him to do me a favor. I didn't say, "I want to hire you." I said, "Do me a favor."
JERRY: That's what a tip is. A tip is money for a favor.
LARRY: No, a favor implies no tip.

—"Seinfeld" (Season Seven, Episode 10)

Fierce: A word used, mostly by gay men, to endorse someone or something.

JEFF: At first I thought it was my imagination, but you're talking really gay. No, no, no, really gay. "Fierce"? Where does "fierce" come from? And everything is this and that!
LARRY: Steve the choreographer says it all the time.
JEFF: You're Steve, the gay choreographer.

—"The 5 Wood" (Season Four, Episode 5)

---

[3] In "The Acupuncturist" (Season Two, Episode 6) Larry accuses his lawyer and anyone else who enjoys casual Fridays in the business world of "encroaching" on his territory. If you work in the business world, you should dress like a business person, not like Larry.

Finders, Keepers: A puzzle. If you lose something of yours, and I find it, is it still yours? Or has it become mine because I found it?

> **Larry:** That's David Schwimmer's watch.
> **Sikh:** No, I found it. It's my watch.
> **Larry:** I know you found it . . . It belongs to David Schwimmer.
> **Sikh:** No, finders keepers.
> **Larry:** No, not finders keepers, that's not right.
>
> —"Opening Night" (Season Four, Episode 10)

Five-Second Rule: The amount of time a healthy man can be in contact with another person before getting an erection.

> **Jeff:** (*asking Larry about the erection he got while hugging Auntie Rae*) How does that happen to you?
> **Larry:** You know, she went over the appropriate amount of time that I can have human contact without getting aroused. I only have five seconds. After that it's out of my control.
>
> —"The N Word" (Season Six, Episode 8)

Flaunt: The act of exposing your bare midriff.

> **Maureen:** Do you know that I have lost sixty-eight pounds in two years?
> **Larry:** That is fantastic. I'm so happy for you.
> **Maureen:** Thank you. I'm very proud of it and I want to flaunt what I've got.
> **Larry:** You can flaunt two-thirds of the day outside the office. And then you got one-third non-flaunt. Do you have to flaunt twenty-four hours? Why not take a break in the flaunt?
>
> —"The Bare Midriff" (Season Seven, Episode 6)

Floor Shit: Flooring materials, such as wood.

> **Krazee-Eyez:** We got the floor, you know what I mean? It's made out of some floor shit, you know what I'm saying?
> **Larry:** Yeah, that's floor shit.
>
> —"Krazee-Eyez Killa" (Season Three, Episode 8)

Flummoxed: The way you claim to have felt when you've "yelled for society" at the wrong time, in the wrong way, toward the wrong person, and/or for the wrong reason. It's a kind of justification for bad behavior: you couldn't help it—you were flummoxed.

> **Larry:** I want to apologize for the whole sponge thing. You know what happened that night, because of the survivor confrontation—it just brought up a lot of stuff about the Holocaust. It's kind of in my DNA, and I was very flummoxed by it. Very flummoxed.
>
> —"The Survivor" (Season Four, Episode 9)

Friend o'Lesbians: A man who is unusually friendly with and trusted by the lesbian community.

Larry: Lesbians love me. They love me . . . Obviously, they talk amongst themselves and the word got out that I am a friend o'lesbians.

—"The Bowtie" (Season Five, Episode 2)

Fuck Hhhyyeeeeewwww: A maximally offensive way to say "fuck you" to a guy named Hugh.

Larry: Fuck Hugh.
Hugh: Fuck you.
Larry: Fuck Hhhyyeeeeewwww.

—"The Nanny from Hell" (Season Three, Episode 4)

Get in That Ass: The way you're supposed to respond to being insulted and threatened by a skinhead.

Leon: You let that man slide today. You've got immediately to get in somebody's ass when that happens to you. You pull that asshole open, step into that asshole, close the door behind you. Take a spray paint can, right? "Larry was here." You spray paint, "Larry was here," "wash me"—all that kind a shit. Fuck his whole asshole up. Eat some snicker bars, throw some paper on the floor, read a newspaper, ball the paper up and throw the newspaper on the floor. Fuck his whole asshole up, know what I'm sayin'? And you open that asshole one more time. Open it again. Open that asshole again. Huhhhhh! Step out his ass. And leave that motherfucker wide open so he know you been there.

—"The Lefty Call" (Season Six, Episode 4)

Gift: A puzzle. If I give you a gift, and you refuse it for some reason, is it no longer a gift for you? Or does it retain its gifthood on account of my initial attempt to give it to you?

Ted Danson: I only gave it back to you because you were being rude about me having to exchange it.
Larry: Well, you still nevertheless didn't accept my gracious gift . . . [4]

—"Chet's Shirt" (Season Three, Episode 1)

Going Down with the Ship: Finishing what you start, whether it's a relationship or a book, regardless of whether you want to, and often *in spite of not wanting to*, merely because you started it.

Larry: I finish things I start. Books, they can be five hundred pages—once I start them, even if I hate it, I'll finish it. I have friends who I can't stand, you know, for like twenty-five years. I'm still friends with them.

---

[4] This same issue comes up in "Beloved Aunt" (Season One, Episode 8) when Larry gives Jeff's mom a pair of sunglasses, but she refuses them because she thinks he intentionally "touched her bosom." There's a big "to-do" over this, and in the end Larry and Jeff have a disagreement: Jeff thinks Larry should nevertheless give the sunglasses to Jeff's mom, but Larry thinks he has been relieved of his gift-giving duty.

PAULA: Why?

LARRY: Because I stay to the end, until they're dead. I go down with the ship. That's what I do. I'm not even the captain; I'm going down with the ship. That's how I want you to think about me: I'm the guy who keeps the captain company.

—"Bat Mitzvah" (Season Six, Episode 10)

Goldfish: A mostly unrewarding responsibility, not a pet.

LARRY: It's like a huge responsibility feeding fish. It's not fun. Think about it, you know, I'm outside, and I gotta go home to feed fish? I mean seriously, who gives a shit?

DOCTOR SCHAFFER: Mr. David, I wanted to talk to you about your girlfriend.

LARRY: You know, they're not pets, really, but yet it's the same responsibility as a pet. But you get nothing back. You watch them? Is that supposed to be fascinating?

—"Funkhouser's Crazy Sister" (Season Seven, Episode 1)

Groat's Disease/Syndrome: A fictional neurological disorder, named after the doctor who discovered it, that causes hyperactivity in children, as if they've had "five cups of coffee at all times" ("The Thong," Season Two, Episode 5). It is also fatal.

MICHAEL RICHARDS: Tell me about the Groat's.

LEON: (*disguised as Danny Duberstein*) Well, everything I ate tasted like peaches. . . . And I forgot how to multiply.

—"The Table Read" (Season Seven, Episode 9)

GTS: Guaranteed tremendous safety, a special feature in some Toyota models.

DANA: I notice this is a GT and the brochure says there's a model called the GTS. Now what is the difference between the GT and the GTS?

LARRY: Okay, the GTS is "guaranteed tremendous safety."

DANA: So, without the "S," it's just "guaranteed tremendous"?

—"The Car Salesman" (Season Two, Episode 1)

Half Get-Up: Only standing up halfway upon meeting someone.

LARRY: Am I supposed to get up? I did sort of a half get-up.

LEWIS: For my niece, I think a full get-up would've . . .

—"Ben's Birthday Party" (Season Four, Episode 2)

Hammock: A metaphor for understanding Larry's inner tranquility.

THERAPIST: I see swings of emotion that disturb me a little bit, Larry.

LARRY: There's no swing. I'm a hammock just gently flowing in the breeze.

—"The Thong" (Season Two, Episode 5)

Having Lunch Together: Ambiguous. Does having lunch together require that people start eating at the same time, or is simply being in each other's presence sufficient?

Lunch guest: I think it would be polite to wait for your food to arrive.

Larry: I think it's kind of impolite to prevent someone who is hungry from eating.

Lunch guest: Yeah, but we're supposed to be having lunch together.

Larry: Do we have to start at the exact same time? I don't get that.

—"The Thong" (Season Two, Episode 5)

Having Said That: An expression used to say what one really believes or wants without having to take responsibility for having said it.

Larry: You say what you really want to say, and then you negate it.

Jerry: "Now having said that"—so what is that? So you win either way?

Larry: A comedian goes up on stage, "you know, you people are a bunch of morons. Having said that, I'm very happy to be here."

—"Seinfeld" (Season Seven, Episode 10)

Heaven: A word that some people use—it would seem inaccurately—to describe the mere fact that they're pleased.

Larry: Everything is "heaven" with him (Ted). The piece of gum he had, "Oh this is heaven!" Had a taste of a chocolate bar, "I'm in heaven." A parking space is "heaven." It's all "heaven"!

—"Ted and Mary" (Season One, Episode 2)

Hoisted on Your Own Petard: What happens when you change or eliminate a social convention, and then suffer unwanted consequences as a result.

Funkhouser: What about your policy? No introductions.

Larry: I know, but there are extenuating circumstances.

Funkhouser: No, you said they were a stupid social convention.

Larry: So I'm hoisted on my own petard?

Funkhouser: Exactly.

—"The Black Swan" (Season Seven, Episode 7)

Homeland: What the vagina is to the penis.

Larry: Let me tell you something, the penis doesn't care about race, creed, and color. The penis wants to get to his homeland. It wants to go home.

—"Palestinian Chicken" (Season Eight, Episode 3)

I'm Feeling Weird: Something you should never say, if it's all you're going to say, in a voicemail.

Larry: What kind of message is that to leave at seven-thirty in the morning? He should have just said what he was feeling weird about. Now I have to think about this all day? I hate messages like that. Either just say "call me back," or tell me why you're feeling weird.

—"AAMCO" (Season One, Episode 7)

Incomplete Dog: What your dog is if you take it for a walk and don't bring a bag for its feces.

Larry: If you're going to have a dog, you have to have a bag.
Woman: I will bring a bag. I didn't bring a bag today. I'm really sorry.
Larry: Because the dog without the bag—it's incomplete. It's a marriage, the bag and the dog. They go together.

—"The Safe House" (Season Eight, Episode 2)

Integrity: Something you can be certain a man has if he is married to a woman who isn't very attractive.

Larry: He's smart. He's good looking. He could have anybody. He chose her.
Jeff: That tells you everything you need to know.
Larry: This guy's got integrity.
Jeff: I trust him now. I trust him completely.

—"The Car Periscope" (Season Eight, Episode 8)

Interesting: A euphemism used to describe your dubiousness when you hear a story you cannot believe.

Larry: Hey, Schwimmer? Did you tell the stewardess my seat wasn't in the upright position?
David Schwimmer: . . . No.
Larry: Hmm, interesting.

—"Opening Night" (Season Four, Episode 10)

Inventor: The meaning of this term is disputed. Larry says he has invented millions of things simply by having ideas for them. Jeff insists that an inventor is someone who implements his ideas: no implementation, no invention.

Larry: I'm an inventor. I have a million ideas for things. I just don't know how to implement . . .
Jeff: Okay, you're an idea man. Go with me on that one. You're an idea man.
Larry: I'm an idea man who comes up with inventions.
Jeff: No, there are no inventions in your world.[5]

—"Car Periscope" (Season Eight, Episode 8)

It Hurts My Neck: A reason a man might give for not performing cunnilingus, when in fact he's just too lazy.

Larry: I like it. I'm just too lazy to do it. It's a whole to-do. It hurts my neck.

—"Krazee-Eyez Killa" (Season Three, Episode 8)

---

[5] Larry's side of this argument is compromised by the fact that he is on record saying, "I'm not an inventor. I'm an improver" ("The Bat Mitzvah," Season Six, Episode 10).

iToilet: "An iPhone application that leads you via your GPS to the nearest acceptable toilet wherever you are in the world"

—"Seinfeld" (Season Seven, Episode 10)

Jane: The name of a hypothetical *daughter* of God whom Larry could worship without feeling gay.

LARRY: Really? See, I could see worshipping Jesus if he were a girl, like if God had a daughter. Jane, I'll worship a Jane. But to worship a guy—it's a little gay, isn't it?

—"The Christ Nail" (Season Five, Episode 3)

Jerry Seinfeld: "He's a eunuch. His testicles were cut off when he was about thirteen because he was in the Beth Shalom Choir. And that's what he wanted to be. He was a choirboy."

—"The Wire" (Season One, Episode 6)

Jews with Trees: Jewish couples who have Christmas trees.

LARRY: Nothing worse than Jews with trees. Two Jews getting trees? They can't let them have their holiday. We have to horn in on their holiday.

—"Mary, Joseph, and Larry" (Season Three, Episode 9)

Juicing: The use of erectile dysfunction drugs to win against a lesbian in a competition for the affections of a bisexual woman.

ROSIE: I know like four decades of women that you've dated. None of them ever, ever talks about your performance . . . What are you juicing, Larry?

LARRY: I have never taken performance-enhancing drugs, ever. Period. No, no, no, no, no, no, no.

—"The Bi-Sexual" (Season Eight, Episode 7)

Kamikaze Pilot: A pilot who *actually dies* by using his plane as a weapon.

LARRY: I'm curious about how you can be a kamikaze pilot and still be alive.

KEVIN NEALON: There's a lot of kamikaze pilots that are still alive.

LARRY: You say that, and I say to you they are not kamikaze pilots.

—"Kamikaze Bingo" (Season Five, Episode 4)

Larry David: The minute I laid eyes him, I said, "This guy is a disaster." He's a storm. He's like a storm that will destroy everything in its path. I mean, he's got this gift. Everything he touches, he dooms. He's a little cyclone, a little tornado . . . (Mel Brooks talking about Larry David)

—"Opening Night" (Season Four, Episode 10)

Larry David and the Hipsters: A Jewish folk band, best known for "The Gefilte Fish Blues" and "My Freakin' Back is Killin' Me and It's Making It Hard to Kvell."

> **CHERYL:** What was the name of your band?
>
> **LARRY:** The Hipsters . . . Larry David and The Hipsters. And then I left The Hipsters and I just became Larry David.
>
> —"The Ski Lift" (Season Five, Episode 8)

Lefty Unhooker: A person who can only remove a woman's bra with his or her left hand. Some speculate that this may be a product of one's formative experiences with bra removal.

> **LARRY:** In terms of unhooking bras, I'm really going to be in trouble. Look at this.
>
> **JEFF:** Why don't you use your right hand?
>
> **LARRY:** I'm a lefty unhooker. Can't unhook righty. It's from the car, I think. When you park. You're making out in the driver's seat. You lean over—it's your left hand that's doing the unhooking.
>
> —"The Hot Towel" (Season Seven, Episode 4)

Lesbian Advantage: The advantage that lesbians have over men in the attempt sexually to satisfy bisexual women. "We don't know what we're doing as much as women know. It's their equipment. They own the equipment" ("The Bowtie," Season Five, Episode 2).

> **LARRY:** Come on, it's over. She's taking her to the Tony's. And let's face it: she's got the lesbian advantage.
>
> —"The Bi-Sexual" (Season Eight, Episode 7)

Level the Playing Field: When you set up a blind man with a woman who wears a burka. He no longer has to cope with the injustice of not knowing what his date looks like while sighted people do.

> **LARRY:** It's quite amazing when you think about it. Nobody knows what she looks like. Everybody is in the same boat as you.
>
> **MICHAEL:** You have leveled the playing field for me, Larry.
>
> —"The Blind Date" (Season Four, Episode 3)

Lingerer: A person who overstays his welcome when you invite him over for dinner.

> **LARRY:** No, we go out. That way we can get rid of him.
>
> **CHERYL:** Is he a talker?
>
> **LARRY:** He's a lingerer.
>
> —"The Group" (Season One, Episode 10)

Liquids Only Rule: An unwritten rule that says you can take liquids, but not food, from someone else's refrigerator without asking for permission.

FUNKHOUSER: What was that whole thing?
LARRY: He goes in my refrigerator? Come on, you don't do that.
FUNKHOUSER: What did he take?
LARRY: Lemonade.
FUNKHOUSER: Liquids are okay . . . You know, I don't mind if you take liquid, but when you take regular food, I have a problem.

—"Funkhouser's Crazy Sister" (Season Seven, Episode 1)

Loss and Responsibility: A puzzle. If you lose something and I find it, but then I lose it again, do I owe you what I lost? Or am I free of any responsibility, since you're no better or worse off than you were before?

DAVID SCHWIMMER: Well, you owe me a watch.
LARRY: What, are you nuts? You didn't even have a watch to begin with, so you're in the same position you were. There's no change.
DAVID SCHIMMER: It's a little different. You had my watch—you had possession of my watch—and now you don't.
MEL BROOKS: He's right. The watch was lost. So it continues to be lost!

—"Opening Night" (Season Four, Episode 10)

Love: A necessary condition for a woman to be willing to have sex with a man.

LEWIS: We're men, and men need it more.
LARRY: No, it's not about that. It's because they are so offended by our genitalia that they have to be in love with us to have it. That's why we can have sex with anyone and they can't.

—"The Bracelet" (Season One, Episode 4)

Magician: Something one is by nature thanks to an inborn potential that other magicians recognize and cultivate. If this weren't true, it's not clear how there could be any magicians, since magicians cannot teach magic tricks to non-magicians and all magic tricks are learned from magicians.

LARRY: You didn't know that trick before the magician taught it to you, right?
STEWART: Yeah.
LARRY: So why did the magician tell you?
STEWART: He can tell that I am a magician.
LARRY: Well, you can tell that I'm a magician.
STEWART: But I'm a magician, just naturally a magician.

—"The Blind Date" (Season Four, Episode 3)

Man-Baby/Man-Child: What you are if you refuse to leave the backseat of a car in order to fill a vacated passenger seat upfront.

LARRY: We could have been there already. Oh, you can't drive with someone in the backseat!
BEN STILLER: You're such a baby. You're a grown man baby.
LARRY: Are you saying I'm a man-child?

—"Ben's Birthday Party" (Season Four, Episode 2)

Married People's Club: The married people of the world, all or most of whom are drawn together by a common misery.

LARRY: Well, welcome back to the married people's club.
JEFF: Oh, we're all so happy.

—"The Nanny From Hell" (Season Three, Episode 4)

Medium Talk: An alternative to small talk that involves discussions about the health of one's marriage and the quality of one's sex life.

HANK: I don't even know how to write cursive anymore.
LARRY: So how's your marriage?
HANK: What the hell? Why would you ask me that?
LARRY: I'm trying to elevate small talk to medium talk.

—"The Hero" (Season Eight, Episode 6)

Meeting: A puzzle. If we meet but don't discuss the agreed upon agenda, have we met? Or do we not meet until we have the meeting we agreed to have?

JASON ALEXANDER: Let's have that meeting.
LARRY: We're having that meeting right now.
JASON ALEXANDER: This isn't a meeting about the show. This is a meeting about having a meeting.
LARRY: I know, but the intention is the same. Don't you understand?[6]

—"Thor" (Season Two, Episode 2)

Misrepresentation: What a bald man does when he hides his baldness with a hat. This is strictly prohibited by the bald code.

LARRY: They'll meet a girl or something, and they'll show up on a date. What are they gonna do? Are they going to take the hat off?
PHIL DUNLAP: Then the girl is going to be like, "I didn't know you were bald."
LARRY: "You misrepresented yourself! You're a liar."

—"The Corpse-Sniffing Dog" (Season Three, Episode 7)

---

[6] The puzzle of "meeting" also comes up on "The Wire" (Season One, Episode 6), when Larry's neighbor feels he hasn't met Julia Louis-Dreyfus *despite having just met her*. "That was terrible. That was maybe an encounter, but that's not a meeting."

Mopey-Dick: A man who is too depressed from a breakup to get out of bed.

> LEON: Who the fuck is Moby-Dick?
> JEFF: *Moby-Dick* is the book, by Melville.
> LEON: Mopey-dick, man. His dick is moping.
> JEFF: Oh, literally mopey-dick?
> —"The Bat Mitzvah" (Season Six, Episode 10)

Munch and Pee: Something you claim to do when you don't trust the person who offers to hold your popcorn while you use the bathroom before a movie.

> GABBY: You're going to take your popcorn to the bathroom? That's disgusting. Don't leave your popcorn in the bathroom with the people and the skeevatz . . .
> LARRY: No, no, I hold onto it! I munch and pee.
> —"Car Periscope" (Season Eight, Episode 8)

Names by Association: A method for organizing your cell phone contacts.

> LARRY: I don't know her last name. She was in my blackberry under Denise Handicap. That's how I remember these names. Don't you do that in your Blackberry? You put names down with jobs, some association so you remember who they are.
> —"Denise Handicap" (Season Seven, Episode 5)

Nice Business: Living the kind of life in which you at least occasionally do nice things.

> LARRY: I did once try and stop a woman who was about to get hit by a car. I screamed, "Watch out!" And she said, "Don't tell me what to do! I tried to save her life and she screamed at me. . . . I got out of the nice business at that point."
> —"The Wire" (Season One, Episode 6)

Niceness: A matter of doing, and not just intending—it's the act that counts, not the thought.

> LARRY: I always think of nice things, but I never act on them. What is that?
> JEFF: It's like you with inventions. You think of inventions. You never do the inventions.
> LARRY: I don't implement. I could do it right now. By God, I'm going to go into that room and do it. I am going to do something nice. Right now!
> —"The Car Periscope" (Season Eight, Episode 8)

No Gifts: Something people say without meaning when they are having a party for themselves. It actually means, "bring a gift or be condemned for failing to."

Cheryl: I thought you said we weren't supposed to bring a present.
Larry: He said, "No gifts." . . .
Larry: Did you guys bring a gift to this thing? He said, "No gifts."
Susie: Nobody means that. You took that seriously?

—"Ben's Birthday" (Season Four, Episode 2)

Norwegian: Someone who is nothing like a Swede, all appearances to the contrary.

Sven: I don't look Swedish, do I? It's a big difference.
Larry: Apparently. What's the difference, may I ask?
Sven: Culture, looks, names, history, food, dancing.
Larry: Are Swedes touchy if you refer to them as Norwegians?
Sven: Why don't you ask a Swede?

—"The 5 Wood" (Season Four, Episode 5)

Numb Vagina: The consequence of a man wearing an "everlast" condom inside out while having sex with a woman.

Jeff: They're designed to go the other way, and then you last and you last.
Larry: Have you ever heard of this before, the numb vagina?
Jeff: We've got bigger problems than a numb vagina.

—"Wandering Bear" (Season Four, Episode 8)

One-Line Idea: Using one line in a busy store to make sure everyone is served no earlier and no later than when it is his turn.

Larry: You have a line problem in this store. The lines move completely disproportionately. You know, there's a way to fix that, too. Like they do in Disneyland—you know how the line snakes around? Go into a deli, you take a number. So it's fair, that's all—'cause you probably don't add up stuff at the same rate. But there's a way to solve it: one line. It's not a crazy idea. They wouldn't have stoned me back a thousand years ago for bringing up the one line idea, because one line everybody feels good. They don't feel they're being cheated.

—"The Ida Funkhouser Roadside Memorial" (Season Six, Episode 3)

Our Money: If you don't work and your spouse's salary is your sole source of income, "our money" is something you can say only for the sake of discussion.

Larry: Well, you can call it "our money," but just for the sake of discussion. He's the one who goes to work and earns the money. You don't work . . .
Susan Braudy: It's not about where it's coming from. It's about what it becomes.
Larry: No, it's completely about where it's coming from.

—"The Corpse-Sniffing Dog" (Season Three, Episode 7)

Outfit Approval: Something a man must get from his wife or girlfriend before she will agree to go to a social function with him.

LARRY: Do you believe my wife made me change clothes before I came here tonight? She didn't like my outfit. I didn't get outfit approval tonight.

—"The Acupuncturist" (Season Two, Episode 6)

Pants Tent: The appearance of an erection caused by excess material in the crotch area of men's pants.

LARRY: I have never seen a bunch up like this in my life. This is like a five-inch bunch up I got here.
CHERYL: Well, you don't have to play with it.
LARRY: Is it a bad thing? Maybe it's not such a bad thing.
CHERYL: Oh, because you want people to think that you constantly have an erection?

—"The Pants Tent" (Season One, Episode 1)

Parkinson's Shake: For Michael J. Fox and his friends, a Parkinson's Shake is an involuntary shaking of the hand or head caused by Parkinson's disease. For Larry, however, a Parkinson's Shake is always deliberate and intended to cause harm, either by expressing disapproval or by causing a soda to explode, and whose nefariousness is concealed by a dishonest appeal to Parkinson's as the cause.

MICHAEL J. FOX: *hands Larry a soda while shaking it.*
LARRY: (*Larry opens soda*) Oh, Jesus Christ! What the Hell? Did you shake that up on purpose?
MICHAEL J. FOX: Parkinson's.

—"Larry vs. Michael J. Fox" (Season Eight, Episode 10)

Patient-Hygienist Confidentiality: An unwritten rule that says it is unethical for a dental hygienist to share her patient's dental health with other people.

LARRY: First of all, number one I don't have any plaque. . . . Number two, she shouldn't be talking about it, that's a breach of patient-hygienist confidentiality.

—"The Weatherman" (Season Four, Episode 4)

Pause Toast: The act of taking toast out of the toaster before it is fully toasted, with the intention of finishing the toasting process at a later time. Whether this can be done is disputed.

LARRY: You don't have to start all over again. You pick up where you left off.
LEON: You can't pause toast.
LARRY: You can pause toast.
LEON: If this toast goes back in that machine, it's going to lose its essence, Larry.

—"The Rat Dog" (Season Six, Episode 6)

Peeing Sitting Down: A rational alternative to peeing standing up.

LARRY: It's more comfortable. When you get up at night you don't have to turn the light on and wake up. And you get to read.

JEFF: What are you reading?

LARRY: . . . Hey, buddy, when you're peeing all over your shoe, I'm learning something.

—"The Weatherman" (Season Four, Episode 4)

Pee Privacy: Something that some men want (i.e. both freedom from being spied on by other men and protection from other men's urine) but only enjoy if there are splash guards between urinals in public bathrooms.

LARRY: How come there's no partitions in the bathroom between the urinals?

TED DANSON: I don't know. I thought we were going to have that.

LARRY: We want a little pee privacy, do we not?

—"The Corpse-Sniffing Dog" (Season Three, Episode 7)

Personal Reasons: Something you can say when it's true, but also when it's not and you don't want to provide a real reason.

LARRY: The caterer cancelled? How come?

CHERYL: Personal reasons.

LARRY: "Personal reasons"? You can get away with anything if you say that. Nobody has to explain themselves. You just have to say, "It's personal."

—"AAMCO" (Season One, Episode 7)

Pig-Parker: A person who takes up more than one parking space in a parking lot and thereby causes a "domino effect."

LARRY: You're a foot over the line. You're taking up two spaces, and the next car is also going to be taking up two spaces. Then you're going to leave, and then that car is going to get blamed. This is chaos. Society can't function like this . . .

MAN: Why don't you stay between the lines of your own goddamn business? Why don't you stay confined within the lines of not being an asshole? 'Cause you're way over that line.

LARRY: The only person who is the asshole here is the "pig-parker."

—"Vow of Silence" (Season Eight, Episode 5)

Plan vs. Confirmation: Larry insists that plans don't require confirmation. Why make plans if you don't intend to keep them? Lewis disagrees: plans aren't set unless they are confirmed.

LEWIS: Well, I will need a confirmation.

LARRY: You're not getting a confirmation. This is the confirmation right now. . . . You're like some kind of government bureaucracy. You've got the plan. You've got the confirmation. You've got a subcommittee. I gotta go through all these levels.

—"Vow of Silence" (Season Eight, Episode 5)

Pointless and Unnecessary Social Convention: The practice of introducing one friend from one part of your life to a group of friends in another part of your life, e.g. while sitting at a restaurant or attending a social function, even though there's virtually no chance they will ever see each other again.

FUNKHOUSER: Why didn't you introduce us?

LARRY: He's from New York. You're never going to see him again for the rest of your life.

FUNKHOUSER: It's the courteous thing to do. . . .

LARRY: He has to know your name and shake your hand? It's a pointless and unnecessary social convention to introduce every single person you know.

—"The Black Swan" (Season Seven, Episode 7)

Pop-In Apology: The kind of apology you give to a deaf person.

LARRY: You want me to come by and make a special trip? I wouldn't think she would want that. I would think they want to be treated like everybody else.

HAL: What do you mean, "they"?

LARRY: Well, deaf people, because they're the only ones who need a special pop-in apology. Every other kind of handicapped person you can apologize to on the phone. Deaf people require that you go to their house.

—"The Rat Dog" (Season Six, Episode 6)

Pop-In/Pop-Out: The sudden and uncontrolled appearance or disappearance of a person in one's masturbation fantasy.

JEFF: You can't control who pops in. She (Cheryl) pops in.

LARRY: She pops in? Why didn't you pop her out?

JEFF: I tried popping her out. She wouldn't pop out.

LARRY: What, she insisted on staying? . . . What the hell are you using my wife for?

JEFF: I thought you'd be flattered?

LARRY: Flattered? I'm fucking nauseous!

—"The Blind Date" (Season Four, Episode 3)

Porn Baby: A young boy with an unusually large penis.

LEWIS: Who's that?

LARRY: That's the kid.

LEWIS: That's the porn baby?

LARRY: That's the porn baby.

—"The Nanny from Hell" (Season Three, Episode 4)

Proclivity for Fat People: Favoritism for fat people.

LARRY: Like you wouldn't hire a fat guy? You don't have a proclivity for fat people? I think you got a strong proclivity for fat people. If a fat guy came in, you wouldn't want to hire him? You would have been all over that fat guy!

—"Grand Opening" (Season Three, Episode 10)

Protesting Math: The refusal to include an additional tip at a restaurant where there is a built-in eighteen percent gratuity, because it requires math.

LARRY: Don't make me do math at the table.
WAITER: So you're protesting math?
LARRY: I'm protesting math.

—"The Black Swan" (Season Seven, Episode 7)

Pussy/Nice Confusion: An error in judgment that occurs when we mistake nice people for "pussies." They appear weak, but that's only because they are nice.

CHERYL: People come to you with their hand out, you can't say no?
LARRY: I have trouble saying no.
CHERYL: You know why? Because you're a pussy.
LARRY: Maybe I'm nice. You have nice/pussy confusion. Maybe I'm just nice.

—"The Acupuncturist" (Season Two, Episode 6)

Pussy On Layaway: Paying for a prostitute's services, even simply to use the carpool lane, the day after those services were rendered.

LARRY: I don't quite have enough cash to pay you tonight. But you know I'm totally good. I'll pay you tomorrow. I'll come to your house—
MONINA: Tomorrow? This ain't motherfucking pussy on layaway.

—"The Carpool Lane" (Season Four, Episode 6)

Red Snapper: A woman's vagina, which may or may not be able to talk.

LARRY: I drove a cab, used to drive around for two hours. I couldn't get a fare. You're telling me you're getting four blowjobs in an hour?
MONINA: Yes, honey, you done picked up the best. Honey, I got a red snapper that talks to you.
LARRY: You know what it's saying? I'm charging way too much.

—"The Carpool Lane" (Season Four, Episode 6)

Republican: A kind of woman with whom Larry cannot have sex.

LARRY: You've got a picture of Bush in your dressing room? You're a Republican?

Cady Huffman: Yes, Larry, I'm a Republican . . .
Jeff: What the fuck were you thinking? A picture of Bush, who gives a flying fuck?

—"Opening Night" (Season Four, Episode 10)

Richard Lewis: "A babbling brook of bullshit!" ("The Bracelet," Season One, Episode 4).

Rivalry: A metaphor for understanding the relationship between a husband and a wife.

Larry: You got yourself a partner! I got a wife. Not exactly a partner. More like a, uh, a rival. You know what I mean? It's a rivalry.

—"Mel's Offer" (Season Four, Episode 1)

Run an Ass into the Ground: Leon's description of a man who divorces a woman after she's no longer in her prime.

Funkhouser: I'm excited. I'm single.
Leon: Get out there and get some new ass, you know what I'm sayin'? You ran that other ass into the ground, right?
Funkhouser: I don't want to talk about my wife like that.
Leon: You ran that ass into the ground, and you're moving on, right?

—"The Divorce" (Season Eight, Episode 1)

Sampling Privilege: The socially acceptable number of samples one can try (no more than one or two) while other customers are waiting behind you.

Larry: Don't abuse your sampling privilege. She abused the sampling privilege. And you know what else? I was watching out for the counter woman as well.
Cheryl: If she had a problem with that woman, don't you think she might say, "excuse me, ma'am"—
Larry: No, because she's always told the customer is right. And in fact, the customer is usually a moron and an asshole.

—"Ida Funkhouser Roadside Memorial" (Season Six, Episode 3)

Schmohawk: A bad driver.

Larry: You know what my father used to call those people? Schmohawks. Did I ever tell you that?
Cheryl: Yeah.
Larry: Did I mention schmohawks to you? Schmohawk. "Hey, schmohawk!" He used to yell that out all the time.

—"Meet the Blacks" (Season Six, Episode 1)

Scrotum-Kabob: The end result of serving kabobs at a dinner party without arranging for a place to dispose of used skewers.

LARRY: I don't like a kabob. I don't know what your feelings are about a kabob, but I'm not a kabob guy. You've got this stick—what do you do? What, do you put it in your pocket? You could stick yourself in the scrotum. Then what do you got? A scrotum-kabob.

—"Ben's Birthday" (Season Four, Episode 2)

Sex for Platonic Friends: The playful touching that friends engage in because they can't have sex with each other but would like to, and so need some sort of substitute.

LARRY: The flirtatious tap . . . that's like sex for platonic friends, because they can't touch each other. It's forbidden, so they're allowed to go like that."

—"The Anonymous Donor" (Season Six, Episode 2)

Sexual Blackmail: The use of private sexual information, such as a partner's preferences or fantasies, as leverage in a divorce.

JEFF: Like sexual . . . There are certain sexual things that I like and I don't want Susie yammering about what they are.

LARRY: This is sexual blackmail.

—"Thor" (Season Two, Episode 2)

Shit Bow: An insincere bow that is dismissive and expresses disrespect.

LARRY: The other night a Japanese fellow apologized to me, but he only went down a few degrees, kind of like that (Larry performs a shallow bow).

JAPANESE MAN IN PARK: Oh, that is not apology to you. No, he was not sorry at all.

LARRY: He wasn't sorry?

JAPANESE MAN IN PARK: No, he a little, uh, dismissive of you.

LARRY: Dismissive? I got a dismissive bow?

Japanese man in park: Yes, a little bit, "shit bow."

—"The Bi-Sexual" (Season Eight, Episode 7)

Shit Where You Eat: The act of dating a woman casually, with no intention of the relationship ending well, when the woman works in any capacity at your favorite restaurant. This can only lead to eating what you have shat.

LARRY: I say that I will eat here again.

LEWIS: Oh, really?

LARRY: Yes, I will be the Edmund Hillary of shitting where you eat.

—"The Smiley Face" (Season Eight, Episode 4)

Shoe-Whore: A shoe salesman who accepts a commission, even though he didn't sell any shoes.

LARRY: How much is the commission? I'll pay you the commission.

SHOE SALESMAN: That is so insulting. How dare you? I am not a shoe-whore.

—"Ted and Marry" (Season One, Episode 2)

Shy/Asshole Confusion: An error in judgment that occurs when we mistake shy people for assholes. They seem rude and judgmental, but they're just shy.

LARRY: I don't know why you call him an asshole. He's not an asshole. He's just shy.

CHERYL: He's not shy. He thinks he's smarter than everybody else. And he sits there and he judges and—

LARRY: No, he doesn't. He's just shy. You've got shy/asshole confusion.

—"The Acupuncturist" (Season Two, Episode 6)

Siamese Twins: White fish and sable.

TED DANSON: You have two fishes in the sandwich?

LARRY: But they blend very well together. They're like Siamese twins, white fish and sable.

—"The Larry David Sandwich" (Season Five, Episode 1)

Sick Sex: The sexual desire aroused by the experience of caring for someone who is sick, or by the experience of being cared for while you are sick.

LARRY: Cheryl was in bed. She had a little temperature, but there was something about it that kind of turned me on. She's sick. She's helpless.

JEFF: I understand. I like it the reverse, when I'm sick.

LARRY: I like it either way. I guess I just like sick sex.

—"The Rat Dog" (Season Six, Episode 6)

Single Life in Eternity: A future for married individuals that seems to be implied by the language used in ordinary wedding vows, which ask people to promise their love for each other until death, whereupon they part.

LARRY: (*responding to Cheryl's unconventional wedding vows*) I guess I had a different plan for eternity. I thought I'd be single, I guess.

CHERYL: I'm sorry. I'm interrupting your single life in eternity?

LARRY: No, I just didn't realize that this relationship carried over after death.

—"The Survivor" (Season Four, Episode 9)

Sin of Omission: A bad thing you "do" *by not doing something*. It's a failure to do what you are supposed to do.

Larry: It's not like I did it on purpose. The thought just didn't even enter my mind. It's not like it entered my mind and I thought, "no, the hell with them." See the difference? Sin of commission/omission. That's a sin of omission, much better than the commission.

—"Ida Funkhouser Roadside Memorial" (Season Six, Episode 3)

Slightly Gay: Some people are gay but don't appear to be; some people are gay and it's obvious that they are; others are gay and they *sort of* appear to be—these people are slightly gay, according to Larry.

Larry: Well, you (Sam) seem slightly gay, and you (Dr. Schaffer) don't. So, I wouldn't be surprised if somebody told me that he (Sam) was gay, but I'm a little surprised when somebody tells me that you're gay. It's no big deal, you know? Is that a crime?

Dr. Schaffer: No, it's not a crime. It's just odd and a little bit offensive.

Larry: I'm sorry if you're offended. I don't think I said anything offensive.

—"Funkhouser's Crazy Sister" (Season Seven, Episode 1)

Smiley Face: An objectionable and unnecessary adornment that some people add to their text messages.

Larry: I told her about the smiley faces. I can't stand it. And everybody uses them!

Jeff: I don't understand.

Larry: What are they going to be in newspapers soon? The *New York Times* headline, "Unemployment Drops."

—"The Smiley Face" (Season Eight, Episode 4)

Snack and Apologize: An act whose moral value is disputed. Some say an apology cannot be sincere if a person offers it while snacking. Others argue that snacking in no way impacts the apology's sincerity.

Yoshi: There's no pistachio crunching and apologizing.

Larry: I respectfully disagree. I've snacked and apologized many times in the past, and everyone has always accepted it quite graciously.

Yoshi: Well, that may be the way you do things in your family, but we don't snack and apologize—

Larry: What, is that a Japanese thing?

Yoshi: No, that's a human thing.

—"Kamikaze Bingo" (Season Five, Episode 4)

Social Assassin: A person you hire, either for pay or via extortion, to say or do what you don't have the courage or the ability to say or do yourself. You hire a social assassin when you feel a brutally honest message *must* be delivered but you don't want to take responsibility for your friend's or family member's hurt feelings.

Larry: He said he'd forget about the money for the car, which is $573, if I tell her to stop saying "lol."

Jeff: You know, in most countries you could get somebody killed for $573.

Larry: I know. By the way, I was this close to telling her the other night.

Jeff: You know what you are? You're a social assassin.

—"Palestinian Chicken" (Season Eight, Episode 3)

Sorry Window: The period of time after a tragedy, such as the loss of a family member, when it's reasonable to expect other people to say they are sorry for your loss.

Larry: With all due respect, don't you think the sorry window has closed on that?

Heidi: The sorry window? I didn't know there was a sorry window.

Larry: Two years and you're still getting "sorry's"? I don't think so. That's a long time for "sorry's." That's like saying "Happy New Year" in October.

—"The Smiley Face" (Season Eight, Episode 4)

Sources: Causes of erections.

Larry: I know the source. I can name sources. Sophia Loren was once a source. I know my sources. Sometimes they're mysterious sources, and I don't know where it comes from. Other times I can pinpoint it.

—"Pants Tent" (Season One, Episode 1)

Stop and Chat: The practice of stopping and having a pointless conversation when simply saying hello, or even just waiving, would be just as good.

Larry: He wanted to do a stop and chat. I didn't want to do a stop and chat.

Jeff: Stop and chat. Where do you come up with these things? Stop and chat.

—"The Massage" (Season Two, Episode 10)

Suicide Call: The person you call when you're thinking about committing suicide.

Larry: Wait, she's going to commit suicide and she calls you?

Lewis: A lot of people call me who are suicidal.

Larry: I don't think you'd be my suicide call.

—"The Safe House" (Season Eight, Episode 2)

Surrogate Etiquette: The unwritten rules governing how one is supposed to treat a surrogate mother at a baby shower.

Cheryl: The shower is for Betty.

LARRY: So she's going to be opening her presents, and the surrogate is going to be standing there like an idiot and she has nothing to open? The whole thing is—What's the surrogate etiquette?

—"The Surrogate" (Season Four, Episode 7)

Survivor: An ambiguous term, referring either to a person who survived the Holocaust, or to a person who was a participant on the reality television show, *Survivor*.

SOLLY: You know nothing about survival. I'm a survivor!
COLBY: I'm a survivor!
SOLLY: I'm a survivor!
COLBY: I'm a survivor!

—"The Survivor" (Season Four, Episode 9)

Sweded: To be tricked by a Swedish lawyer whose scam is to convince you he is Jewish, because he knows you believe the stereotype that Jewish lawyers are the best.

LARRY: I got Sweded. . . . So did you know Berg was a Swede? . . . He's so devious.

—"The Divorce" (Season Eight, Episode 1)

Switzerland: Have you heard of Switzerland? It's a country in Europe and they don't like to fight. They let everybody do their fighting for them while they ski and eat chocolate.

—"The Doll" (Season Two, Episode 7)

Take a Pop: A way for a Christian Scientist to take medication without betraying her faith. If she just pops it in, it's okay!

DEBORAH: (*Lewis's Christian Scientist girlfriend*) I don't take medication.
LARRY: Just pop it in.
DEBORAH: Pop it in? That's a betrayal of my faith. . . .
LARRY: No one's watching, pop! Take a pop!

—"The Benadryl Brownie" (Season Three, Episode 2)

Talk Lefty: Talking on the phone using the ear you aren't accustomed to using for phone calls. Some people cannot do this.

LARRY: You want me to talk lefty?
DR. SCHAFFER: Yeah, just talk lefty.
LARRY: I have a hard time talking lefty on the phone. Everything comes out wrong. It's like throwing lefty—I can't do it. I'm not myself. I feel different, strange, like I'm not me. I'm not comfortable talking lefty.

—"The Lefty Call" (Season Six, Episode 4)

Tap Me on the Shoulder: All a woman has to do when she wants sex with her husband or boyfriend, because he wants it all of the time.

LARRY: Just assume that I want it all the time, so whenever you want it, just tap me on the shoulder. Otherwise I'll be making moves all the time. Do you want that? Do you want somebody just mauling you all the time?

—"The Group" (Season One, Episode 10)

Tapped Out: A man's inability to have sex immediately after masturbating.

CHERYL: Why can't you do it tonight? Remember, the other night, you said all I have to do is tap you on the shoulder and you're ready.

LARRY: I'm kind of tapped out.

—"The Group" (Season One, Episode 10)

Tennis Grunt: A sound that some tennis players make as they hit the ball.

LARRY: You grunt on every shot. Every shot you hit you, "Uhhh!" "Uhhh." You make this disgusting noise. You don't hear it?

CHERYL: No.

LARRY: . . . It sounds like pigs fucking.

—"Club Soda and Salt" (Season Three, Episode 3)

The Technique to Firing: You act as if it is not bad news.

LARRY: There's a technique to firing. . . . Bad news has to be delivered in a casual way, like it's not bad news. If you deliver bad news like it's bad news, it's going to be bad news. If you deliver bad news like it's not a big deal, then it's not a big deal.

—"Denise Handicap" (Season Seven, Episode 5)

Titmouse: What a man calls a mouse when he is obsessed with women's breasts.

CHERYL: Why do you call it a titmouse?

LARRY: Because that's what you call it.

CHERYL: Who calls it that?

LARRY: A lot of people call it that.

CHERYL: Oh, my God. You're obsessed with tits.

—"Ben's Birthday Party" (Season Four, Episode 2)

Tongue Sign: An ambiguous movement of the tongue that can indicate an interest in sex or a mouth full of cotton.

LARRY: Get together? You and me? Really?

DALILAH THE HYGIENIST: Am I being too forward? Because when you were at the office, you gave me the tongue sign.

LARRY: Tongue sign? I was just really trying to get cotton out my mouth.

—"The 5 Wood" (Season Four, Episode 5)

Too Saucy: The explanation you can, but perhaps shouldn't, give to a professional cook when you don't like his cooking.

> **JOSH:** What was wrong with it?
> **LARRY:** A little saucy. A little too saucy.
> **JOSH:** "Saucy"?
> **LARRY:** Yeah, kind of saucy.
> **JOSH:** Was there anything else?
> **LARRY:** Meh, not really.
>
> —"Club Soda and Salt" (Season Three, Episode 3)

Topsy-Turvy: A strategy for turning the tables on an interviewer during an interview.

> **LARRY:** You flip it. Now he's trying to impress you.
> **LEON:** Turn that shit around on him.
> **LARRY:** Turn it around on him.
> **LEON:** Topsy-turvy that motherfucker.
> **LARRY:** Yeah, yeah, yeah!
>
> —"The Rat Dog" (Season Six, Episode 6)

Toupe-People: Bald men who hide their baldness with toupées.

> **LARRY:** I'm surprised Hitler didn't round up the toupée-people. If I'm going to be a sick megalomaniac, to round up people who I hated, they would be on my list.
>
> —"The Corpse-Sniffing Dog" (Season Three, Episode 7)

The Ultimate form of Consolation: Sex.

> **CHERYL:** What are you doing?
> **LARRY:** What?
> **CHERYL:** You're turning consolation into sex?
> **LARRY:** Well, that's the ultimate form of consolation.
>
> —"Lewis Needs a Kidney" (Season Five, Episode 5)

Unwritten Law of Dry Cleaning: "Sometimes you get home and you have something that isn't yours, and sometimes something of yours gets taken. That's just the unwritten law of dry cleaning.

> —"The Anonymous Donor" (Season Six, Episode 2)

Unwritten Rules: The set of rules governing society that we know but typically don't know that we know. They aren't written down, and they often go unrecognized until someone points them out. These rules govern how much caviar one takes at a dinner party, how many kinds of ice cream one can sample at an ice cream shop while others are waiting, where the sign-in sheet belongs in the doctor's office, and much more.

> **LARRY:** She was breaking the rules. She wasn't following the rules of society.

CHERYL: (*exasperated*): What rules?
LARRY: The unwritten rules that we have as we go about our day.

—"Ida Funkhouser Roadside Memorial" (Season Six, Episode 3)

Upstream: The act of walking up the street, against traffic, to get in front of another person who is also waiting for a cab.

LARRY: Hey! Hey! What are you doing? I'm standing here. I was here first.
WOMAN GETTING INTO CAB: I don't care. I'm getting the cab.
LARRY: What, you're upstreaming me?
WOMAN GETTING INTO CAB: Everybody upstreams, you idiot. You don't stand there like a jackass.
LARRY: That's anarchy! We need some rules!

—"Car Periscope," Season Eight, Episode 8

Vanilla Bullshit Cappa-Thing: A café latte.

LARRY: And I'll have a vanilla . . . one of the vanilla bullshit things . . . some vanilla bullshit cappa-thing. Whatever you got. I don't care.

—"Shaq" (Season Two, Episode 8)

Verbal Texting: Speaking as if you were writing a text message on a cell phone.

LARRY: If you were going to laugh out loud, why aren't you laughing out loud? Why say it? Why not just laugh?
ILENE: I am laughing. That's what that is. It's me—that's laughing.
LARRY: No, you're saying, "L-o-l," you're verbal texting.

—"Palestinian Chicken" (Season Eight, Episode 3)

Waiter: Someone who waits an unreasonable amount of time for food at a restaurant, and then resorts to serving himself.

WAITER: Where did this food come from?
LARRY: I brought it here.
WAITER: Do you understand, I am the waiter.
LARRY: Yet we were the ones who were doing the waiting, so we became the waiters.

—"The Hero" (Season Eight, Episode 6)

Wait for Dessert Rule: An unwritten rule that says you cannot leave a party until after dessert has been served.

FUNKHOUSER: You left my party before dessert. How can you do that? It's not proper etiquette.
LARRY: I don't subscribe to the wait for dessert rule.

—"The Bowtie" (Season Five, Episode 2)

Wear an Outfit Till Its Completion: Leaving formal clothes on after you have left the funeral or wedding that required them.

JEFF: Why are you still wearing the tie? You don't have to wear it anymore. If I didn't have to I wouldn't.

LARRY: Well, as long as you've got the outfit on, you might as well just wear it till its completion. Maintain the outfit.

—"Beloved Aunt" (Season One, Episode 8)

Whisper Lunch: The type of lunch you have in a restaurant where the table placement forces you to share your space with strangers.

LARRY: I can't even talk. I can't say anything in here.

LEWIS: Direct it right to me.

LARRY: You gotta have a whole whisper lunch. It's a whisper lunch.

—"The Nanny from Hell" (Season Three, Episode 4)

Wrong Person: The person who is thought to have revealed another person's secret, when in fact it was someone else. Sadly, these situations end badly for the "wrong person," while the "right person" gets away with betraying his friend's trust.

LARRY: I think you need to tell him who you heard it from, otherwise he could think the wrong person told you, and that would be bad.

WANDA: Bad for who?

LARRY: For that wrong person.

WANDA: Larry, I don't give a fuck about the "wrong person." This doesn't make any sense—

—"Krazee-Eyez Killa" (Season Three, Episode 8)

Yarmulke Alert: The panic that precipitates when a devout Jewish man's yarmulke falls onto the floor.

LARRY: Hey! You dropped your yarmulke! Oh my God! Yarmulke alert! Oh! Sirens. Yarmulke on the floor!

—"Palestinian Chicken" (Season Eight, Episode 3)

Yelling for Society: Living as Larry does: making a point of informing people when they've violated an unwritten rule, questioning why things are done the way they are, offering suggestions for how things might be done differently…

LARRY: I'm yelling for society, for everybody! It's not just me!

—"The Safe House" (Season Eight, Episode 2)

You're Not Happy: Something you can say when you want to break up with someone whose family member just passed away. The amount of time you have to wait before you can say this varies depending on which family member died.

LARRY: If it was her mother, I'd say you have to go back on the plane and wait maybe six days, a week. For an aunt? For an aunt who doesn't even live where you live whom you don't see that often, I think you could do it when you get home.

CRAIG: What should I say?

LARRY: Just tell her you're not happy. That's very good, that works.

—"Beloved Aunt" (Season One, Episode 8)[7]

---

[7] We would like to thank Sean Petranovich, Keith Marshall, and Misha Chkhenkeli for providing very useful feedback on an earlier draft of this glossary.

Bald and Un-Bald Brothers and Sisters

Vincent Altamore, who drew our cover picture of Larry David, has been a freelance illustrator for over twenty-five years, and delights in stretching the features of the rich and famous. You can find more of his work on his blog, <vincentaltamore.blogspot.com>. He lives by the rule, Nolite te Bastardes Carborundorum, and resides in Morris Plains, New Jersey (not that that's anything to be proud of).

Robert R. Clewis is author of *The Kantian Sublime and the Revelation of Freedom* (2009) and teaches at Gwynedd-Mercy College in Pennsylvania. He has taken *Curb Your Enthusiasm*'s advice to heart and has his enthusiasm duly curbed. In fact, he doesn't care about anything anymore. Not even the show.

Taine Duncan is currently Assistant Professor of Philosophy at the University of Central Arkansas. She teaches courses on race, class, and gender, and fancies herself to be a little bit of the ever-optimistic bleeding heart that is Cheryl. She has a lithograph of Larry David hanging in her dining room to look each visitor squarely in the eye.

Robert Farrow, occasionally described as '245 pounds of twisted steel and drop-your-bony-butt-to-the-curb appeal', is a philosopher and technologist in the Institute of Educational Technology at The Open University. Rob holds a PhD in philosophy from the University of Essex and can be found online as philosopher1978. He hates himself, but it has nothing to do with being Jewish.

Chad Flanders is an assistant professor of law at Saint Louis University, where he teaches criminal and constitutional law. He's the author of articles and essays on punishment, election law, and the philosophy of Adam Smith. Both David and Chad received their PhD's at the University of Chicago. Neither have sandwiches named after them.

Natalie Fletcher has the delectable pleasure of teaching philosophy to teenagers at John Abbott College in Montreal. She's the director of Brila Youth Projects (www.brila.org), a Philosophy-for-Children (P4C) initiative that promotes critical thinking and social responsibility through creative inquiry workshops and digital magazine production. You couldn't pay her enough to try "The Larry David Sandwich"—talk about a ginormous salad-bowl of wrong!—but she's all for binging on delicious sponges . . . especially when they double as crash pads.

Andrea Lehn is a freshman in the Honors Program studying Biomedical Engineering and Chemistry at The George Washington University. What does *Curb Your Enthusiasm* have to do with either of these subjects? Well, . . . nothing. Andrea's convinced that she'll be able to complete the problem sets she put off while writing the glossary for this book after she puts the finishing touches on her time machine. Her mother is happy that she's paying for $4 espresso beverages instead of funding Andrea's time machine, which will take priority . . . someday. Andrea's liver violently opposes, but once that time machine is complete, she will travel back to kick the habit—if there's time after convincing Larry and Jeff to invest in her time machine instead of that silly car periscope.

Anna Mudde is currently Visiting Assistant Professor of philosophy at Campion College (University of Regina) on the Canadian prairies. If you've never schlepped to Saskatchewan, she's here to tell you: it's a schlep. She specializes in epistemology, ontology, feminist philosophy, philosophy of technology, and Simone de Beauvoir. Her newest project is about living as experimentation.

Simon Mussell studied at the University of Sussex and works on twentieth-century social and political theory, aesthetics and cultural studies. He currently idles in the seaside town of Brighton, England. As a perpetually poor student, Simon would routinely abuse his sampling privileges in order to eat well. Today, he vociferously pops bubble-wrap and campaigns for the egalitarian respect of wood. His next project, 'The Five-Inch Bunch Up and its Discontents', will warn colleagues of the risks involved in wearing loose-fitting corduroy pants while teaching. A significant amount of his time is dedicated to the avoidance of unwanted stop and chats, truly a task without end.

Sean Petranovich is a PhD student in philosophy at Loyola University Chicago, and completed his BA and MA in philosophy at the University of New Mexico. Petranovich is often guilty of humming parts of the *Curb Your Enthusiasm* soundtrack to supplement ordinary moments in his day, and has difficulties restraining himself from calling people "Schmohawks" while driving. While he was initially only drawn to *Curb* as a means for picking up golf tips, Petranovich was hooked by the show's messages of kindness and moral purity.

ROBERT PIERCEY is Associate Professor of Philosophy at Campion College in Regina, Saskatchewan. He works on contemporary European philosophy and is the author of two books: *The Crisis in Continental Philosophy* and *The Uses of the Past From Heidegger to Rorty*. Rob enjoys sponge cake, milk and coffee mixed together, and wine that tastes a little like a tree.

MARK RALKOWSKI is an assistant professor of Philosophy and Honors at The George Washington University. He is the author of *Heidegger's Platonism* and a variety of articles on topics in the history of philosophy. Ralkowski respects Jesus and the Buddha, but what he'd really like to know, and what he'd really like people to ask before they make decisions, is *What would Larry do?* No doubt you're dubious, but who knows? It might just make you and the rest of us ebullient and hammock-like, gently swaying in the wind.

JAMES ROCHA is an assistant professor of Philosophy and Women and Gender Studies at Louisiana State University. He specializes in Kant, race, feminism, and applied ethics. One key part of his job is teaching students to never follow the unwritten rules of society without question such as the unwritten rule that you can't take flowers from a roadside memorial even if you need them to placate your wife. Wait, maybe that's a pretty, pretty, pretty good rule. Well, question even that one, and then decide based on what's most rational. That's the Kantian way—and the Larry David way.

JAMES RODWELL teaches in the School of Art History and Philosophy at the University of Essex. Amongst other things, he works on Kierkegaard and post-Kantian philosophy of religion. All his sins are sins of omission.

DAVID SVOLBA will frequently call Chad Flanders while waiting for the doctor, *using the doctor's phone*. Chad is nonplussed by this. David is a philosophical journeyman, having taught philosophy at the University of Illinois at Chicago, at the Jesuit University in Krakow, Poland, and most recently at Fitchburg State University, where he has accepted a tenure-track job teaching philosophy. He has written on the work of Harry Frankfurt and on *The Big Lebowski*.

JOSEPH WESTFALL steals forks from restaurants. He is an Associate Professor of Philosophy at the University of Houston-Downtown, and the author of *The Kierkegaardian Author: Authorship and*

Performance in Kierkegaard's Literary and Dramatic Criticism (2007), in addition to numerous articles on issues of authorship, identity, irony, and the arts in nineteenth- and twentieth-century European philosophy. He is also nothing like Joseph Westfall.

BEKKA WILLIAMS is a PhD candidate at the University of Wisconsin-Madison, where she's completing a dissertation exploring the relationship between group obligations and individual obligations. She works for the Institutional Review Board at her university, where she tries to help make sure that medical researchers follow the rules. And most semesters, Bekka also teaches undergraduate philosophy—primarily Ethics classes, in which she tries to convince her students that there really is something to "all this morality stuff." Bekka finds that teaching undergraduates involves the perfect amount of social interaction: While she doesn't like talking to people she *knows*, students she has no problem with.

KEVIN ZANELOTTI is an assistant professor of philosophy at McKendree University. His research focuses on nineteenth-century German philosophy, applied ethics, and the pedagogy of philosophy. He has published articles on Spinoza, Fichte, and strategies for teaching philosophy to undergraduates. As the sole member of a one-person philosophy department, his teaching focuses on, well, *everything*. As a balding person, he shares Larry David's disdain for the arrogance of the full-haired majority and contempt for self-hating baldies everywhere.

Index

Curb Seasons and Episodes